Roadmap Strategies for Startups Series
TRADEMARK PROTECTION AND PROSECUTION

Roadmap Strategies for Startups Series

HOW-TO AND DO-IT-YOURSELF SERIES

BY ANN CARRINGTON

Business Structures and Incorporation

Trademark Protection and Prosecution

Writing Winning Business Plans and Investor Presentations

Meet the Author and Publisher at https://www.AuthorsDoor.com

Roadmap Strategies for Startups Series

TRADEMARK PROTECTION AND PROSECUTION

HOW-TO AND DO-IT-YOURSELF SERIES

ANN CARRINGTON

AuthorsDoor Group

an imprint of The Ridge Publishing Group

Copyright © 2021 by Ann Carrington
All rights reserved. Published by AuthorsDoor™ Group,
an imprint of The Ridge Publishing Group

The name and house mark, logo, and all other AuthorsDoor Group related marks depicted representing AuthorsDoor Group, whether registered or unregistered, are trademarks or servicemarks of The Ridge Publishing Group
www.RidgePublishingGroup.com

No part of this publication may be reproduced, or stored in a retrieval system, or transmitted in any form or by any means, electronic, mechanical, photocopying, recording, or otherwise, without written permission of the publisher. For information regarding permissions, contact The Ridge Publishing Group, Attention Permissions Department at contact@RidgePublishingGroup.com.

LIMITED OF LIABILITY DISCLAIMER OF WARRANTY: While the publisher and author have used their best efforts in preparing this book, they make no representations or warranties with respect to the accuracy or completeness of the contents of this book and specifically disclaim any implied warranties of merchantability or fitness for a particular purpose. No warranty may be created or extended by sales representatives or written sales materials. The advice and strategies contained herein may not be suitable for your situation. The publisher and author are not engaged in rendering professional services, and you should consult a professional where appropriate. Neither the publisher nor author shall be liable for any loss of profit or any other commercial damages, including but not limited to special, incidental, consequential or other damages. This book was prepared for general information and as a checklist of certain laws applicable to corporations in general. This book does not purport to cover all of the laws and related issues applicable to businesses in particular. The publisher and author undertake no responsibility to provide updates to this book.

Carrington, Ann
Trademark Protection and Prosecution / by Ann Carrington

Summary: A comprehensive book on trademarks, including sample filings. Because trademark rights in the U.S. are based on use, when a trademark is not used or is used incorrectly, the mark may be deemed abandoned. Avoid the risk of loss of rights!

ISBN 978-1-884573-90-3 (Softcover)

[1. Trademarks – Non-fiction. 2. Business Law – Non-fiction. 3. Intellectual Property – Non-fiction. 4. Branding – Non-fiction. 5. Legal – Non-fiction.] I. Title. II. Series.

Revised Edition: April 2021

Printed in the United States of America

TABLE OF CONTENTS

1	Trademark Intelligence	1
2	Overview of Trademark Law	8
3	Trademark Program	17
4	Trademark Protections	35
5	Trademark Infringement	46
6	Trade Dress	65
7	Trade Name	73
8	Trademark Prosecution Process	85
9	The Drawing Page	142
10	Foreign Registration	164
11	Trademark Maintenance	193
12	Trademark Portfolio	232
13	Trademarks and Licensing	250
14	Trademark Assignments	273
15	Trademark Enforcement	280
About the Author and Publishers		288

Roadmap Strategies for Startups Series

TRADEMARK PROTECTION AND PROSECUTION

CHAPTER 1

TRADEMARK INTELLIGENCE

In the eyes of the public, the trademarks or service marks of a business symbolize the quality, reliability and excellence of a company's products and services. These marks help not only to maintain the company's identity and reputation among its customers and vendors but also serve to differentiate a business from its competitors. Thus, a company's growing list of marks constitutes a valuable component of the company's marketing strategy. The value of these business marks resides in the goodwill, which is generated as they are used and become increasingly identified with a company's standards of quality, technical excellence and business credibility.

Historically, trademarks are not a recent addition to the commercial landscape. In fact, the trademark laws in force today are based upon the commercial usage of trademarks dating back thousands of years. For example, dating back more than 2,500 years ago, skilled Greek potters were applying distinctive trademarks to their amphora's. Another example, more than 2,000 years ago, craftsmen were pressing their marks into the bricks from which Rome was built. Subsequently, at a very early stage in the history of civilization, trademarks were being applied to goods as a kind of guarantee that they were of a standard that could be relied upon and trusted by a customer. Today, just as in the ages of classical Greece and Rome, a trademark or service mark is a badge of quality that serves to identify and differentiate goods and services.

Principal Register

The Principal Register is the primary trademark register of the United States Patent and Trademark Office (USPTO). When a mark has been registered on the Principal Register, the mark is entitled to all the rights provided by the Trademark Act of 1946. The advantages of owning a registration on the Principal Register include the following:

TRADEMARK PROTECTION AND PROSECUTION

- ❖ Public notice of your claim of ownership of the mark;
- ❖ A legal presumption of your ownership of the mark and your exclusive right to use the mark nationwide on or in a connection with the goods or services listed in the registration;
- ❖ The ability to bring an action concerning the mark in federal court;
- ❖ The use of the U.S. registration as a basis to obtain registration in foreign countries;
- ❖ The ability to record the U.S. registration with the U.S. Customs and Border Protection (CBP) Service to prevent importation of infringing foreign goods;
- ❖ The right to use the federal registration symbol ®; and
- ❖ Listings in the USPTO's online database.

Trademarks and Service Marks

A trademark is a brand name. A trademark includes any word, phrase, symbol or design, or any combination, "used" or "intended to be used" to identify and distinguish the source of the goods or services of one party from those of others. A service mark is the same as a trademark except that it identifies and distinguishes the source of a service rather than a product. Normally, a mark for goods appears on the product or on its packaging, while a service mark appears in advertising for the services of a business.

Although federal registration of a mark is not mandatory, it has several advantages as stated above. Consequently, if you claim rights to use a mark, you may use the "TM" (trademark) or "SM" (service mark) designation to alert the public to your claim of ownership of the mark, regardless of whether you have filed an application with the USPTO. However, you may only use the federal registration symbol "®" after the USPTO actually registers a mark, and not while an application is pending.

Collective Membership Marks

Collective membership marks are marks adopted for the purpose of indicating membership in an organization such as a union, professional society, or fraternity. It does not identify or distinguish goods or services. The owner of the mark exercises control over the use of the mark; however, because the sole purpose of a membership mark is to indicate membership, use of the mark is by members.

Collective Marks

Collective trademarks and service marks are marks adopted by a collective organization (cooperative, an association, or other collective group or organization) for use by its members to indicate the source of the goods and services it's selling and distinguishing those goods and services from those of non-members. The organization cannot sell goods or services, but may advertise or promote the goods or services under the mark. These marks, owned by a group are very similar to certification marks (owned by an individual).

Certification Marks

A certification mark is any word, phrase, symbol or design, or a combination thereof used by one person other than its owner to certify that the goods or services of others have certain characteristics. An owner of a certification mark cannot use the mark in connection with his or her own goods or services. The owner must oversee other's use of the mark and prohibit others from using the mark for purposes other than certifying or from falsely certifying the existence of characteristics that the owner's products or services lack (control the mark). An owner of a certification mark may not discriminately refuse to certify goods or services that satisfy its stated objective standards for certification.

Geographic Certification Marks

Geographic certification marks are private intellectual property rights and therefore their owners deserve a level of protection for these marks against infringement and unfair competition that is not available through misleading advertising laws or labeling regulations. In most cases, government agencies charged with investigating misleading labeling claims are not looking for whether the unauthorized use of the term is infringement, but merely whether the consumer is misled by the information on the label. In many cases, this means that unauthorized users can overcome a claim of misleading advertising by merely putting dispelling information on the label, including the country of actual manufacture or a notice that "this produce is not affiliated with X." While such a practice may overcome misleading advertising claims, the unauthorized use still has the effect of diminishing the value of the geographic certification mark and its ability to identify the source of the goods or its certified characteristics to consumers. This is the value that intellectual property laws protect, and thus, dispelling information will not overcome a claim of infringement when the consumers are likely to be confused as to existence of some link between the owner and unauthorized parties using the mark.

Moreover, registration with the USPTO of a certification mark entitles the owner to use the federal registration symbol ® whenever the mark is used, thereby providing clear notice to the public and to competitors regarding the exclusive claim to the mark by the owner. Also, a USPTO registration allows the owner to record the registration with U.S. Customs and Border Protection, which will block infringing imports.

Trade Names

A trade name is the name by which a legal entity (such as a corporation) does business and is known to the public, its suppliers, its customers and its creditors. For companies, the trade name is usually the business name. For example, Aauvi® is a registered trademark of Aauvi Group, Inc. Aauvi is the trade name for Aauvi Group, Inc.

House Marks

A house mark can simply be a shortened mark derived from a company's trade name and frequently is used as an abbreviated way of representing the company's name in advertising literature, news releases, etc. For example, Aauvi House is the house mark of Aauvi House Publishing Group.

In addition, a house mark is frequently used in conjunction with other company trademarks. A house mark identifies the company or division that is the maker or seller of the product or offeror of a service. It can also be used to identify a particular grouping of products such as a product line. For example, Aauvi House offers books from several of its imprints (JNJ Publishing, Rags to Riches Entertainment, Pragmatic Press, etc.).

Design Marks

Logos are registrable trademarks. The word "logo" is a frequently used abbreviation for the world "logotype." A logotype is a unique graphical symbol which may appear in combination with, or consist entirely of, stylized letters which function much as a visual trademark for authenticating the origin of a company's products or services in advertising literature. The following is an example of the Aauvi House logo:

TRADEMARK INTELLIGENCE

Sound Marks

Sound can be granted trademark registration protection as long as it is distinctive, and not merely functional. For example, General Electric Broadcasting Co. applied to register "SM" for the source made by a ship's bell clock for a radio broadcasting station break. Registration was refused because GE failed to prove adequate secondary meaning. Nonetheless, sounds are not per se unregistrable. If it is a unique, distinctive, different or arbitrary sound, it can be registered without further evidence of secondary meaning.

Scent Marks

A scent can also be granted trademark registration as long as it is distinctive, and not merely functional. For example, *In re Clarke*, plaintiff tried to register yarn that had a distinctive floral fragrance. The USPTO refused registration claiming that the scent did not function as a registrable trademark because it did not identify or distinguish plaintiff's goods from those of others. Here, plaintiff proved secondary meaning by advertising nationwide as the source of sweet, scented embroidery products – also, a unique nature of the product. Subsequently, plaintiff has the registration only for this particular scent in connection with the yarn, not all scented yarn.

Supplemental Register

The Supplemental Register is a secondary trademark register for the USPTO. It allows for registration of certain marks that are not eligible for registration on the Principal Register, but are capable of distinguishing an applicant's goods or services. Marks registered on the Supplemental Register receive protection from conflicting marks and other protections, but are excluded from receiving the advantages of certain sections of the Trademark Act. The excluded sections are listed in 15 U.S.C. Section 1094.

If the applicant seeks registration on the Supplemental Register, the application should state that registration is requested on the Supplemental Register. If no register is specified, the USPTO will presume that the applicant seeks registration on the Principal Register. To register a mark on the Supplemental Register, applicants must either be using the mark or filing under Trademark Act Section 44 based on a foreign registration.

Slogans

Slogans are registrable on the Supplemental Register. That is, a slogan can be registered and protected if it functions to identify and distinguish the registered trademark owner's goods or services from those of others. A slogan must be distinctive. If merely descriptive, the slogan must have acquired a secondary meeting to be protected. A slogan's length is relevant to its ability to act as a registered trademark. For example, longer slogans are harder to understand when read casually and without careful study or diminishes the uniqueness and distinctiveness of the phrase which are essential to its function.

Surnames

Surnames are registrable on the Supplemental Register. That is, a surname can be registered and protected if it has acquired, through usage a secondary meaning. If a surname is registered and someone else wishes to register their surname, the courts must apply a balancing test: (i) rights of the first user against second user who wishes in good faith to use his or her family name; (ii) to avoid confusion, one may add initial or first name to surname or disclaimer to registered trademark; (iii) if secondary user in bad faith (riding on coattails), then registration will be denied; and (iv) court will also weigh personal property right for oneself to use his or her name in business against the public's right to be free from any confusion resulting from the concurrent use of similar names.

Corporate Identity

A business's trademarks and service marks are visible emblems of the company's "corporate identity" and, when viewed, should bring to mind that corporate style, product quality, technology leadership, management character and even corporate personality that make the company such a distinct entity in its industry. Because the corporate identity plays such a crucial role in reinforcing the recognition of (and preference for) the company's products and services, the company's trademarks and service marks provide an increasingly powerful sales tool in the commercial marketplace. To protect the value of these marks, they must be used correctly. In fact, the use of these marks in advertisements, corporate press releases, and technical papers and even in newspaper or magazine articles can either strengthen the validity of a company's marks – or help destroy them.

Thus, your company's trademarks or service marks are important and valuable corporate assets and, as such, should be treated and used with care. To preserve the company's rights in its trademarks or service marks all company marks must be used properly and consistently. If the rules of proper trademark or service mark usage are not observed, the marks could be weakened or lost. By contrast, through correct usage, the value and strength of your company's marks will actually increase with time.

Trade Dress

Trade dress falls under the umbrella of corporate identity. Trade dress is the total image of a product, the overall impression created, not the individual features. Test for trade dress protection include: (i) acquired secondary meaning; (ii) feature is non-functional; and (iii) consumers are likely to confuse the owner's product with the infringer's product. For example, a registered trademark may consist of a color pattern if the pattern is distinctive, rather than functional or merely ornamental; also, color may be registered if acquired secondary meaning. Thereafter, use of color so as to cause confusion as to goods or services source may be unfair competition.

Consequently, there are a limited number of colors in the universe. To permit one, or a few producers to use colors as registered trademarks would deplete the supply of usable colors to the point where competitor's inability to find a suitable color will put that competitor at a significant disadvantage. Courts argue doctrine of functionality would prevent this from happening. Color can be protected if it is linked in the public's mind as a particular product with a source.

CHAPTER 2

OVERVIEW OF TRADEMARK LAW

A trademark or service mark is different from a patent or a copyright. A patent is a limited duration property right relating to an invention, also granted by the USPTO in exchange for public disclosure of the invention. A copyright protects works of authorship, such as writings, music, and works of art that have been tangibly expressed. Unlike patents and trademarks, copyrights are registered through the U.S. Copyright Office, a division of the Library of Congress.

Establishing Trademark Rights

Trademark rights arise from either (1) actual use of the mark, or (2) the filing of a proper application to register a mark in the USPTO stating that the applicant has a bona fide intention to use the mark in commerce regulated by the U.S. Congress. Federal registration is not required to establish rights in a mark, nor is it required to begin use of a mark. However, federal registration can secure benefits beyond the rights acquired by merely using a mark. For example, the owner of a federal registration is presumed to be the owner of the mark for the goods and services specified in the registration, and to be entitled to use the mark nationwide.

There are two related but distinct types of rights in a mark: the right to register and the right to use. Generally, the first party who either uses a mark in commerce or files an application in the USPTO has the ultimate right to register that mark. The USPTO's authority is limited to determining the right to register. The right to use a mark can be more complicated to determine. This is particularly true when two parties have begun use of the same or similar marks without knowledge of one another and neither has a federal registration. Only a court can render a decision about the right to use, such as issuing an injunction or awarding damages for infringement. It should be noted that a federal registration can provide significant advantages to a party involved in a court proceeding. The USPTO cannot provide advice concerning rights in a mark. Only a private attorney can provide such advice.

Unlike copyrights or patents, trademark rights can last indefinitely if the owner continues to use the mark to identify its goods or services. The term of a federal trademark registration is ten years, with ten-year renewal terms from the grant date of registration. However, between the fifth and sixth year after the date of initial registration, the registrant must file an affidavit setting forth certain information to keep the registration alive. If no affidavit is filed, the registration is canceled.

Laws & Rules Governing Federal Registration

The federal registration of trademarks is governed by the Trademark Act of 1946, as amended, 15 U.S.C. Section 1051 et seq.; the Trademark Rules, 37 C.F.R. Part 2; and the Trademark Manual of Examining Procedure.

Types of Applications for Federal Registration

An applicant may apply for federal registration in three principal ways. (1) An applicant who has already commenced using a mark in commerce may file based on that use (a "use" application). (2) An applicant who has not yet used the mark may apply based on a bona fide intention to use the mark in commerce (an "intent-to-use" application). For the purpose of obtaining federal registration, commerce means all commerce, which may lawfully be regulated by the U.S. Congress, for example, interstate commerce or commerce between the U.S. and another country. The use in commerce must be a bona fide use in the ordinary course of trade, and not made merely to reserve a right in a mark.

Use of a mark in promotion or advertising before the product or service is actually provided under the mark on a normal commercial scale does not qualify as use in commerce. Use of a mark in purely local commerce within a state does not qualify as "use in commerce". If an applicant files based on a bona fide intention to use in commerce, the applicant will have to use the mark in commerce and submit an allegation of use to the USPTO before the USPTO will register the mark. Additionally, under certain international agreements, an applicant from outside the United States may file in the United States based on an application or registration in another country.

A United States registration provides protection only in the United States and its territories. If the owner of a mark wishes to protect a mark in other countries, the owner must seek protection in each country separately under the relevant

TRADEMARK PROTECTION AND PROSECUTION

laws. The USPTO cannot provide information or advice concerning protection in other countries.

Other Types of Applications

In addition to trademarks and service marks, the Trademark Act provides for federal registration of other types of marks, such as certification marks, collective trademarks and service marks, and collective membership marks. These types of marks are relatively rare. For forms and information regarding the registration of these marks, contact the USPTO or an attorney.

Use of the "TM," "SM" and "®" Symbols

Anyone who claims rights in a mark may use the ™ (trademark) or ˢᴹ (service mark) designation with the mark to alert the public to the claim. It is not necessary to have a registration, or even a pending application, to use these designations. The claim may or may not be valid. The registration symbol, ®, may only be used when the mark is registered in the USPTO. It is improper to use this symbol at any point before the registration issues. As a practical matter, omit all symbols from the mark in the drawing you submit with your application; these symbols are not considered part of the mark.

Who May File an Application?

The application must be filed in the name of the owner of the mark, usually an individual, corporation or partnership. The owner of a mark controls the nature and quality of the goods or services identified by the mark. The owner may submit and prosecute its own application for registration, or may be represented by an attorney. The USPTO cannot help you select an attorney.

The question of whether an application may be filed in the name of a minor depends on your state's law. If the minor may validly enter into binding legal obligations, and may sue or be sued, in the state in which he or she is domiciled, the application may be filed in the name of the minor. Otherwise, the application must be filed in the name of a parent or legal guardian, clearly setting forth his or her status as a parent or legal guardian. An example of the manner in which the applicant should be identified in such cases is: "John Smith, United States citizen, (parent/legal guardian) of Mary Smith."

Foreign Applicants

Applicants not living in the United States must designate in writing the name and address of domestic representative – a person residing in the United States "upon whom notices of process may be served for proceedings affecting the mark." The applicant may do so by submitting a statement that the named person at the address indicated is appointed as the applicant's domestic representative under Section 1(e) of the Trademark Act. The applicant must sign in this statement. This person will receive all communications from the USPTO unless an attorney in the United States represents the applicant.

If you have dual citizenship, then you must indicate which citizenship will be printed on the Certificate of Registration.

Searches for Conflicting Marks

An applicant is not required to conduct a search for conflicting marks prior to applying with the USPTO. However, it is advisable to conduct a search before filing your application. In evaluating an application, an examining attorney conducts a search and notifies the applicant if a conflicting mark is found. The application fee, which covers processing and search costs, will not be refunded even if a conflict is found and the mark cannot be registered.

To determine whether there is a conflict between two marks, the USPTO determines whether there would be likelihood of confusion, that is, whether relevant consumers would be likely to associate the goods or services of one party with those of the other party as a result of the use of the marks at issue by both parties. The principal factors to be considered in reaching this decision are the similarity of the marks and the commercial relationship between the goods and services identified by the marks. To find a conflict, the marks need not be identical, and the goods and services do not have to be the same.

The USPTO does not conduct searches for the public to determine if a conflicting mark is registered, or is the subject of a pending application, except as noted above when acting on an application. However, there are a variety of ways to get the same type of information. First, you may search the USPTO's Trademark Electronic Search System (TESS) database free of charge before filing. Second, you may wish to hire a private trademark search company, or an attorney who deals with trademark law to perform the search and assess the results for you. Alternatively, you can search the database at a Patent and Trademark Resource Center (PTRC). The USPTO cannot provide advice about possible conflicts between marks.

TRADEMARK PROTECTION AND PROSECUTION

Where to Send the Application and Correspondence

If not filing online with the USPTO and using the United States Postal Service, the application and all other correspondence should be addressed to:

>Commissioner for Trademarks
>P.O. Box 1451
>Arlington, Virginia 22313-1451

If using other delivery services such as Federal Express, United Parcel Service, and DHL, the application and all other correspondence should be addressed to:

>Trademark Assistance Center
>Madison East
>Concourse Level Room C 55
>600 Dulany Street
>Alexandria, VA 22314

The applicant should indicate its telephone number on the application form. Once a serial number is assigned to the application, the applicant should refer to the serial number in all written and telephone communications concerning the application.

It is advisable to submit a stamped, self-addressed postcard with the application specifically listing each item in the mailing, that is, the written application, the drawing, the fee, and the specimens (if appropriate). The USPTO will stamp the filing date and serial number of the application on the postcard to acknowledge receipt. This will help the applicant if any item is later lost or if the applicant wishes to inquire about the application. The USPTO will send a separate official notification of the filing date and serial number for every application about two months after receipt.

OVERVIEW OF TRADEMARK LAW

SAMPLE PATENT OR TRADEMARK POSTCARD

Express Mail No. _____	First Class Mail ( )
Date Mailed _____	
Serial No. _____	Filed _____
Inventor _____	
For _____	

( ) Affidavit/Declaration	( ) Fee Address Indication Form
( ) Amendment ( ) Response	( ) Fee Calculation
( ) Application ___ pages	( ) Issue Fee Transmittal
( ) ___ claims ___ drawing sheets	( ) Notice of Appeal
( ) Assignment ( ) Cover Sheet	( ) Oral Hearing Request/Confirm
( ) Brief (in triplicate)	( ) Petition to Extend Time ___ months(s)
( ) Declaration & Power of Attorney	( ) Petition under 27 C.F.R. ___
( ) Executed ( ) Unexecuted ( ) Copy	( ) Power of Attorney
( ) Declaration of Inventor(s)	( ) by Assignee ( ) Associate ( ) with Revocation
( ) Executed ( ) Unexecuted ( ) Copy	( ) Request for Correction of Filing Receipt
( ) Design Application	( ) Sequence Listing w/Computer Readable and Paper Copy
( ) Disclaimer ( ) Disclaimer Fee	( ) Small Entity Status
( ) Disclosure Statement ( ) Form PTO-1449	( ) Status Letter
( ) w/refs. ( ) w/o refs.	( ) Transmittal Letter
( ) Drawings, Formal	
Sheets ___ Figures ___	

Other: _____

File No. _____ Sender: _____

The Registration Process

Filing Date – Filing Receipt

The USPTO is responsible for the federal registration of trademarks. When an application is received, the USPTO reviews it to determine if it meets the minimum requirements for receiving a filing date. If the application meets the filing requirements, the USPTO assigns it a serial number and sends the applicant a receipt about two months after filing. If the minimum requirements are not met, the entire mailing, including the filing fee, is returned to the applicant.

Examination

About four months after filing, an examining attorney at the USPTO reviews the application and determines whether the mark may be registered. If the examining attorney determines that the mark cannot be registered, the examining attorney will issue a letter (called an "Office Action") listing any grounds for refusal and any corrections required in the application. The examining attorney may also contact the applicant by telephone if only minor corrections are required. The applicant must respond to any objections within six months of the mailing date of the Office Action, or the application will be abandoned. If the applicant's response does not overcome all objections, the examining attorney will issue a final refusal. The applicant may then appeal to the Trademark Trial and Appeal Board, an administrative tribunal within the USPTO.

A common ground for refusal is likelihood of confusion between the applicant's mark and a registered mark. Marks that are merely descriptive in relation to the applicant's goods or services, or a feature of the goods or services may also be refused. Marks consisting of geographic terms or surnames may also be refused. Marks may be refused for other reasons as well.

Publication for Opposition

If there are no objections, or if the applicant overcomes all objections, the examining attorney will approve the mark for publication in the Official Gazette, a weekly publication of the USPTO. The USPTO will send a Notice of Publication to the applicant indicating the date of publication. In the case of two or more applications for similar marks, the USPTO will publish the application with the earliest effective filing date first. Any party who believes it may be damaged by the registration of the mark has thirty days from the date of publication to file an opposition to registration. An opposition is similar to a formal proceeding in the federal courts, but is held before the Trademark Trial and Appeal Board. If no opposition is filed, the application enters the next stage of the registration process.

Certificate of Registration or Notice of Allowance

If the application was based upon the actual use of the mark in commerce prior to approval for publication, the USPTO will register the mark and issue a Certificate of Registration about twelve weeks after the date the mark was published, if no opposition was filed.

If, instead, the mark was published based upon the applicant's statement of having a bona fide intention to use the mark in commerce, the USPTO will issue a Notice of Allowance to either (1) use the mark in commerce and submit a Statement of Use, or (2) request a six-month Extension of Time to File a Statement of Use. The applicant may require additional extensions of time only as noted in the instructions on the back of the extension form. If the Statement of Use is filed and approved, the USPTO will then issue the Certificate of Registration.

OVERVIEW OF TRADEMARK LAW

Filing Requirements

Before completing an application, read the instructions carefully and study the examples provided. Errors or omissions may result in the denial of a filing date and the return of application papers, or the denial of registration and forfeiture of the filing fee. To receive a filing date, the applicant must provide all the of the following:

- ❖ Application form;
- ❖ A drawing of the mark on a separate piece of paper;
- ❖ The required filing fee; and
- ❖ If the application is filed based upon prior use of the mark in commerce, three specimens for each class of goods or services. The specimens may be identical, or they may be examples of three different uses showing the same mark.

Application Form

To apply for a trademark or service mark, or other type of mark an initial application form must be completed, choosing from the five application forms available:

1. Trademark/Servicemark Application, Principal Register;
2. Trademark/Servicemark Application, Supplemental Register;
3. Certification Mark Application, Principal Register;
4. Collective Membership Mark Application, Principal Register; or
5. Collective Trademark/Servicemark Application, Principal Register.

The application must be filed in English. A separate application must be filed for each mark the applicant wishes to register. Likewise, if the applicant wishes to register more than one version of the same mark, a separate application must be filed for each version. For line-by-line sample instructions for filling out a sample application form, see *Trademark Prosecution* chapter.

Drawing

The "drawing" is a clear image of the mark applicant seeks to register. The USPTO uses the drawing to upload the mark into the USPTO search database and to print the mark in the Official Gazette and on the registration certificate. There are two types of drawings: (1) standard character and (2) special form. For more information on the different types of drawings see *Trademark Prosecution* chapter.

TRADEMARK PROTECTION AND PROSECUTION

Filing Fee

Effective September 26, 2011 the USPTO published a lengthy fee schedule. The following fees are excerpts therefrom:

- Application for registration, per international class (paper filing) – $375

- Application for registration, per international class (electronic filing, TEAS application) – $325

- Filing a Statement of Use, per class – $100

- Filing a Request of a Six-month Extension of Time for Filing a Statement of Use, per class – $150

- Application for renewal, per class – $400

Visit the USPTO website for current and all fees.

Specimen

A specimen is a sample of how you actually use the mark in commerce on your goods or with your services. A specimen shows the mark as your purchasers encounter it in the marketplace (e.g., on your labels or on your website).

Filing Electronically

The USPTO's Trademark Electronic Application System (TEAS) allows you to fill out and file an application form online, paying by credit card, electronic funds transfer, or through an existing USPTO deposit account. TEAS can also be used to file other documents including a response to an examining attorney's Office Action, a change of address, an allegation of use, and post registration maintenance documents.

For example, file the application and all other documents electronically through the TEAS. Carefully review all documents before filing to make sure all issues have been addressed and all the necessary elements are included. Authorize email correspondence and promptly inform the USPTO through the TEAS of any change in correspondence address, including your email address. Then, check the status of your application every three- to four-months using the Trademark Applications and Registrations Retrieval (TARR) database. If the USPTO has taken any action, you may need to respond promptly. All USPTO actions are available for viewing using the Trademark Status and Document Retrieval (TSDR) database.

CHAPTER 3

TRADEMARK PROGRAM

As a further definition, in both a legal sense and according to the dictionary, a trademark can be defined as: word(s), name(s), acronym, slogan, graphical symbol, device or even a melody – or any combination of these elements – that have been adopted by a manufacturer, retailer or service provider for use in connection with its products or services to identify their origin and to differentiate them from the products or services of competitors.

Generally, trademarks that come quickly to mind do so largely as a result of the successful marketing efforts of their owners. For example, trademarks that are "acronyms" may include: IBM for International Business Machines, HP for Hewlett Packard or NCG for Northern California Graphics. On the other hand, trademarks that consist of "graphical symbols", for instance, might include: the rainbow-colored apple (with the bite taken out of it) for Apple Computer. Less obvious, but just as common in the consumer marketplace, are trademarks that are "devices" such as: the star and circle hood ornament (and even the radiator grill) of the Mercedes Benz or the distinctive hourglass shape of a Coca-Cola Coke bottle.

Another trademark subset is the "house mark" which is the mark that a company applies to the broad spectrum of its products and or services. "Aauvi®" is the Aauvi Group, Inc. house mark. Yet another distinct subset would be those marks expressed as graphical symbols or logotypes (often called "logos" for short). Logos are distinctive pictorial representations adopted by companies for quick visual identification of products, product literature, product packaging or even the letterhead on official stationery. The Aauvi logo is composed of an upside-down and right-side-up double A (the "AA") in broken circular formation with a horizontal bar inside the broken circle connecting the double-As (the "circle"). The following is an example of the Aauvi logo:

Weak and Strong Trademarks

The selection of new company trademarks is usually at the prerogative of your company's marketing, sales and product development personnel who tend to evaluate a potential mark by its suggestiveness, sound, uniqueness and customer appeal. However, the exercise of selecting a new trademark can turn into a legal nightmare if the implications of trademark law are not also a part of this selection criterion.

It is fundamental of trademark law that the first user of a particular trademark has "priority" over all others who might later seek to use that mark (or a confusingly similar mark) in conjunction with similar goods or services. Such a trademark – if any other company has never used it before – is said to be "unique". Unique marks are "strong" marks in the sense that (by definition) they will not cause consumer confusion in the marketplace. Unfortunately, unique trademarks are becoming increasingly rare as the catalog of marks in commercial use continues to grow.

Being the first to use a particular trademark is not an absolute guarantee of trademark strength. The actual meaning, form and content of the trademark itself will greatly affect its own legal viability. As a result, trademarks must be selected with an eye to their inherent distinctiveness. The courts have determined that the more "distinctive" a trademark is, the greater protection it will be given. The courts grant greater protection to distinct trademarks because distinct marks best serve the consuming public in making purchasing decisions and in avoiding marketplace confusion. Depending on their relative distinctiveness, trademarks will receive different degrees of protection ranging from the legally "unassailable" to the legally "unavailable".

For example, an improperly selected trademark may be unenforceable against subsequent users and may, in fact, be enjoined (prohibited from further use). Unfortunately, such legal entanglements usually surface only after considerable

TRADEMARK PROGRAM

financial and marketing effort has been invested in a selected trademark and only after the mark has begun to achieve wide customer recognition. Thus, one of the primary objectives of a company's trademark program is to provide a reasonably comprehensive review of trademark law so that your company and its employees considering the adoption of new trademarks will select both distinct and viable new marks.

The following is a hierarchy of the more commonly recognized categories of trademark distinctiveness arranged from the strongest marks to the weakest. Strong marks will receive a higher level of protection against potential infringement than will relatively weak marks. To the fullest extent possible (or commercially feasible), all company trademarks should be selected from within the strongest category available.

- **Fanciful Trademarks**. Fanciful trademarks are marks that in and of themselves have no meaning – either as words (in English or any other language), phonetic equivalents or as abbreviations. Fanciful trademarks are often called "coined" marks because they are created (or minted) without reference to a dictionary, textbook or any other source. Fanciful trademarks are the most distinctive and therefore the strongest possible marks and will be afforded the greatest legal protection. Examples of fanciful marks include: "Aauvi," "Starbucks," "Exxon," "Verizon," "Cingular" and "Kodak".

- **Arbitrary Trademarks**. Arbitrary trademarks are always protected without any proof of secondary meaning. Arbitrary trademarks are composed of words, phrases or abbreviations that may be found in commonly available sources such as dictionaries or textbooks and which have easily understood meanings. However, such meanings have no relationship to the products or services with which they are associated. Arbitrary trademarks are also considered by the courts to be distinctive marks and they will also receive extensive legal protection. Examples of arbitrary marks include: "Nickelodeon" for its definition as "an early movie theater charging an admission price of a nickel" has no direct relation to a cable television channel for children.

  "Apple" is another example of an arbitrary mark. Obviously, whether a mark is arbitrary or not depends upon its context. Whereas "Apple" as applied to computer products is arbitrary, if applied to a fruit grower that mark would be descriptive.

TRADEMARK PROTECTION AND PROSECUTION

❖ **Suggestive Trademarks.** Suggestive trademarks are entitled to registration with little to no proof of secondary meaning. Like the previously described arbitrary trademarks, suggestive trademarks are composed of words, phrases, abbreviations, etc. which have well defined meanings. However, unlike arbitrary trademarks, these meanings are considered to be at least indirectly descriptive (or "suggestive") of some feature of the product or service. But some exercise of the imagination is still required to mentally connect the mark to the product or service. Although suggestive marks are also accepted and enforced by the courts, they are more frequently subject to legal challenge by third parties.

Examples of suggestive marks include: "Greyhound" for bus services and "Jaguar" for automobiles, with both marks suggesting the speed of their products, both of which are used for transportation. Other examples include "Playboy" for a men's magazine focusing upon women, "7-Eleven" for a convenience store that was originally open from 7:00 a.m. to 11:00 p.m. and "Coppertone" is suggestive of suntan lotion.

❖ **Descriptive Trademarks.** Descriptive trademarks can be registered if secondary meaning is proved. Descriptive trademarks are composed of words, phrases, abbreviations, etc. that have specific meanings. However, unlike arbitrary or suggestive marks, these meanings describe some salient feature of the relevant product or service. Descriptive marks are considered to be weak and only become legally enforceable after years of use. Examples of such trademarks include: "Vision Center" for a business offering optical goods and services, "Oatnut" for bread containing oats and nuts and "Computerland" for a computer store.

❖ **Generic "Trademarks".** Generic trademarks occur when a trademark used to identify a single product is also used to identify a whole class of similar products. They are terms that have eventually become a part of the common vernacular to describe the very products that they once sought to distinguish. Thus, generic "trademarks" are the proverbial "bone yard" for once viable and even quite strong trademarks that were lost through neglect, misuse and/or abuse. Examples of generic marks include: "aspirin," "escalator," "milk," "trampoline" and "zipper".

TRADEMARK PROGRAM

Secondary Meaning

In order to establish secondary meaning, one must show that the primary significance of the term in the minds of the consuming public is the source, not the product. Factors relevant to determine secondary meaning include amount and manner of advertising, volume of sales, length and manner of use, direct consumer testimony, and consumer surveys. Ways to show secondary meaning include exclusive and continuous use for five years; collective evidence (any way) of the public's perception; and distinctive trade dress. On the other hand, you don't have evidentiary presumption when you have an unregistered mark. Also, mark will not be found to have secondary meaning if packaging is common, for instance, pillow-shaped package.

Properly Maintaining Trademarks

Assuming that your company has adopted trademarks that are both unique and distinctive, the best way to protect those marks is to use them – and that means both to use them widely and to use them wisely. In fact, probably the most common means by which trademarks can be lost are through lack of use (or "abandonment" in the parlance of trademark law) or through misuse. The loss of a trademark due to abandonment is easy to understand. The courts will not prevent the adoption of a mark by a subsequent user if the original user no longer utilizes the mark. However, the loss of a trademark through misuse is not quite so straightforward. Basically, a trademark will receive the widest possible protection from the courts if the mark is used in compliance with a few simple but hard-and-fast rules of proper usage. Rules of usage include:

- ❖ When a trademark is used in printed materials, always distinguish the mark in relation to other words in the body of the text. The objective of this rule is to emphasize the trademark so as to enhance its visibility. To this end, trademarks are frequently distinguished by being printed in capital letters within the text of a document or using the symbols "®" or "™" at the end of the mark.

- ❖ Always adhere strictly to the use of the correct form of a trademark. This rule should be followed whether the trademark is an acronym, a word, words, or a graphic design. Accordingly, verbal trademarks should not be modified by abbreviations, translations or connection (by a hyphen or otherwise) to other words or trademarks. All logos should be reproduced in strict compliance with the established graphical form and in the correct colors.

TRADEMARK PROTECTION AND PROSECUTION

❖ Always use the trademark as an uninflected (unaltered) adjective. In other words, a trademark should not be used as either a noun or a verb in a sentence. Nor should a trademark be made into a plural, a possessive, or otherwise modified. Thus, a trademark should be used only as an adjective that is followed by the "generic" noun best describing the product or service to which it refers.

A distinct trademark of long-standing and proper use is granted almost absolute legal protection. The key to proper trademark usage lies in "consistency". If a trademark is used consistently and correctly – with the same spelling and in the same grammatical format – that mark's strength will not be diluted and, in fact, will grow over time. By contrast, a descriptive or improperly used trademark is granted little if any protection. This result follows in large part from the value that a particular trademark has or can be expected to acquire in the consuming public's decision-making processes when evaluating competing products. It should be remembered that the object of the courts is to protect the consumer and not to protect the trademark itself.

Registration of Trademarks

In the United States, trademark rights are acquired from the moment marked products enter into the stream of commerce (i.e., are first sold). These "automatic" trademark rights are granted as "common law" rights – that is, they are not derived from statutory laws but are based on a long series of court decisions. Although these common law trademark rights do not require a formal act of trademark "registration" to become enforceable, the legal protection these marks will receive is much less certain and not nearly as broad as those secured via a state or federal registration of the mark. As a practical matter, federal registration of a trademark proves the best means of trademark protection available.

Federal protection of trademarks can only be achieved through the formal registration of a mark with the USPTO. Although federal trademark registration provides the trademark owner with many valuable rights, securing these rights is frequently a difficult, time-consuming and costly task. In large part, the difficulty in achieving federal trademark registration lies in the requirement that the USPTO carefully scrutinize trademark applications to determine each mark's uniqueness, distinctiveness and suitability for use in commerce. In fact, it has recently been estimated that over 80% of the applications filed for federal trademark registration are initially rejected by the USPTO. However, the proper selection of distinctive trademarks can greatly enhance the chances of achieving

TRADEMARK PROGRAM

a satisfactory and economical federal registration. As a rule, the greater the ingenuity and deliberation required associating the trademark with the product or service, the easier the task of registering that mark will be.

Federal trademark registration is initiated when a formal application and the requisite filing fee are submitted to the USPTO. Registration will be granted if the examiners in the USPTO determine that the trademark being applied for: (i) is not confusingly similar to an already registered trademark, (ii) is reasonably distinctive, and (iii) complies with certain specific statutory requirements as to content. The statutory content requirements prohibit the registration of trademarks that are: miss-descriptive, deceptive and scandalous or falsely suggest a connection to well-known persons or institutions.

As a matter of statutory procedure, before formally registering a trademark, the USPTO will publish the mark for "opposition". If the trademark remains unopposed during this opposition period (thirty days) by any persons or corporations who might object to its use, the mark will be "allowed" and entered in the "Principal Register" of the USPTO. Federal registration of a trademark is subsequently attained when the USPTO issues the trademark owner a "Certificate of Registration". The "Certificate of Registration" will grant the trademark owner the exclusive right to use the mark with respect to certain categories or classes of goods and services designated by the owner.

Identification of Goods and Services Manual

The Identification of Goods and Services Manual (ID Manual) lists identifications of goods and services and their respective classifications that the USPTO examining attorneys will accept without further inquiry if the specimens of record support the identification and classification. The listing is not exhaustive, but is intended to serve as a guide to both examining attorneys in acting on applications and to filers in preparing applications. Using language directly from the ID Manual helps avoid objections by examining attorneys concerning "indefinite" identifications of goods or services; however, applicants must assert actual use in commerce or a bona fide intent to use the mark in commerce for the goods or services specified. Therefore, even with a definite identification, examining attorneys may inquire as to whether the identification chosen accurately identifies the applicant's goods or services.

A failure to list the goods or services correctly with which you use your mark, or intend to use your mark, may prevent you from registering your mark; therefore, proper selection from the ID Manual is critical.

TRADEMARK PROTECTION AND PROSECUTION

Another resource is the International Schedule of Classes of Goods and Services. This is a listing, by class, of all of the headings for the international classes. It also identifies some of the most common items falling within the class, and includes explanatory notes indicating what the class specifically does and does not include. Note: Under U.S. Trademark law, class headings by themselves are not acceptable for registration purpose. The specific items of goods and or services must be listed.

Registers

A trademark that has been accepted by the USPTO for publication in the Principal Register will provide the owner with numerous legal advantages in preventing subsequent infringement of the mark. Among the more important advantages are:

- Federal registration puts all potential infringers on notice that the trademark has been claimed. Thus, the courts will not look favorably on an argument that a subsequent user (i.e., infringer) innocently adopted the mark.

- The mark is given a presumption of validity if later challenged in court. If the USPTO has accepted a mark for registration, arguments by others that the mark is overly "descriptive", etc. will not carry much weight.

- Registration entitles the owner to sue in the federal court system to protect the mark. Without prior federal registration, a trademark owner can only resort to state courts to enforce or preserve a mark and, as a general rule, the remedies available for trademark infringement in state courts are limited.

- Registration entitles the owner to recover lost profits, damages (treble damages if the infringement were determined to have been willful), the costs of litigation and even criminal penalties (where counterfeiting is proven).

- Registration enables the trademark owner to have the United States Customs stop the importation of goods bearing an infringing mark and to order such goods destroyed.

At the end of five years of unchallenged federal registration in the Principal Register, a registered trademark achieves legally "incontestable" status and is no longer subject to challenge by third parties. A registered trademark will remain protected for a term of ten years – provided that the owner offers the USPTO the occasional required proof of continued use. After the expiration of the initial ten-year registration period, registration may be repeatedly renewed for subsequent ten-year periods – for as long as the owner continues to use the mark.

Before 1988, federal registration of trademarks could only be applied for after the mark had been used in interstate commerce. Unfortunately, back then; if problems arose during the registration process, valuable time, energy and investment in an unregistrable mark might have already been wasted. Now, however, applications for federal registration can be filed with the USPTO before the mark has actually been used. Under these new "intent to use" registration provisions, a trademark owner can seek registration (and subsequent publication of opposition) prior to investing heavily in the marketing effort associated with a trademark that may ultimately be either unregistrable or strenuously opposed by one or more competitors. The "intent to use" registration procedure will reserve a trademark for up to three years before proof of actual use will be required to complete registration.

Registration of a trademark is also possible in the USPTO's Supplemental Register. Although registration in the Supplemental Register is more easily obtained from the USPTO because there is minimal review of the mark by the USPTO examiners, the ensuing legal protections are much less expansive than those afforded to marks appearing in the Principal Register.

The Proper Marking of Trademarks

As discussed earlier, a trademark owner gains certain "common law" rights to a mark commencing immediately upon first use of the mark. To enhance the enforceability of these common law trademark rights, and to put potential infringers on notice that the trademark has been claimed, an unregistered trademark should always be followed with the superscript "^{TM}". However, the use of this superscript is not required each and every time the mark is used throughout a printed publication. It is only a requirement that the superscript be used when the mark first appears within the body of the written text. Additionally, a clear annotation or footnote located in a convenient spot (following the text in a printed publication or in a lower corner of advertising literature) should specifically attribute ownership of the mark.

A federally registered trademark – and only a federally registered trademark – should be followed by the statutory trademark notice symbol "®". As with unregistered trademarks, the superscript need be used only with the trademark when first encountered in the body of the written text. Additionally, as with the common law superscript "®", a footnote should indicate that the trademark has been registered by the owner. Using the symbol "®" as a superscript with a trademark that is not listed on the Principal Register is a federal offense.

Accordingly, whenever a trademark is first encountered in the text of a document or wherever a mark used in isolation on product packaging or advertising literature, it should be followed by the appropriate superscript – the "TM" for unregistered marks or the "®" for registered marks. Additionally, a footnote, conveniently located somewhere on the document or in the text, should attribute the trademark to its owner. For example, if the registered trademark "AAUVI" were used in the text of a printed article, it would be written "AAUVI®" or "Aauvi®" when first used and be followed by a footnote to the effect that "Aauvi is a registered trademark of Aauvi Group, Inc."

International Trademark Registration

Each foreign country has its own set of trademark laws. These laws are frequently unique and perplexing and may be starkly different from our own. For example, while many countries are much stricter than the United States in refusing to register "descriptive" trademarks (e.g., Japan and Taiwan), some countries register all submitted marks without any review (e.g., France and Spain). While many foreign countries require neither the formal registration of trademarks nor the subsequent identification of registered trademarks (e.g., German and Belgium), some countries actually impose penalties for failure to identify registered marks (e.g., Mexico and Spain).

Additionally, many foreign countries require the identification of trademarks with symbols other than the "®" or "TM" superscript used in the United States. For example, in many Latin American countries the superscript indicating trademark registration is "MR" for "Marca Registrada" and use of the "®" is of no significance. Thus, for labels, packaging, advertising literature, etc. prepared for use in specific foreign countries, advice and clearance should be sought from attorneys specialized in intellectual property law before printing marketing materials using any company trademarks.

Trademark Program Implementation

The purpose of a trademark program is to set forth a series of easy to follow step-by-step, company procedures to be used in the selection and approval of new company trademarks. Such procedures should be established to provide company employees with a "road map" of the trademark application process in the selection of distinctive and registrable company trademarks. A good understanding and adherence to such procedures will help ensure that a company's trademarks are viable and distinct before submitting a trademark application to the USPTO.

The procedures discussed in this section should be followed by all businesses seeking to establish a new company trademark. For a number of legal reasons, unauthorized trademarks will not be acceptable as designated company trademarks. For example, failing to control the size of the company trademark portfolio by keeping a limit on the number and variety of official company trademarks is self-defeating. Hence, an overabundance of different trademarks, will weaken the mark impact of both old and new company trademarks. Additionally, improperly screened trademarks may become the target of expensive legal challenges.

Selecting New Trademarks

If the applicant in selecting a "candidate" trademark exercises a reasonable degree of care, the probability is good that the mark will successfully complete the company application cycle. Care in selecting a new trademark should focus on two overlapping areas of general concern – one area is the marketing appeal of the mark and the other area is the legal viability of the mark.

From a sales and marketing perspective, a trademark should be selected based on a number of business and grammatical criteria including:

- ❖ Being easy to read and pronounce.
- ❖ Being easy to remember.
- ❖ Not being confusingly similar to the marks of others.
- ❖ Having positive implications for the product.
- ❖ Being consistent with previously adopted company trademarks.

Special consideration should be given to choosing trademarks that fit with the company's already selected trademark styles or patterns. For example, new marks that start with an acronym or where the letters are given double use are favored because they can help reinforce the recognition of similar marks. Additionally, avoid contractions or combinations of pre-existing company marks when selecting trademarks. Such new trademarks are deemed to be "dilutive" of the older marks from which they are derived. Likewise, avoid the use of modifiers such as "…plus", "ultra…" or "mini…" etc. which are also dilutive of the marks to which they are affixed. Thus, potential trademarks such as "Aauvi-plus" or "ultra-Aauvi" are undesirable.

TRADEMARK PROTECTION AND PROSECUTION

A trademark should be selected only if it is both "unique" and "distinctive". Thus, the most desirable company trademarks are those that are not similar in sight, sound or meaning to any other company's marks – regardless of the products with which they are associated. Additionally, the most desirable trademarks are "coined" marks or marks that rank high on the so called "distinctiveness scale" as discussed earlier.

Trademark Application Form

After an appropriate "candidate" trademark has been selected, the next step in the trademark acquisition process is to complete an in-house trademark application form. Such application form should be drafted to elicit all the information needed to justify (and expedite) management approval of a new trademark.

SAMPLE INTERNAL NEW TRADEMARK APPLICATION FORM AND INSTRUCTIONS

New Trademark Application Form

Application number: _____

Date: _____

1. Trademark requested: _____

2. Alternative trademarks, if any: _____
(If a logo and/or distinctive print style are described, please illustrate on separate piece of paper and attached.)

3. Name of requestor: _____
   Title: _____ Department: _____
   Telephone: _____ Mail stop: _____

4. Reason for requesting this trademark: _____
   _____
   _____

5. Goods or services with which trademark will be used: _____
   _____
   _____

6. Date of anticipated first use of trademark: _____

7. Countries of intended trademark use: United States: ☐ Yes ☐ No
   Others: _____

TRADEMARK PROGRAM

8. Other comments or relevant information: _____

_____
_____
_____

9. Trademark illustration (from part 1.)

10. Signatures

Signature of requestor   Date

Signature of Vice President   Date

Trademark Committee: Trademark Search   ☐ Yes   ☐ No
                        U.S. Registration   ☐ Yes   ☐ No
                        Foreign Registration ☐ Yes   ☐ No

Instructions for Completing the Company Trademark Application Form

1. Carefully type or print the trademark being requested and list any alternate trademarks in exactly the style, form and spelling desired. Please pay special attention to the use of capital letters, spaces, hyphens, slashes, etc. If a logo and/or distinctive script are desired, an accurate pictorial representation should be made either on the space provided in the application form or on a separate blank sheet of paper which should be attached to the Application Form.

2. Fill in all the requestor contact information.

3. Briefly state the reasons for requesting this new trademark: such as, "to support marketing efforts for new product."

4. Identify the specific products or services with which the proposed trademark will be used. Also, give the anticipated date of first sale of the products or services (including date of first "beta site" shipments). This date will be important in

TRADEMARK PROTECTION AND PROSECUTION

> deciding whether or not to register the mark under the federal "intent to use" trademark registration provisions.
>
> 5. Indicate the countries into which the products or services will be marketed and/or sold in volume.
>
> 6. Provide any additional information concerning the new trademark that you feel is relevant, such as specifically recommending certain foreign registrations or pointing out a need for urgent action due to anticipated use of the mark by others.
>
> 7. Please sign and date the Application Form on its reverse side and have it approved and signed by your reporting Vice President.
>
> 8. Please submit the completed Application Form to your legal counsel. If you should have any questions concerning the completion of this form (or its status after submission) please call the intellectual property counsel for assistance.

The application form should be completed as accurately and comprehensively as possible because copies of the form are usually circulated among the members of a trademark committee for formal approval. Assuming some indeterminate lead time will be required before final authorization is received from the trademark committee – especially if a trademark search or federal "intent to use" registration is to be undertaken – the application form should be submitted at least sixty days prior to anticipated new product introductions. Keep in mind, if a "candidate" trademark is found to be unregistrable due to prior use or disapproved on other grounds, then time must be allowed to repeat the trademark approval cycle before the new product is launched.

To expedite the approval of a product or service-related trademark, the applicant should also consider listing one or two alternate marks in the space provided in the application form. Because the outcome of a trademark search is essentially unpredictable, the creator of the mark should not become too attached to his or her initial mark. Consider there are already hundreds of thousands of trademarks registered at the federal level. Additionally, many hundreds of thousands of marks are already claimed as common law trademarks. Thus, the chances of picking an "unused" trademark on the first shot are not particularly good.

This same application form should be used when selecting names for company subsidiary businesses. Although not strictly speaking, corporate name trademarks are subject to many of the same legal and business requirements to be considered with approving company trademarks. The application form should also be used when seeking additional foreign registrations or expanded U.S. registrations for pre-existing company trademarks. The application form should also be used to formally "de-select" or "abandon" pre-existing marks no longer in use by the company.

Trademark Committee

As part of the trademark program, the company should establish and in-house trademark committee. After the New Trademark Application Form has been completed it should be delivered to your legal counsel. There it will be reviewed for completeness and circulated among the members of the company's trademark committee. The trademark committee should be composed of three or four senior managers, including representatives of the company's domestic and foreign sales and marketing team and the company's intellectual property counsel. The trademark committee is charged with evaluating trademark applications from a business, marketing and legal perspective.

The members of the trademark committee should examine "candidate" trademarks to confirm that they are acceptable from a company marketing perspective, are consistent with other marks already in the company trademark portfolio and conform to general legal guidelines. If a mark is found to provide value to the marketing effort and justify the expense, the trademark committee should usually authorize a formal trademark search to ascertain whether there are any prior users of the mark. A trademark search can cost more than five hundred dollars and require up to two weeks to complete. The interpretation (and evaluation) of the results of a trademark search may require the exercise of a good degree of subjective judgment. If the search results are not clear, the creator of the new trademark should be contacted directly by the intellectual property counsel for an assessment of the relative risks to be encountered if the mark were to be adopted.

The trademark committee should also perform a cost-benefit analysis of any trademarks for which U.S. and or foreign registrations are requested. Because the costs involved in registering a U.S. trademark can exceed hundreds and even thousands of dollars (per subject matter classification) and the cost of merely filing an application for foreign registration can exceed a similar amount (per subject matter classification), the committee may elect to forego initial registration of the mark. If the trademark committee authorizes a U.S. or foreign registration of a trademark, it should also determine under which product classifications the marks will be registered (i.e., mobile applications, mobile systems, services, etc.). If a mark is not deemed suitable for immediate registration (or to be unregistrable for some reason), the trademark committee may nonetheless authorize the mark for inclusion in the company's trademark portfolio where it should be maintained as an unregistered mark to be used with the "TM" superscript.

Trademark Status Reports

A trademark status report should provide a complete listing of all of a company's trademarks as of its effective date. The trademark listing should include those company trademarks registered in the United States, those marks claimed as trademarks in the United States, and those marks registered throughout the world. The status report should be the "official" compilation of a company's trademarks. If a mark does not appear on the list, it should not be considered as a company's trademark. To add trademarks to the list, the trademark application procedures set forth earlier should be initiated.

Only those trademarks specifically designated as having been registered in the United States should be denoted with the symbol "®". All other claimed company trademarks should be denoted with the symbol "TM". Foreign jurisdictions use a number of different superscripts/symbols to denote registration and legal counsel should be contacted prior to use of registered marks in these countries to determine the correct trademark superscript/symbol to be used.

It is important to note that the trademarks set forth in a status report appear exactly in the form that they should appear in print. For example, "IBM" should never be used as "I.B.M." or "Ibm" or "ibm" when being used as the corporate trade name. If a trademark uses upper and lowercase letters, then only those upper and lowercase letters should be used when referencing the trademark. Likewise, the Aauvi numerical trademarks should appear just as listed and not modified. For example, in the case of the "AGI5000" trademark, it is improper to use: "AGI 5000", "AGI-5000", etc.

The status report should be updated each calendar quarter and distributed internally accordingly.

TRADEMARK PROGRAM

SAMPLE INTERNAL TRADEMARK STATUS REPORT

Quarterly Trademark Status Report		02/01/2021	
1. Trademarks registered in the United States, which should be used with a symbol "®":			
1.1 Aauvi			
2. Trademarks claimed in the United States, which should be used with a symbol "TM":			
2.1 Aauvi Group-based Trademarks:			
	AGI	AauviGroup	
	Aauvicom	MacAauvi	
2.2 Aauvi House-based Trademarks			
	Aauvi House	FHPG	JNJPG	R2R
	AHPG	JNJ	R2Rentertainment	R2RPG
2.3 Aauvi Numerical Trademarks:			
	Aauvi5000		
3. Trademarks registered in foreign jurisdictions, which should be used with a local registration mark:			
3.1 Argentina: None			
3.2 Canada: None			
3.3 China: None			
3.4 France: None			
3.5 Germany: None			
3.6 Greece: None			
3.7 Hong Kong: None			
3.8 Ireland: None			
3.9 Italy: None			
3.10 Japan: None			
3.11 Philippines: None			
3.12 South Korea: None			
3.13 Spain: None			

TRADEMARK PROTECTION AND PROSECUTION

3.14 Switzerland: None
3.15 Taiwan: None

Conclusion

In summary, the primary purpose of a company's trademark program is to ensure the acquisition and protection of company trademarks. Your company has already invested considerable financial resources in enhancing the visibility and "goodwill" associated with its existing trademarks. The guidelines for trademark usage that follow will serve to encourage correct trademark usage and to facilitate uniformity in trademark use throughout the company. Additionally, the guidelines for trademark selection herein are intended to assure the selection of strong new trademarks. It is essential that such guidelines be observed since your company's existing trademarks can easily be lost through misuse and new marks must be legally viable if they are to survive.

Your company has or should have developed a valuable portfolio of distinctive trademarks, including potentially extensive registrations of some or many of your company's trademarks throughout the world. The protection and preservation of your trademarks requires vigilance on the part of each and every employee. You must all remain alert to any perceived misuse – either within the company or by others – of your company's trademarks. To that end, if any employee becomes aware of a possible incorrect or unauthorized use of your company's trademark, or the use of a mark confusingly similar to a company's trademark, your legal counsel should be notified immediately. Only by remaining vigilant can you ensure that your company trademarks will retain their value – both for you and for your customers.

Of course, in the day-to-day business affairs of a company, trademark issues or problems may arise which were neither envisioned nor covered herein. In these instances, please contact an intellectual property attorney directly. The attorney should work diligently to assist you in resolving any trademark issues that may arise.

CHAPTER 4

TRADEMARK PROTECTIONS

The incorrect use of a company trademark may result in the loss of that mark by rendering it unenforceable against infringers. To avoid the loss of company trademarks, the rules of trademark usage set forth in this section will be briefly reiterated by focusing on specific 3Com trademarks. 3Com Corporation, one of the undisputed leaders of the highly competitive computer networking industry, has invested significant time and resources to protect and promote its trademarks and service marks, equating them with the same high standards of quality that distinguish the 3Com product line.

While trademarks are important for establishing and protecting corporate and product identity, they are fragile rights that can be lost through misuse. Trademarks must be used properly and consistently, otherwise the trademark risks become generic, making the mark impossible to enforce (as happened with aspirin, cellophane, zipper and many others).

Trademarks on the Web

Given that the Internet is a highly visible medium in much of the world, it's vital that your company trademarks are treated according to trademark guidelines. Since the courts look to these Web sites to determine how a company treats their trademarks, proper usage is essential. For instance, you should treat each web page or article as if it will be read independently. That is, attribute trademarks on the first prominent reference, typically the headline, as well as the first occurrence in copy, per web page. For example, if you are posting 3Com trademarks on a Web site other than 3Com's, your section should include a trademark block attributing the 3Com marks referenced in your document, or it should include a link, which attributes all 3Com trademarks.

TRADEMARK PROTECTION AND PROSECUTION

Global Registration of Trademarks

It is 3Com's policy to register its trademarks throughout the world, when appropriate, to maximize control over the use of their trademarks and to prevent unauthorized use by third parties. Similarly, your company will need to decide where you will register your own company trademarks.

Trademark Usage Guidelines

Apply the following general trademark rules to all company trademarks:

- ❖ **Never use the trademark in a fashion that risks making the term "generic."** In order to protect a trademark by law, you must use it appropriately. An infamous example of a trademark that became generic through inappropriate use was Bayer Corporation's former trademark, "aspirin." Since the trademark "aspirin" was consistently used without the proper noun "pain reliever" following it, "aspirin" became the generic term for "pain reliever" and, therefore, became unprotectable by law.

- ❖ **Always use trademarks as adjectives, followed by an appropriate descriptive noun.** Trademarks used as nouns risk becoming generic, sacrificing the trademark status. For example, "The Palm VII™ organizer uses a fast, wireless connection to allow you to easily make electronic transactions" is correct usage. However, "The Palm VII™ uses a fast, wireless connection to allow you to easily make electronic transactions" is incorrect usage.

- ❖ **Attribute each trademark with its appropriate symbol at least once in each piece.** The appropriate trademark symbol must appear on the first prominent reference, typically a headline, and again on first reference in body copy. It's not necessary to repeat the designation throughout the rest of the document. However, do attribute trademarks on first occurrence within sidebars, charts, tables, graphs and slides, since these elements have greater potential to be read or placed independently.

- ❖ **How to incorporate Trademark Symbols into Documents.** See the following table to locate ™ and ® symbols on your keyboard or menu options for the software application listed. If you use a different application, check the user manual or the onscreen Help menu (if available) for information regarding trademark symbols. Always superscript the symbols using the appropriate command. If the

TRADEMARK PROTECTIONS

formatted ™ and ® symbols aren't available to you, simply use parentheses to denote the trademark designation: (TM) or (R).

Software Application	™	®
Microsoft Word for Apple Macintosh	Hold the option key while typing "2"	Hold the option key while typing "r"
Microsoft Word for PC/Windows	Go to the insert pull-down menu and choose Symbol; select ™ from the table and click insert	Go to the insert pull-down menu and choose Symbol; select ® from the table and click insert
HTML	&#153;	&#174;

❖ **Be consistent and always use trademarks and brand names in the ways they were intended to be used.** Use a trademark only in the form in which it has been registered or is being claimed. It's important that all parties involved in developing communications tools be consistent in their use of trademarks.

To maintain the integrity of a trademark, never use in a possessive, plural, hyphenated, or abbreviated form, and never alter by adding letters or numbers. Always use the proper spelling, punctuation, capitalization, or format, such as italics or boldface.

❖ **Never use trademarks as possessives.** For example, "The Palm IIIx™ organizer's shirt pocket size is a great selling feature" is proper usage. However, "The Palm IIIx's™ shirt pocket size is a great selling feature" is incorrect usage.

❖ **Never use trademarks in a plural form.** For example, "Use the HomeConnect™ solutions for your networking needs" is proper usage. However, "Use the HomeConnects™ solutions for your networking needs" is incorrect usage.

❖ **Never hyphenate a trademark.** For example, "Enhanced HotSync® technology enables remote synchronization" is correct usage. However, "Enhanced HotSync®-enabled systems can synchronize remotely" is incorrect usage.

❖ **Never alter a trademark.** For example, "use an EtherLink® network interface card in your computer" is correct usage. However, "EtherLinkize® your computer" is incorrect usage.

TRADEMARK PROTECTION AND PROSECUTION

- **Always use the proper capitalization of a trademark.** For example, "AirConnect™ wireless PC Card" is correct usage. However, "Airconnect™ wireless PC Card" is incorrect usage.

- **Never abbreviate a trademark in such a way that the noun is left out.** For example, "Palm V™ connected organizer" is correct usage. However, "Palm V™" is incorrect usage.

- **Always use lowercase letters for the generic noun following the trademark.** For example, "Bigpicture® video phone" is correct usage. However, "Bigpicture® Video Phone" is incorrect usage.

- **Avoid putting descriptions between a trademark and its noun.** For example, 8-slot or 4-slot NETBuilder II® system" is correct usage. However, "NETBuilder II® 8-slot or 4-slot system" is incorrect usage.

- **Always attribute the ™ or ® correctly.** For example, "U.S. Robotics® modem" is correct usage. However, "U.S. Robotics modem®" is incorrect usage.

- **Differentiate a trademark (brand name) from the company trade name.** For example, "3Com" can be used as a trademark (brand name) or a trade name, which is the name of a company used to identify the company rather than its products or services. In this instance, you would use the ® trademark symbol when using "3Com" as a trademark or brand name. For example, "XYZ company announces the purchase of new 3Com® servers" (trademark and brand name).

  Never use the ® trademark symbol when using "3Com" as part of the legal corporate name. For example, "3Com® Corporation" is incorrect usage. 3Com Corporation is correct usage.

Trademark Legend

Always use a trademark attribution line, also called a legend or acknowledgement. For example, if your material contains references to 3Com, U.S. Robotics, PathBuilder, and other products, the acknowledgment line should read:

> Copyright © 1999 3Com Corporation. All rights reserved. 3Com, the 3Com logo, Megahertz, and U.S. Robotics are registered trademarks and FDDLink, More connected. and PathBuilder are trademarks of 3Com Corporation. All other

TRADEMARK PROTECTIONS

company and product names may be trademarks of their respective companies.

Third-Party Trademarks

Every company should respect all third-party trademarks. If you use another company's trademark, it's not necessary to use the trademark symbol within the text unless a specific contract dictates otherwise. However, always attribute the specific owner in the attribution section at the end of the document. For example, "Windows is a registered trademark of Microsoft Corporation." Always follow with a generic umbrella statement if applicable, for example, "All other company and product names may be trademarks of their respective companies."

Logos and Taglines

Existing logos should always be reproduced from an electronic template or logo stat sheet, which dictates the placement of the trademark symbol. For example, treat the 3Com "More connected.™" tagline as a complete thought. Use the tagline to emphasize a point, but avoid incorporating the phrase into common, everyday usage. In short:

- Do not italicize the words, More connected
- Use an uppercase "M" and a lowercase "c"
- Use a period after "connected"
- Use a ™ symbol after the period
- Do not use within a sentence as this is a tagline
- Always remember to attribute in the legal attribution line
- Use periods as opposed to hyphens, i.e., 3Com. More connected.™ Not, 3Com-More connected.™

For example, "3Com connects more businesses and people to information and resources in more ways than any other networking company" is correct usage. Another example, "For large enterprises, small to mid-size companies, providers, and individual users around the globe, 3Com means connectivity. 3Com. More connected.™" is also correct usage. However, "3Com builds more connected solutions for its customers" is incorrect usage. Another example, "We recognize the needs of businesses as they move to the more connected networks of the future" is also incorrect usage.

TRADEMARK PROTECTION AND PROSECUTION

Examples of Proper Usage

The following examples of proper usage are again based on the 3Com Corporation trademarks. However, any company investing in trademarks and branding should do the same for their trademark portfolio.

Incorrect	Rule	Correct
Configurations using 3-Com-based products.	Never hyphenate a trademark.	Configurations using 3Com® products.
Widgeteer software is compatible with the Palm V.™	Always use a generic noun with a trademark.	Widgeteer software is compatible with the Palm V™ connected organizer.
3Com® Corporation announces a new U.S. Robotics® modem.	Never use a symbol when using "3Com" as part of the legal corporate name.	3Com Corporation announces a new U.S. Robotics® modem.
XYZ company announces the purchase of new 3Com servers.	Use a trademark symbol when using "3Com" as a brand name. If you can mentally use "brand" after 3Com, you are using the name as a brand name as opposed to using it as the company name.	XYZ company announces the purchase of new 3Com® servers.
You can access the dynamic infrared beaming feature on the Palm IIIs™.	Never use trademarks in a plural form.	You can access the dynamic infrared beaming feature on the Palm III™ organizers.
3Com announces its award-winning CoreBuilder® High-Function Switch for LAN routing.	Don't capitalize the generic noun, as the emphasis should be placed on the brand, not the noun.	3Com announces its award-winning CoreBuilder® high-function switch for LAN routing.
The Impact® IQ modem is easier to install than the xyz modem.	Never abbreviate a trademark as it must be used consistently in the way it was intended to be used.	The 3ComImpact® IQ modem is easier to install than the xyz modem.
Hotsyncing your data ensures a two-way data exchange between your PC and the product.	Never alter a trademark (a trademark is never a verb).	Synchronization, using HotSync® technology, allows two-way data exchange between your PC…
Use a Megahertz PC Card modem.	Use a trademark symbol on first reference.	Use a Megahertz® PC Card modem.
The PathBuilder's key selling feature is…	Never use trademarks as possessives.	The PathBuilder™ platform's key selling feature is…
TNM software.	Never turn a trademark into an acronym. Not only does the acronym dilute the brand, it could be another company's registered trademark.	Transcend® network management software.

TRADEMARK PROTECTIONS

The new OfficeConnect® delivers flexible, high-speed solutions for small offices.	Never use a trademark as the noun or 3Com risks losing the trademark.	New OfficeConnect® switches deliver flexible, high-speed solutions for small offices.
The magazine cited the U.S. robtoics® modem as the best.	Always use the proper capitalization of a trademark.	The magazine cited the U.S. Robotics® modem as the best.
PACE-enabled® network interface cards enhance…	Never use a hyphen in conjunction with a trademark.	Network interface cards with PACE® technology enhance…
The SuperStack II NETBuilder® router is price competitive.	When compound trademark uses occur, apply the appropriate trademark symbol ™ or ® to both trademarks.	The SuperStack® II NETBuilder® router is price competitive.
Transcend Networking® framework.	Place symbols correctly. "Networking" is not part of the registered trademark.	Transcend® networking framework.
CoreBuilder® 12-slot chassis.	Avoid placing descriptors between a trademark and its noun.	12-slot CoreBuilder® chassis.
SuperStack® II Hub 10 hubs get positive praise at the world's most attended tradeshow this month.	When a product name includes the generic noun, it's not necessary to repeat the noun.	SuperStack® II Hub 10s get positive praise at the world's most attended tradeshow this month.
HomeConnect™ NC.	Avoid using acronyms as the noun; the generic noun must tell the consumer what the product (brand) is or does.	HomeConnect™ network interface card.
3Com® delivers third-party Web software to U.S. Robotics® modem users.	Never use a trademark symbol on "3Com" when using the name as a trade name.	3Com delivers third-party Web software to U.S. Robotics® modem-users.
TokenLink® network interface card.	Never abbreviate a full trademarked name.	TokenLink Velocity® network interface card.

Trademarks and Nouns List

Your trademark portfolio should offer a complete listing of your company's trademarks, service marks, and suggested nouns for each. Again, since trademark status is highly volatile and prone to frequent revision your trademark portfolio will also need to be frequently revised. Note: "brand," "mark," "name," and "trademark" are always appropriate nouns; "service" is an appropriate noun for any service mark.

The following examples of proper usage are again based on 3Com trademarks – this is a partial list. However, any company investing in trademarks and branding should do the same for their trademark portfolio.

3Com Trademarks	Bigpicture®	HandFax™

TRADEMARK PROTECTION AND PROSECUTION

3Com®
brand
logo

3Com Connected™
logo
program
system
PC
brand

3ComImpact®
IQ ISDN modem
modem
product
terminal adapter

3Com networking Partners®
program

3Com Park® (logo only)
logo

3Star®
program

3Wizard®
certificate
training program

AccessBuilder®
access concentrator
ATM Access Manager
hardware
multiplexer
product

camera and capture card
videoconferencing system
video phone

BootWare®
software

Boundary Routing®
architecture
system architecture
technology

BRASICA™
chip set
technology

Connections™
CD-ROM

CoreBuilder®
switch
chassis
hardware
hub
network
platform

Courier™
modem

DynamicAccess®
technology
network performance manager
LAN agent
network edge monitor
mobile connection manager

software

HandPhone™
software

HiPer™
access router card
technology

HomeConnect™
network interface card
PC digital camera
video application launcher

HotSync®
software
technology

iMessenger™
application

Impresario™
management software
software

LANsentry®
packet decoder
statistical monitoring device

3Com Service Marks

3Com Care℠
service

3Com Facts℠
fax information service

3Source℠
CD-ROM subscription

42

TRADEMARK PROTECTIONS

remote access module server	VPN encryption software	EdgeWare^{SM} service
AirConnect™ wireless PC card wireless PCI card wireless access point device	**EdgeServer™** card integrated NT server	**Express^{SM}** support package
	EtherCD™ CD-ROM	**Guardian^{SM}** support package
AllPoints® LAN card wireless PC Card	**EtherDisk®** software	**InfoPAK^{SM}** support package
ATMDisk™ software	**EtherLink®** network interface card	**Service Partner^{SM}** service
ATMLink™ Network interface card	**FDDILink™** network interface card	**SupportPAK^{SM}** service
AutoIQ™ software	**Graffiti®** software	**Towne Square^{SM}** service
	HardWare™ software	**3Com Tagline** More connected.™

Trademark Application Guidelines

Guidelines to trademark use should apply to all written and electronic documents produced by employees and or others who represent the company's products and services. Examples of documents to which trademark rules apply:

- ❖ Company marketing material (e.g., brochures, booth graphics, promotional giveaways)
- ❖ All written correspondences to customers (i.e., memos from sales representatives, technical notices, in service materials)
- ❖ Company website
- ❖ E-mails to customers or contacts
- ❖ Commercial invoices
- ❖ Payment reminders
- ❖ Packaging, boxes, labels and devices
- ❖ Employment advertisements

TRADEMARK PROTECTION AND PROSECUTION

❖ Business cards, letterhead, fax letterhead, etc.

Examples of documents to which trademark rules may not necessarily apply, include notes, or other internal messages created within the company, which are not designed to formally represent the company and its products (i.e., daily work done by employees, meeting notes, etc.). Note: "Official" company internal documents such as training records, policies and procedures, and work instructions should follow trademark guidelines.

Legend Application Guidelines

The legend should appear with every authorized use of a company's trademarks. The legend should contain only those marks in which the company is claiming trademark rights to and which have been cleared by your legal counsel. Additionally, if a licensee is using your company trademark, in addition to including the legend, the licensee should identify itself as a licensee by specifying the relationship between itself and your company. For example, Aauvi Group, Inc.'s trademarks are used by Aauvi House Publishing Group under license.

Trade Name Application Guidelines

Do not confuse the Aauvi® trademark with use of the company name, Aauvi Group, Inc. A trade name is the name used to identify a business, partnership or enterprise. It refers to all aspects of a business, including the quality of its products or services and its reputation in the business or financial community.

Unlike trademarks, trade names are proper nouns and can be used in the possessive form and do not require use of a generic term. Trademark symbols such as "®" or "™" should not be used in connection with trade name use.

Correct example:

❖ Aauvi Group, Inc. must take steps to protect its trademarks.

Incorrect example:

❖ Aauvi® is introducing a new line of accessories.

Use of Third-Party Trademarks Application Guidelines

Third party trademarks can be used to identify that third party's goods and services. They cannot be used to identify your company's goods and services. The third party's ownership of its trademarks must be acknowledged by either of the methods listed below:

TRADEMARK PROTECTIONS

❖ Use the trademark accompanied by a footnote which indicates ownership, as follows: "*insert* Third Party mark is a trademark of *insert* Third Party trade name" or

❖ After listing your company's trademarks, state: "All other trademarks referenced are the property of their respective owners."

It is important to establish and follow guidelines for using company trademarks (for example, do not use the mark as a noun or verb) when using third party marks. When in doubt, you should consult with a trademark attorney, when using another's trademarks to avoid infringing another's rights.

CHAPTER 5

TRADEMARK INFRINGEMENT

What infringes a trademark? It is infringement for someone else to use the same or a confusingly similar term on the same geographical area, or in some cases, within a natural area of expansion. Under federal and state law, an unauthorized use of a trademark constitutes an infringement if it creates a likelihood of consumer confusion as to the source or sponsorship. Societal interests include: (i) shields the public from misleading information in the marketplace; (ii) prevents unjust enrichment of the infringer; and (iii) protects the trademark owner, thereby harming the owner's reputation among the consuming public.

Likelihood of Confusion

To win an infringement suit, plaintiff must show:

- ❖ Use in common, or a reproduction, counterfeit, copy or colorable imitation of a registered mark, that is likely to cause confusion, or to cause mistakes or to deceive.

- ❖ *Borden Ice Cream v. Borden Condensed Milk* – no infringement found because ice cream and milk are not competing goods.

- ❖ *Aunt Jemima case* – second circuit court found that Aunt Jemima's pancake syrup infringed Aunt Jemima's pancake batter. Thus, non-competing goods may be found to be infringing.

Infringement occurs in two ways: (1) Prevents a defendant's use of a confusingly similar mark that may cause consumers to buy defendant's goods when they meant to buy plaintiff's (diversion of sales). (2) Damage to goodwill – noncompeting goods, but defendant has a confusingly similar mark that suggests affiliations with the plaintiff that does not exist and leads consumers into assigning blame on the plaintiff for the poor quality.

Tests for infringement include: (i) whether the defendant's use of the mark is likely to cause an appreciable number of consumers to be confused about the source affiliation or sponsorship of goods; or (ii) whether the use creates a likelihood that consumers will associate the defendant's goods with the plaintiff. Do not assume a side-by-side comparison by the consumer of plaintiff and defendant's goods. A defendant's intent to cause confusion is strong evidence that confusion is likely. Also, in infringement cases, what matters is the evidence the parties set forth and how they make their case. It is very fact determinative.

The "Polaroid" Factors

Under the *Polaroid* case, it found eight factors for evaluating likelihood of confusion between non-identical goods or services:

1. Strength of plaintiff's trademark;

Analysis: The stronger plaintiff's mark, the more likely it is that consumers seeing the defendant's allegedly similar mark will be confused about its source.

2. Degree of similarity between plaintiff's and defendant's marks;

Analysis: (a) Similarity of appearance – usually dealing with picture or design marks. A court will look at the overall impression created by each mark. (b) Similarity of sound – focuses on how the mark sounds phonetically. Important because very often consumers never actually see the mark, but only hear it. (c) Similarity of meaning – mental image evoked by marks may overpower any differences between them in sound or appearance, leading to a finding of likelihood of confusion. These are confusingly similar because they evoke similar images in the consumers' minds. Note: If the mark looks or sounds familiar, but presented in a way that is distinctive, courts will not find confusion even if they are for similar goods. If you have a brand name in addition to the product name very obviously displayed on the label, likelihood of confusion will be reduced.

3. Proximity of the products or services;

Analysis: Ask; are plaintiff and defendant's goods likely to be sold in the same or same kind or same area of stores?

4. Likelihood that plaintiff will bridge the gap;

Analysis: Ask; how likely plaintiff will begin selling the products or services which the defendant is trying to sell with a similar trademark? Even if the plaintiff has no immediate plan to sell the same kind of goods or services through use of the mark, the court may still consider the plaintiff's interest in reserving the option to use the mark on such goods or services in the more distant future.

5. Evidence of actual confusion;

Analysis: It is not necessary to prove that the defendant's use causes a likelihood of confusion. If available, however, such evidence could be highly persuasive.

6. Defendant's good faith in adopting the mark;

Analysis: When the goods are not directly competitive, the court will weigh the equities of each parties use. If the defendant didn't intentionally copy to "cash in" on the plaintiff's goodwill and has expended significant amounts of money in promoting its mark, a court will be more hesitant to provide relief to the plaintiff. Consequently, if there is bad faith, there is a presumption of actual confusion.

7. Quality of defendant's product or service; and

Analysis: If both parties use their marks on the same or related types of services, then there is a greater likelihood of confusion.

8. Sophistication of the buyers.

Analysis: Ask; what is the market of consumers? The more sophisticated the potential purchasers and the more costly the goods or services, the more careful and discriminating the purchasers will be and the less likely the chance they will be misled or confused.

Note: This list does not exhaust other possibilities. The court may have to take still other variables into account. Also, none of the factors is dispositive.

Relevant Public/Secondary Confusion

Secondary confusion or post-sale confusion is when the purchaser is not confused about what he or she is buying (knows that it is an imitation), but other people (potential purchasers) seeing the goods in the purchaser's possession after the sale may be confused about their source. This could lead to injury of the producer's goodwill.

Even if a consumer is not actually confused at the point of sale, this will not change the likelihood that others will associate the copy with the original, whether at the point of sale or post-sale. Courts care about the purchaser and subsequent viewers of the product (potential purchasers). Pre-post sale is a matter of discretion to the courts. Attorneys will attempt to persuade the court to look at the moment of confusion in which their client will win.

Reverse Confusion

The public comes to assume that the senior user's products are really the junior user's or that the former has become somehow connected to the latter. The result is that the senor user loses the value of the mark in its product identity, corporate identity, control over its goodwill and reputation, and ability to move into new markets.

Even after you find that the theory of reverse confusion applies, you still need to find if there exists legal likelihood of confusion. The intent fact of likelihood of confusion analysis is essentially irrelevant in a reverse confusion case because by definition the defendant is not palming off or attempting to cause confusion of source. Therefore, in reverse confusion cases, the courts rarely look at bad faith.

Contributory Infringement

A person may be found to be vicariously liable for another's trademark infringement if he or she has assisted in the infringement by: (1) Inducing infringement – intentionally suggesting either directly or impliedly that the other person infringed the plaintiff's mark and the other does infringe. For example, manufacturer suggests to retailer substitute his or her goods for another's similar goods to customers who ask for the others by name. If the retailer does this, he or she is an infringer and by the manufacturer asking to do this, he or she is a contributory infringer. (2) Knowingly aiding infringement – when a defendant sells goods to another knowing or having reason to know that the buyer will use the goods in direct infringement of the plaintiff's mark.

One has no duty to actively discover infringing activities, but once you have actual knowledge of infringement, if you fail to prevent it, you will be liable for contributory infringement.

Statutory Defenses/Incontestability

A mark that has been in continuous use for five consecutive years will obtain "incontestability" status upon the registrant's filing of an affidavit to that effect that truthfully states that there has been no final decision adverse to the registrant's claim of ownership of a registered trademark and that there is no proceeding presently pending involving the registrant's right in the registered trademark. Incontestability gives the registrant an advantage in an infringement action (regardless of whether the registrant is the plaintiff or the defendant), though not as great an advantage as the name might suggest. For the most part, the incontestable registered trademark is subject to all the same challenges and defense as a registered trademark that had not attained incontestability status. Arguments against incontestability include generic, abandoned, fraudulent registration or improper use of a certification registered trademark.

Defenses to incontestably registered marks include: (i) fraudulent acquisition of trademark; (ii) abandonment; (iii) use of the trademark to misrepresent source; (iv) fair use defense; (v) limited territory defense; (vi) prior registration by defendant; (vii) use of trademark to violate antitrust laws; or (viii) equity. Note that functionality is not on this list. That is, a functionality defense cannot be raised against incontestably registered marks.

Fair use – owners of a descriptive trademark may prohibit others from using the descriptive trademark if it causes a likelihood of confusion. However, they may not assert monopoly rights in the descriptive meaning of their trademark. A defendant is free to use the descriptive trademark in a strictly descriptive capacity to describe his or her own product or its geographical origin or to identify its producer. Courts usually consider three factors: (1) What is the manner in which the defendant uses the trademark product or service – is the word or symbol prominently featured or secondary to the other words? (2) Is the defendant using the trademark in good faith? (3) Is the defendant's use likely to cause confusion? If factors one and two indicate a fair use, the court may tolerate a greater chance of consumer confusion.

Remedies

Civil remedies available under the federal law and most state laws include: (i) An injunction against future infringement; (ii) The infringer's profits; (iii) Damages for past infringement suffered by the owner of the mark (which may be trebled under the federal law); (iv) Destruction of all material bearing the infringing mark; (v) The costs of the action and, in exceptional cases, reasonable attorney's fees; (vi) Punitive damages; and (vii) Pre-judgment interest. Also, criminal penalties may be available under the Trademark Counterfeiting Act of 1984.

Lawful Unauthorized Use

Collateral use of a trademark is proper with full disclosure. Includes use in situations involving rebottled, repackaged, repaired, reconditioned, service outlets, dealerships, and replacement parts. Also includes comparative advertising. However, full disclosure is necessary. For example, an original product is reconditioned and sold used. Courts have held, even though second-hand dealer may get some advantage from the trademark, their use is wholly permissible so long as the manufacturer is not identified with the inferior qualities of the product resulting from wear and tear or the reconditioning by the dealer. Full disclosure gives the manufacturer all the protection to which he or she is entitled.

Promotional Products

Without any authorization (like as a licensee) and without disclaimer, the courts will find bad faith. For example, whether the authorized, intentional duplication of a professional hockey team's symbol on an embroidered emblem, to be sold to the public as a patch for attachment to clothing, violates any legal right of the team to exclusive use of that symbol, the courts held the team has an interest in its own individualized symbol and the team was entitled to legal protection against such unauthorized duplication. In another court decision, the courts presumed that at least a sufficient number of purchasers would be likely to assume, mistakenly, that defendant's shirts had some connection with the official sponsors, and thus held unlawful.

Comparative Advertising

Collateral use also includes the use of a mark to make truthful statements in comparison in advertising. The use is proper as long as it does not misrepresent or cause confusion as to the source of product. However, comparative advertising is not a complete defense. It is possible to use competitor's name in its advertising, but it will be in violation if misleading or confusing. If not truthful (misleading) then comparative advertising is actionable.

Parodies

Parodies are permitted. A parody is a form of artistic expression that is protected by the 1st Amendment. Parody is a humorous form of social commentary and literary criticism. A parody must convey two simultaneous and contradictory massages: that it is the original, but also that it is not the original and is instead a parody. Survey evidence is used to prove actual confusion. Very compelling evidence is required. Courts look to see if defendant made it clear to consumers that it was a parody.

Trademarks as Speech

1st Amendment confers a measure of protection for the unauthorized use of trademarks when that use is a part of the expression of a communicative message. Fair use may be used when: (i) even though they are intentionally copied and registered, as long as they aren't being used for a trademark purpose, it is okay to use; (ii) comparative advertising; (iii) describe the product or service which relates to the plaintiff's; (iv) collateral use – nominative use; (v) textual reference – comparative advertising; (vi) names; (vii) geographic location; and (viii) functionality (separate defense).

Trademark Disputes

Trademark infringement is a violation of the exclusive rights attaching to a trademark without the authorization of the trademark owner or any licensees (provided that such authorization was within the scope of the license). Infringement may occur when one party, the "infringer," uses a trademark which is identical or confusingly similar to a trademark owned by another party, in relation to products or services which are identical or similar to the products or services which the registration covers. Inasmuch, an owner of a trademark may commence legal proceedings against a party which infringes its registration. In many countries, but not in the United States, which recognizes common law trademark rights, a trademark which is not registered cannot be "infringed" as such, and the trademark owner cannot bring infringement proceedings. Instead, the owner may be able to commence proceedings under the common law for passing off or misrepresentation, or under legislation which prohibits unfair business practices. In some jurisdictions, infringement of trade dress may also be actionable.

Demand Letter

Before filing a lawsuit, you should begin by writing a demand letter. A demand letter is the key to getting your dispute off the ground and into court. The demand letter is a layperson's version of a legal complaint. In it, you state what your dispute is and why you want to handle it in court. The demand letter must also contain the amount for which you are suing or the specific relief you seek. You submit this letter to the person with whom you have the dispute.

Start a demand letter with a brief history of the dispute. Explain why there has been no agreement so far. While your opponent may know exactly what happened, a judge or court clerk who may end up reading it will not. Organize it chronologically, but be brief, polite, concise and specific about what you want and what your next step will be if the problem is not resolved.

Avoid threatening or disparaging the other person. Do not use language that will convey your frustration or anger. Creating a negative mood will only lessen your chances of reaching an agreement. The idea of the demand letter is to show

TRADEMARK INFRINGEMENT

the other person you are serious and give them the chance to consider their legal choices. It is not an opportunity to insult them or create an adversarial relationship. If the dispute ends up in court, remember that the same judge who will hear your case will read your demand letter. This is another reason to keep it objective and professional.

There is no minimum or maximum length for a demand letter. However, shorter is better. It should only be long enough to clarify your intent. A letter that gets to the point will show your opponent that you are serious about the lawsuit. The less you give them to read, the better it will be. Finally, make and keep several copies of the letter for yourself and to use in any future court appearances.

SAMPLE INFRINGEMENT DEMAND LETTER

Mr. _____
Title
Company Name
Street Address
City, State and Zip code

Re: XYZ Registered Trademark "XXX" in classes 9 and 10

Dear Mr. _____,

Attached are copies of XYZ's U.S. registrations for the trademark XXX®. The mark was registered in the U.S. on 28 January 2010 in classes 9 and 10. The mark is also registered in the European Community, Switzerland, Norway and other countries.

Also attached is a copy of marketing information published in the United States by your ABC division for your AAA™ product. We have highlighted your use of our registered trademark.

As your AAA™ product is in the same market and performs the same functions as XYZ's YYY® infant hearing testing product, your use of our registered trademark XXX® with reference to your AAA™ product will inevitably create confusion in the marketplace.

XYZ therefore respectfully requests that your company and all of its affiliates and subsidiaries immediately cease all usage of our XXX® trademark in at least all referenced jurisdictions.

If you have any questions, we are certainly available to discuss this matter with you. However, given the requirements of trademark law, we cannot wait very long for your compliance with our request to cease all use of this registered trademark.

We look forward to hearing from you no later than [one month from date of mailing].

Sincerely,

Your Name

TRADEMARK PROTECTION AND PROSECUTION

Your Title
Your Company Name

Domain Name Disputes

The Uniform Domain-Name Dispute-Resolution Policy (UDRP) is a process established by the Internet Corporation for Assigned Names and Numbers (ICANN) for the resolution of disputes regarding the registration of Internet domain names. The UDRP currently applies to all: .aero, .asia, .biz, .cat, .com, .coop, .info, .jobs, .mobi, .museum, .name, .net, .org, .pro, .tel and .travel top-level domains, and some country code top-level domains.

When a registrant chooses a domain name, the registrant must "represent and warrant," among other things, that registering the name "will not infringe upon or otherwise violate the rights of any third party," and agree to participate in an arbitration-like proceeding should any third party assert such a claim.

A complainant in a UDRP proceeding must establish three elements to succeed:

- ❖ The domain name is identical or confusingly similar to a trademark or service mark in which the complaint has rights;

- ❖ The registrant does not have any rights or legitimate interests in the domain name; and

- ❖ The registrant registered the domain name and is using it in "bad faith."

In a UDRP proceeding, a panel will consider several non-exclusive factors to assess bad faith, such as:

- ❖ Whether the registrant registered the domain name primarily for the purpose of selling, renting, or otherwise transferring the domain name registration to the complainant who is the owner of the trademark or service mark;

- ❖ Whether the registrant registered the domain name to prevent the owner of the trademark or service mark from reflecting the mark in a corresponding domain name, if the domain name owner has engaged in a pattern of such conduct; and

- ❖ Whether the registrant registered the domain name primarily for the purposes of disrupting the business of a competitor; or

- ❖ Whether by using the domain name, the registrant has intentionally attempted to attract, for commercial gain, Internet users to the registrant's website, by creating a likelihood of confusion with the complainant's mark.

The goal of the UDRP is to create a streamlined process for resolving such disputes. It was envisioned that this process would be quicker and less expensive than a standard legal challenge. The cost to hire a UDRP provider to handle a complaint often starts around $1,000 to $2,000.

If a party loses a UDRP proceeding, in many jurisdictions it may still bring a lawsuit against the domain name registrant under local law. For example, the administrative panel's UDRP decision can be challenged and overturned in a U.S. court of law by means of e.g., the Anticybersquatting Consumer Protection Act. If a domain name registrant loses a UDRP proceeding, it must file a lawsuit against the trademark holder within ten days to prevent ICANN from transferring the domain name.

SAMPLE DOMAIN NAME INFRINGEMENT DEMAND LETTER

Mr. _____
Title
Company Name
Street Address
City, State and Zip code

Re: <u>XYZ Registered Trademark "XXX" in classes 9 and 10</u>

Dear Mr. _____,

It has recently come to the attention of XYZ, Inc. that you are operating a website at the address www.XYZ.com. It appears that you are offering on this website Internet search services aimed at individuals who use medical software for hand-held computers.

Since at least as early as October 2010, XYZ has advertised, promoted and sold computer software for medical professionals under the mark XYZ. For more details about XYZ's current product line, go to www.XYZ.com. As a result, the XYZ trademark has become well known to consumers and the industry as identifying our client's products. On September 15, 2010, XYZ filed an application for registration of the XYZ trademark with the United States Patent & Trademark Office ("USPTO"), which has since issued. XYZ's use and registration of the XYZ trademark predates by several years your registration of the www.XYZ.com domain name.

Given the above facts, we strongly believe that you wrongfully represented that the www.XYZ.com domain name did not infringe upon or otherwise violate the rights of any third party when you registered the www.XYZ.com domain name and, thus, that registration was made in bad faith. This conclusion is further supported by several UDRP decisions which demonstrate that you have a history of making such bad faith registrations of domain names.

TRADEMARK PROTECTION AND PROSECUTION

XYZ therefore requests that you immediately transfer the www.XYZ.com domain name to XYZ. If you refuse to do so, XYZ will take swift and appropriate action in response to your infringement of its valuable trademark rights.

Sincerely,

Your Name
Your Title
Your Company Name

SAMPLE COMPLAINT

COMPLAINT TRANSMITTAL COVERSHEET

Attached is a Complaint that has been filed against you with the World Intellectual Property Organization (**WIPO**) Arbitration and Mediation Center (the **Center**) pursuant to the Uniform Domain Name Dispute Resolution Policy (the **Policy**) adopted by the Internet Corporation for Assigned Names and Numbers (**ICANN**) on October 24, 1999, the Rules for Uniform Domain Name Dispute Resolution Policy (the **Rules**), and the WIPO Supplemental Rules for Uniform Domain Name Dispute Resolution Policy (the **Supplemental Rules**).

The Policy is incorporated by reference into your Registration Agreement with the Registrar(s) of your domain name(s), in accordance with which you are required to submit to and participate in a mandatory administrative proceeding in the event that a third party (a **Complainant**) submits a complaint to a dispute resolution service provider, such as the Center, concerning a domain name that you have registered. You will find the name and contact details of the Complainant, as well as the domain name(s) that is/are the subject of the Complaint in the document that accompanies this Coversheet.

You have no duty to act at this time. Once the Center has checked the Complaint to determine that it satisfies the formal requirements of the Policy, the Rules and the Supplemental Rules, it will forward an official copy of the Complaint to you. You will then have 20 calendar days within which to submit a Response to the Complaint in accordance with the Rules and Supplemental Rules to the Center and the Complainant. Should you so desire, you may wish to seek the assistance of legal counsel to represent you in the administrative proceeding.

- The **Policy** can be found at http://arbiter.wipo.int/domains/rules/
- The **Rules** can be found at http://arbiter.wipo.int/domains/rules/
- The **Supplemental Rules**, as well as other information concerning the resolution of domain name disputes can be found at http://arbiter.wipo.int/domains/rules/
- A **model Response** can be found at http://arbiter.wipo.int/domains/respondent/index.html

Alternatively, you may contact the Center to obtain any of the above documents. The Center can be contacted in Geneva, Switzerland by telephone at +41 22 338 8247, by fax at +41 22 740 3700 or by e-mail at domain.disputes@wipo.int.

TRADEMARK INFRINGEMENT

You are kindly requested to contact the Center to provide the contact details to which you would like (a) the official version of the Complaint and (b) other communications in the administrative proceeding to be sent.

A copy of this Complaint has also been sent to the Registrar(s) with which the domain name(s) that is/are the subject of the Complaint is/are registered.

By submitting this Complaint to the Center, the Complainant hereby agrees to abide and be bound by the provisions of the Policy, Rules and Supplemental Rules. ***Before the:***

WORLD INTELLECTUAL PROPERTY ORGANIZATION ARBITRATION AND MEDIATION CENTER

XYZ, Inc. Street Address City, State and Zip code	
Complainant	**Disputed Domain Name:**
-v-	xyz.com xyzs.com
ABC, Inc. Street Address City, State and Zip code	
Respondent	

COMPLAINT
(Rules, Para. 3(b))

I. Introduction

1. This Complaint is hereby submitted for decision in accordance with the Uniform Policy for Domain Name Dispute Resolution, adopted by the Internet Corporation for Assigned Names and Numbers (**ICANN**) on August 26, 2020 (the **Policy**), the Rules for Uniform Domain Name Dispute Resolution Policy, approved by ICANN on October 24, 2020 (the **Rules**) and the WIPO Supplemental Rules for Uniform Domain Name Dispute Resolution Policy (the **Supplemental Rules**).

II. The Parties

A. The Complainant
(Rules, para. 3(b)(ii) and (iii))

2. The Complainant in this administrative proceeding is XYZ Inc., a California corporation, with its principal place of business at [street address and city], California, United States of America [zip code].

3. The Complainant's contact details are as follows:

    Address: Your Name
              XYZ, Inc.
              Street Address

TRADEMARK PROTECTION AND PROSECUTION

                        City, State and Zip code
                        United States of America
          Telephone: _____
          Fax: _____
          E-mail: _____

4.   The Complainant's preferred method of communications directed to the Complainant in the administrative proceeding is as follows:

        Electronic-only material
        Method: e-mail
        Address: _____
        Contact: _____

        Material including hardcopy
        Method: Post/courier
        Address: XYZ, Inc.
                      Street Address
                      City, State and Zip code
                      United States of America
        Contact: _____

B.   **The Respondent**
(Rules, para. 3(b)(v))

5.   According to the concerned registrar's Whois database, the Respondent in this administrative proceeding is ABC, Inc., [street address, city and state], United States of America [zip code]. Copies of the printouts of the WHOIS database searches for the two domain names at issues, conducted on December 30, 2010 and January 12, 2011 respectively, are provided as Annex 1.

6.   All information known to the Complainant regarding how to contact the Respondent is as follows:

        ABC, Inc.
        Street Address
        City, State and Zip code
        United States of America
        Telephone: _____
        Email: _____

III.   **The Domain Names and Registrar**
(Rules, para, 3(b)(vi) and (vii))

7.   This dispute concerns the domain names identified below:

        xyz.com
        xyzs.com

8.   The registrar with which the domain names are registered is:

        Company Name
        Street Address
        City, State and Zip code
        Telephone: _____

TRADEMARK INFRINGEMENT

Email: _____; _____

IV. Jurisdictional Basis for the Administrative Proceeding
(Rules, paras. 3(a), 3(b)(xv))

9. This dispute is properly within the scope of the Policy and the Administrative Panel has jurisdiction to decide the dispute. The registration agreement, pursuant to which the domain names that are the subject of this Complaint are registered, incorporates the Policy. The domain name xyz.com was registered on December 15, 2009 and the Uniform Dispute Resolution Policy was incorporated in the registrar's services agreement at that time. The domain name xyzs.com was registered on September 15, 2010 and the Uniform Dispute Resolution Policy was incorporated in the registrar's services agreement at that time. A true and correct copy of the domain name dispute policy that applies to the domain names in question is provided as Annex 2 to this Complaint.

10. In addition, in accordance with Policy, Paragraph 4(a), the Respondent is required to submit to a mandatory administrative proceeding because:

(1) The domain names are identical or confusingly similar to a trademark or service mark in which the Complainant has rights; and

(2) The Respondent has no rights or legitimate interests in respect of the domain names; and

(3) The domain names were registered and are being used in bad faith.

V. Factual and Legal Grounds
(Policy, paras. 4(a), (b), (c); Rules, para. 3)

11. This Complaint is based on the following grounds:

A. COMPLAINANT'S TRADEMARK XYZ

- Complainant XYZ, Inc. ("XYZ" or "Complainant") was founded in 2010 and now is a leading provider of computer software databases related to drug information, drug formularies, infectious diseases, diagnostics and other health-care related topics. XYZ' databases are used by physicians and other health care professionals in the course of rendering care to their patients and can be easily downloaded onto handheld computers or personal digital assistants, or can be accessed through an Internet account.

- XYZ has a network of more than 470,000 subscribers, including more than one in four U.S. physicians, students at every U.S. medical school, and hundreds of thousands of other allied healthcare professionals, who use XYZ mobile and online clinical reference and support solutions daily.

- XYZ has been widely acknowledged for its accomplishments and successes, and copies of exemplary articles from such publications as *Medical Economics, PC Magazine, Forbes, Newsday, Wall Street Journal* and *The New York Times* recognizing high regard for XYZ and its products are attached hereto as Annex 3.

- The high quality and value of XYZ's products is widely recognized by individuals and entities in the health care field, as demonstrated in part by the commitment of Harvard Medical School, the University of Pennsylvania School of Medicine and Duke University Health System, the nation's leading medical schools, to provide their students with access to XYZ databases.

TRADEMARK PROTECTION AND PROSECUTION

XYZ's products have also received positive reviews, appearing in the Journal of the American Journal of Medicine, Advance News Magazines for Nurse Practitioners, and the Indiana University School of Medicine Scope Newsletter, as well as other publications. See Annex 4.

- In addition, XYZ has also received awards and accolades from the computer industry, recognizing the excellence of its products. For example, in 2011, XYZ was recognized as one of the best healthcare solutions for Windows Mobile devices by the editors of PC Magazine; in 2011, XYZ received the "eHealth Impact Award" at the eHealth Institute's annual Developers' Summit for making the greatest positive impact on health and/or health care; and in 2010, XYZ received two PalmSource "Powered Up" awards -- Best Enterprise Solution and Best Overall Solution -- for its innovative software applications. See Annex 5.

- XYZ has a considerable presence on the Internet as evidenced by its primary website, <www.XYZ.com>. In particular, the XYZ website contains information about the company, its products, industry solutions, technology, services, press room, events, and so on. The XYZ website is also the primary distribution channel for the company's software and databases. Copies of exemplary pages from the <www.XYZ.com> website are attached hereto as Annex 6.

- The XYZ trademark is coined and therefore is an arbitrary and strong trademark.

- XYZ is the owner of numerous registrations for trademarks incorporating the word XYZ in connection with computer software and related services:

Country/ Registration No.	Mark	Registration Date
United States 1,234,567	XYZ	August 13, 2009
United States 1,234,568	XYZ DX	November 15, 2009
United States 1,234,569	XYZ HONORS	April 20, 2010
United States 2,896,170	XYZ MEDTOOLS	October 19, 2011
European Union 1234567	XYZ	August 20, 2010
European Union 2234567	XYZ MEDTOOLS	November 26, 2011
Israel 123456	XYZ	June 7, 2010
Japan 1234567	XYZ	December 2, 2010

Copies of the above-listed registration certificates are attached hereto as Annex 7.

TRADEMARK INFRINGEMENT

- Complainant has used and continues to use the mark XYZ extensively. The mark XYZ is distinctive, and is understood and associated by consumers throughout the world as Complainant's mark, denoting its products, services, and business.

B. **THE THREE ELEMENTS OF PARAGRAPH 4(A) OF THE POLICY ARE CLEARLY PRESENT HERE.**

1. **THE <XYZ.COM> AND <XYZS.COM> DOMAIN NAMES ARE CONFUSINGLY SIMILAR TO THE XYZ TRADEMARK.**

- XYZ believes that Respondent registered the <XYZ.com> domain name at issue on November 13, 2009. Sometime thereafter, Respondent introduced its <www.XYZ.com> website which references medical software and resources, including drug and prescription information, as well as software and hardware products related to personal digital assistants. A copy of a printout from this website is attached hereto as Annex 8.

- The <XYZ.com> domain name is virtually identical to Complainant's mark XYZ, with the only difference being the deletion of the letter "s." Thus, the two terms are confusingly similar.

- XYZ believes that Respondent registered the <XYZS.com> domain name at issue on September 1, 2010. Sometime thereafter, Respondent introduced its <www.XYZS.com> website which references medical software and resources, including drug and prescription information, as well as software and hardware products related to personal digital assistants. A copy of a printout from this website is attached hereto as Annex 9.

- The <XYZS.com> domain name is virtually identical to Complainant's mark XYZ, with the only difference being the addition of the letter "s." Thus, the two terms are confusingly similar.

- In this regard, numerous decisions under the ICANN policy recognize that this conduct, commonly referred to as "typo squatting," creates a virtually identical and/or confusingly similar mark to the Complainant's trademark under paragraph 4(a)(i) of the Policy. *See, e.g., Bang & Olufsen a/s v. Unasi Inc.*, WIPO Case No. D2005-0728 (September 7, 2005) § 6A (finding that <bag-olufsen.com>, <bagolufsen.com>, <bang-olusen.com> and <bangolusen.com> are confusingly similar to Bang & Olufsen's mark); *Autosales Inc., dba Summit Racing Equip. v. Domain Active Pty. Ltd.*, WIPO Case No. D2004-0459 (September 3, 2004) § 6A (finding the domain names <summitracin.com> and <wwwsummitracing.com> confusingly similar to Complainant's marks); *CareerBuilder, LLC v. Azra Khan*, WIPO Case No. D2003-0493 (August 5, 2003) § 6A (finding the domain name <careeerbuilder.com> confusingly similar to CareerBuilder's trademarks and service marks); *Wachovia Corp. v. Carrington*, WIPO Case No. D2002-0775 (October 2, 2002) § 6A (finding that <wochovia.com>, <wachvia.com> and <wachovai.com> are confusingly similar to the trademark WACHOVIA; *America Online, Inc. v. Johuanthan Invs., Inc.*, WIPO Case No. D2001-0918 (September 14, 2001) § 6 (finding the domain name <aollnews.com>

TRADEMARK PROTECTION AND PROSECUTION

confusingly similar to trade and service marks in which AOL has rights, namely <aolnews.com>); *Backstreet Prods., Inc. v. Zuccarini*, WIPO Case No. D2001-0654 (August 24, 2001) § 8A (finding, *inter alia*, the domain names <backsreetboys.com> and <backstreetboyz.com> virtually identical and confusingly similar to the Backstreet Boys' mark); *AltaVista Co. v. Yomtobian*, WIPO Case No. D2000-0937 (October 13, 2000) § 6 (finding the domain names <altabista.com> and <altaista.com> confusingly similar to the trademark Alta Vista); *Encyclopaedia Britannica, Inc. v. Zuccarini*, WIPO Case No. D2000-0330 (June 7, 2000), § 3 (finding the domain name <encyclopediabrittanica.com> virtually identical and confusingly similar to Encyclopedia Britannica's mark). Copies of these and all cases cited in this Complaint are attached hereto as Annex 10.

2. **RESPONDENT HAS NO RIGHTS OR LEGITIMATE INTERESTS IN THE <XYZ.COM> AND <XYZS.COM> DOMAIN NAMES.**

- Respondent is not a distributor or licensee of Complainant. Indeed, Respondent has no relationship with Complainant whatsoever. Complainant has never given its permission or consent to Respondent to use Complainant's well-known trademark XYZ or any other of Complainant's intellectual property.

- Complainant is informed and believes and thereon alleges that Respondent does not own any trademark registrations for or applications to register the marks XYZ or XYZS and that Respondent has not been commonly or otherwise known by the names, "XYZ" or "XYZS."

- Thus, Respondent has no rights or legitimate interest in either the "XYZ" or XYZS" name.

3. **RESPONDENT HAS REGISTERED AND IS USING THE <XYZ.COM> AND <XYZS.COM> DOMAIN NAMES IN BAD FAITH.**

- Respondent deliberately uses both the www.XYZ.com and www.XYZS.com domain names in an attempt to attract, for commercial gain, Internet users to its websites, by creating a likelihood of confusion with the Complainant's mark as to the source, sponsorship, affiliation, or endorsement of its websites. Respondent registered the domain names at issue to improperly suggest sponsorship by Complainant of Respondent's website.

- In particular, the type of content which Respondent displays on both the www.XYZ.com and www.XYZS.com websites demonstrates that Respondent is aware of the uses connected with the XYZ trademark. Respondent has listed links to what it describes as "popular categories," each of which relate to Complainant's business of providing downloadable software concerning information regarding medications and insurance coverage but which are not associated with Complainant. Those searches include: XYZ Rx, Palm Software, Medical, Drug Information, Pharmacy, Rxfree, Drugs, XYZS, Medical Software, Palm, and the like, as well as links to other categories. See Annexes 8 and 9.

TRADEMARK INFRINGEMENT

- Misspellings alone, such as that used by Respondent, "are sufficient to prove bad faith under paragraph 4(b)(iv) of the Policy because Respondent has used these names intentionally to attract, for commercial gain, Internet users to his website by creating a likelihood of confusion with the Complainant's mark." *AltaVista Co. v. Yomtobian*, WIPO Case No. D2000-0937 (October 13, 2000).

- Furthermore, Respondent's bad faith is evident by its pattern of conduct in repeatedly using other's misspelled trademarks to attract traffic to its websites. *See, e.g., Mimran Group, Inc. v. LaPorte Holdings*, WIPO Case No. D2005-1016 (December 22, 2005); *NBTY, Inc. v. LaPorte Holdings*, WIPO Case No. D2005-0835 (September 30, 2005); *Sodexho Alliance v. LaPorte Holdings*, WIPO Case No. D2005-0287 (July 2, 2005); *Adorama, Inc. v. LaPorte Holdings, Inc.*, WIPO Case No. D2005-0240 (June 1, 2005); *DaimlerChrysler Corp. et al. v. LaPorte Holdings, Inc.*, WIPO Case No. D2005-0143 (April 1, 2005); *DaimlerChrysler Corp. et al. v. LaPorte Holdings, Inc.*, WIPO Case No. D2005-070 (April 13, 2005); *Matrix Group Ltd., Inc. v. LaPorte Holdings, Inc.*, WIPO Case No. D2005-0059 (April 7, 2005); *Medco Health Solutions, Inc. v. LaPorte Holdings, Inc.*, WIPO Case No. D2004-0800 (December 22, 2004); *Credit Industriel et al. v. LaPorte Holdings, Inc.*, WIPO Case No. D2004-1110 (March 31, 2005); and *Questar Corp. v. LaPorte Holdings, Inc.*, National Arbitration Forum Claim Number: FA0510000573940 (November 28, 2005). Copies of these cases are included in Annex 10.

- Based on the foregoing, it is clear that Respondent has no rights or legitimate interests in the domain names. It is clear that Respondent uses Complainant's well-known trademark to attract Internet users to Respondent's websites and, by so doing, creates a likelihood of confusion with the complainant's mark as to the source, sponsorship, affiliation, or endorsement of the registrant's websites. As such, Respondent registered and uses the domain names in bad faith.

VI. Remedies Requested
(Rules, para. 3(b)(x))

12. In accordance with Paragraph 4(i) of the Policy, for the reasons described in Section V above, the Complainant requests the Administrative Panel appointed in this administrative proceeding issue a decision that the contested domain names be transferred to the Complainant.

VII. Administrative Panel
(Rules, para. 3(b)(iv))

13. The Complainant elects to have the dispute decided by a single-member Administrative Panel.

VIII. Mutual Jurisdiction
(Rules, para. 3(b)(xiii))

14. In accordance with Paragraph 3(b)(xiii), the Complainant agrees to submit, only with respect to any challenge that may be made by the Respondent to a decision by the Administrative Panel to transfer or cancel the domain names that are the subject of this Complaint, to the jurisdiction of the courts where the principal office of the concerned registrar is located.

TRADEMARK PROTECTION AND PROSECUTION

IX. Other Legal Proceedings
(Rules, para. 3(b)(xi))

15. No other legal proceedings have been commenced or terminated in connection with or relating to the domain names which are the subject of this Complaint.

X. Communications
(Rules, para. 3(b)(xii); Supplemental Rules, para. 4(b))

16. A copy of this Complaint and Annexes, together with the cover sheet as prescribed by the Supplemental Rules, has been sent or transmitted to the Respondent on February __, 2012 by U.S. Postal Service, to [company name, street address, city and state], United States of America [zip code].

17. A copy of this Complaint, has been sent or transmitted to the concerned registrar on February __, 2012 by U.S. Postal Service to [company name, street address, city and state], United States of America [zip code].

XI. Payment

18. As required by the Rules and Supplemental Rules, payment in the amount of USD $1500.00 by check made payable to World Intellectual Property Organization accompanies the paper copy of this complaint.

XII. Certification
(Rules, para. 3(b)(xiv))

19. The Complainant agrees that its claim and remedies concerning the registration of the domain names, the dispute, or the dispute's resolution shall be solely against the holder of the domain names and waives all such claims and remedies against (a) the WIPO Arbitration and Mediation Center and Panelists, except in the case of deliberate wrongdoing, (b) the concerned registrar(s), (c) the registry administrator, (d) the Internet Corporation for Assigned Names and Numbers, as well as their directors, officers, employees, and agents.

20. The Complainant certifies that the information contained in this Complaint is to the best of the Complainant's knowledge complete and accurate, that this Complaint is not being presented for any improper purpose, such as to harass, and that the assertions in this Complaint are warranted under the Rules and under applicable law, as it now exists or as it may be extended by a good-faith and reasonable argument.

Respectfully submitted,

_____

Your Name
Your Company Name

Date: February __, 2021

CHAPTER 6

TRADE DRESS

Trade dress is another form of intellectual property. It is a legal term of art that generally refers to characteristics of the visual appearance of a product or its packaging (or even the design of a building) that signify the source of the product to consumers. Trade dress is a cousin of trademark; not just a shape, but it must be a physical embodiment of some type and accompany goods. It is different from a design patent, which has only a fourteen-year life and covers only the specific product and may have some element of functionality. Applying for a design patent on the trade dress will absolutely defeat the trade dress.

Trade Dress Rights

The previous chapters have addressed trademarks and service marks – words, names, symbols, devices, and combinations thereof. While the trademark search may reveal that the mark is available, you may be using the mark in ways that are neither envisioned nor addressed in the foregoing analysis. For example, you may be using the mark on labels, packages, advertising, and in various other ways. Very likely the mark in these materials will be surrounded by artwork and other components, both written and visual. This collection of components, which together constitute the manner in which the mark is presented to the market, is often termed "trade dress."

Trade dress has been referred to as the "total image of the business." Trade dress may be considered generic if it is a mere refinement of a commonly adopted and well-known form of ornamentation, or a common basic shape or design, even if it has not before been refined in precisely the same way before. In addition, even if a trade dress feature of the actual product is found to have secondary meaning, other factors can lead to a finding of lack of confusion. Therefore, it is critical that anyone asserting that trade dress protects an entire line of different products must explain the specific common elements sought to be protected with sufficient detail to identify when a competitor would be infringing as opposed to incorporating generic features in a particular product design.

Lanham Act

In the United States, like trademarks, a product's trade dress is legally protected by the Lanham Act, the federal statute which regulates trademarks and trade dress. Trade dress protection is intended to protect consumers from packaging or appearance of products that are designed to imitate other products; and to prevent consumers from buying one product under the belief that it is another. For example, the shape, color, and arrangement of the materials of a children's line of clothing can be protectable trade dress (though, the design of the garments themselves is not protected), as can the design of a magazine cover, the appearance and décor of a chain of Mexican-style restaurants, and a method of displaying wine bottles in a wine shop.

Under section 43(a) of the Lanham Act a product's trade dress can be protected without formal registration with the USPTO. In relevant part, section 43(a) states the following:

> "Any person who, on or in connection with any goods or services, or any container for goods, uses in commerce any word, term, name, symbol, or device, or any combination thereof, or any false designation of origin, false or misleading description of fact, or false or misleading representation of fact, which: (A) is likely to cause confusion, or to cause mistake, or to deceive…as to the origin, sponsorship. Or approval of his or her goods, services, or commercial activities by another person, or (B) in commercial advertising or promotion, misrepresents the nature, characteristics, qualities, or geographic origin of his or her or another person's goods, services, or commercial activities, shall be liable in a civil action by any person who believes that he or she is likely to be damaged by such act."

This statute allows the owner of a particular trade dress ("container for goods") to sue an infringer (a person or entity who illegally copies that trade dress) for violating section 43(a) without registering that trade dress with any formal agency or system (unlike the registration and application requirements for enforcing other forms of intellectual property, such as patents). It is commonly seen as providing "federal common law" protection for trade dress (and trademarks).

Thus, the Lanham Act, in Section 43(a), provides a cause of action for the use of any symbol or device likely to cause confusion as to the origin of goods. This language has been held to include "trade dress" a category that originally included only the packaging of a product, but in recent years has been expanded by many courts of appeals to encompass the product design. The Supreme Court has held that trade dress must be shown to be distinctive, whereas trade dress of a product's design must always be shown by acquired distinctiveness.

The Court has observed that, "the Lanham Act does not exist to reward manufacturers for their innovation in creating a particular device; that is the purpose of the patent law and its period of exclusivity." The Lanham Act, furthermore, does not protect trade dress in a functional design simply because an investment has been made to encourage the public to associate a particular functional feature with a single manufacturer or seller. In other words, a functional feature is not protected as trade dress even if the owner could prove secondary meaning.

It certainly seems desirable, when addressing trademark rights and their use, to take under advisement the importance of the manner in which marks are used on products or in connection with services in the marketplace. A mark that is otherwise available for your use might, by virtue of its trade dress, infringe the right of another.

Hence, if you are going to employ packaging or other devices that are patterned after or are otherwise similar to the trade dress employed by a competitor, you should be warned that the result might well be held to violate trade dress rights of the competitor and be encouraged to evaluate this possibility further before proceeding to finalize packaging and other marketing materials.

Formal Registration

Trade dress may be registered with the USPTO in either the Principal Register or the Supplemental Register. Although registration is not required for legal protection, registration offers several advantages. In the Principal Register, a registrant gains nationwide constructive use and constructive notice, which prevent others from using or registering that registrant's trade dress (without contesting the registration). Further, a registrant in the Principal Register gains incontestable status after five years, which eliminates many of the ways for another party to challenge the registration. Registration under the Supplemental Register allows the registrant to protect its trade dress in foreign countries, although the protections are much more limited than protections under the Principal Register in the U.S.

TRADEMARK PROTECTION AND PROSECUTION

Distinctiveness

To gain registration in the Principal Register or common law protection under the Lanham Act, a trade dress must be "distinctive." This means that consumers perceive a particular trade dress as identifying a source of a product.

Claimed trade dress in the product design – as opposed to product packaging – context can no longer be "inherently distinctive;" it must acquire distinctiveness through "secondary meaning." *Wal-Mart Stores, Inc. v. Samara Brothers, Inc.* Here, the court ruled that distinctiveness through secondary meaning means that although a trade dress is not distinctive on its face, the use of the trade dress in the market (the "goodwill" of the trade dress) has created an association between the trade dress and a source in the mind of the consumer.

Although the law is evolving, as it stands now, product packaging (including packaging in very general terms, such as a building's décor) may be inherently distinctive. However, product design, that is the design or shape of the product itself, may not be inherently distinctive, and must acquire secondary meaning to be protected.

Marks Consisting of a Configuration of a Product

In *Wal-Mart*, the United States Supreme Court held that while packaging may sometimes be distinctive, a configuration of a product can never be inherently distinctive; therefore, it is registrable only upon a showing of secondary meaning. The Court noted that product design almost invariably serves purposes other than source identification, and that consumers are aware that even the most unusual product design (e.g., a cocktail shaker shaped like a penguin) is intended not to identify the source, but to make the product itself more useful or appealing.

Therefore, the examining attorney must refuse to register, on the Principal Register, a mark that consists of a configuration of a product or portion thereof, unless the applicant establishes that the mark has acquired distinctiveness under Section 2(f). The examining attorney must issue this refusal in all applications seeking registration of a product design, regardless of the basis of the application. The ground for refusal is that the proposed mark consists of a non-distinctive configuration of the goods or portion thereof, and thus does not function as a mark under sections 1, 2, and 45 of the Lanham Act.

Examples:

❖ If a Section 1(b) applicant seeks to register the configuration of a barbecue grill and the goods are "barbecue grills," even absent a use amendment, in the first Office Action the examining attorney must refuse registration because the asserted mark is not inherently distinctive.

❖ If in a Section 44(e) application the record shows that the mark sought to be registered is the configuration of an automobile grille and the goods are "automobiles," in the first Office Action the examining attorney must refuse registration because the asserted mark is not inherently distinctive.

If the product configuration is not de jure (i.e., concerning law) functional, the mark may be registered on the Supplemental Register, or, if the applicant shows that the product configuration has acquired distinctiveness, on the Principal Register under Section 2(f).

Marks Consisting of Product Packaging for Goods or Trade Dress for Service

The Court's decision in the *Wal-Mart* case was limited to product design marks. Therefore, if the proposed mark consists of product packaging for goods or trade dress for services, the examining attorney should apply current practice and determine whether the mark is inherently distinctive. If it is not, the examining attorney must refuse registration on the ground that the proposed mark is not inherently distinctive under Sections 1, 2 and 45 for trademark applications, or under Sections 1, 2, 3 and 45 for service mark applications.

"A mark is inherently distinctive if its intrinsic nature serves to identify a particular source," cited *Wal-Mart*. To determine whether a mark is inherently distinctive, the examining attorney must consider whether the proposed mark is:

❖ A "common" basic shape or design;

❖ Unique or unusual in the field in which it is used;

❖ A mere refinement of a commonly-adopted and well-known form of ornamentation for a particular class of goods viewed by the public as a dress or ornamentation for the goods;

❖ Capable of creating a commercial impression distinct from the accompanying words.

TRADEMARK PROTECTION AND PROSECUTION

The courts have also held, while the designs applicant seeks to register may be unique in the sense that we have no evidence that anyone else is using designs which are identical to them, they are nonetheless not inherently distinctive. The courts have also held, novel tubular lights used in connection with bowling alley services would be perceived by customers as "simply a refinement of the commonplace decorative or ornamental lighting" and would not be inherently regarded as a source indicator.

Unlike applications for product designs, applications for product packaging for goods or trade dress for services based on Section 1(b) of the Lanham Act generally will not be refused registration on the ground of non-distinctiveness until the applicant has filed an amendment to allege use or statement of use.

Regardless of basis, if the proposed mark is inherently distinctive and is not de jure functional it may be registered on the Principal Register. If the proposed mark is not inherently distinctive and is not de jure functional the mark may be registered on either the Principal Register under Section 2(f) or the Supplemental Register.

Example:

- ❖ A section 44(e) applicant seeks to register the configuration of a perfume bottle and the goods are "perfume." If the examining attorney determines that the bottle shape is inherently distinctive and is not de jure functional, it may be registered on the Principal Register.

Color Marks

Color marks consist solely of one or more colors used on goods or in connection with services. In *Wal-Mart*, the court stated that color marks are never inherently distinctive. Therefore, the examining attorney must refuse to register a color mark on the Principal Register unless the applicant establishes that the mark has acquired distinctiveness under Section 2(f). The examining attorney must issue this refusal in all color mark applications, regardless of the basis of the application. For Section 1(b) applications, the examining attorney must issue the refusal even if the applicant has not filed an amendment to allege use or statement of use. The ground for refusal is that the color is not inherently distinctive and thus does not function as a trademark under Sections 1, 2 and 45, or does not function as a service mark under Sections 1, 2, 3 and 45.

Functionality

To gain registration in the Principal Register or common law protection under the Lanham Act, a trade dress must not be "functional." That is, the configuration of shapes, designs, colors, or materials that make up the trade dress in question must not serve a utility or function outside of creating recognition in the consumer's mind. For example, even though consumers associated a distinct spring design for wind resistant road signs with a particular company, the spring design was not protectable for trade dress purposes because the springs served the function of withstanding heavy wind conditions.

What is considered "functional" depends upon the specific product or thing sought to be protected. For example, the color red in a line of clothing may not be functional (and thus part of protectable trade dress) whereas the same color on a stop sign would be functional because the color red serves the function of putting drivers on alert (and thus would not be part of a protectable trade dress).

Marks that Are Functional

When an applicant applies to register a product design, product packaging for goods, trade dress for services, or color, in addition to determining whether the proposed mark is inherently distinctive, the examining attorney must determine whether the mark is de jure (i.e., concerning law) functional. If the proposed mark is de jure functional, it cannot be registered on either the Principal Register or the Supplemental Register.

To determine if a proposed mark is de jure functional, the examining attorney must consider how the asserted mark is used. Generally, in a Section 1(b) application the examining attorney will not issue a refusal on the ground that the mark is de jure functional until the applicant has filed an amendment to allege use or statement of use.

Electronic Interfaces and Websites

Although the exact parameters of protection are still uncertain, courts are beginning to allow trade dress protection for the overall "look and feel" of a website. In *Blue Nile, Inc. v. Ice.com, Inc.*, the plaintiff sued the defendant for copying the overall "look and feel" of plaintiff's retail jewelry websites, including the design of plaintiff's search pages. Although the court ordered more factual development before it could rule definitively on the issue, the court did hold that it was possible for the look and feel of the websites to have trade dress protection if the plaintiff's copyright claims did not already cover those parts. In *SG Services, Inc. v. God's Girls, Inc.*, the court denied trade dress protection for the plaintiff's website because the plaintiff did not demonstrate that the website was non-functional or distinctive. This case shows the court's willingness to consider trade dress protection for a website, even though the court did not find protection in this case. It is notable, however, that the *SG Services* court did not look at the overall "look and feel" of the website, but rather, at specific characteristics (such as color) of the website that the plaintiff claimed were infringed.

Although the future of trade dress protection for websites is still very unclear, much thought has been given to this area and it will likely continue to be an actively developing area for courts and litigants.

CHAPTER 7
TRADE NAME

A trade name, also known as a trading name or a business name, is the name, which a business trades under for commercial purposes, although its registered, legal name, used for contracts and other formal situations, may be another. For example, the company Panda Chemical Manufacturers, Inc. may use the more friendly name Panda Pharmaceuticals when it holds itself out to the public. In this example, Panda Pharmaceuticals is the trade name. The registration of trade names and marks is not legally required, but is an accepted business practice.

Choice of Name

Choosing a business name is one of the most important decisions you will make and is the first step in branding your business. A business name is different from your trademarks, service marks, logos, and slogans. Trademark law protects product names, logos, and trade names, even some slogans as trademarks or service marks. Copyright law protects written works, works of art, and other creative works. Patent law protects inventions and designs. Business law, however, does not fully guarantee you the exclusive use of your business name. To get close to exclusivity, you have to be first, you have to be national, and you have to be alert.

The most common misunderstanding about business names is about reserving, registering, and protecting business names. You can't reserve a business name or have exclusive use completely. Think of a business name as a lot like a personal name, many people often have the same name. So too, the first John Smith can't stop all other persons named John Smith from using that same name. Just like XYZ Restaurant can't make XYZ Hardware Store change its name, and XYZ Hardware Store in San Francisco can't sue XYZ Hardware Store in Manhattan.

The confusion starts because business names are registered by different authorities in different places, and on different levels.

- ❖ The first and simplest business name is your own name, which might be enough for John Smith using John Smith Publishing. This kind of business name normally does not require any additional paperwork.
- ❖ The second level of business names is called DBA for "doing business as" which is commonly used for sole proprietorships comprising an individual, husband and wife, or partnership. Registering a Fictitious Business Name statement within your county government gives an individual the right to operate under a business name with bank accounts, checks, etc. if yours is the first business in the county with that name. Consequently, there might still be a Chrysalis Restaurant as a DBA in any other counties within any given state.
- ❖ The third level of business name is the corporation, including C corporations, S corporations, and limited liability companies. The corporation is registered at the state level by filing charter documents within its state. Subsequently, no two corporations can have the exact same name in that state. Then again, there might be a Chrysalis Restaurant in other states.

Although duplicate business names are possible and common, you do still have the right to protect and defend your own business name by registering your business name with the United States Patent and Trademark Office (USPTO). In the U.S., a registered trademark or trade name trumps a non-registered first use defense within the U.S. However, in many other countries, first use trumps a registered trademark or trade name creating more confusion with our growing global economy.

Business Name Considerations

First impressions count and the business name you choose is initially the only thing customers and suppliers know about you. For example, it projects important messages to customers, staff, and suppliers, making it a critical aspect towards success. Your business name also casts a certain brand image and should reflect the personality of the organization in a way that appeals to the target market, making it suitable for the company and its target group.

Your domain name is equally as important as your business name and should also have strong business characteristics. Finding a descriptive name, which can be typed easily and quickly into the address bar of the Internet browser, is not

TRADE NAME

always easy. If they are not already taken, they are usually very long. However, one should attempt to find a descriptive name, as it offers some advantages for the Google ranking and users will know instantly what to make of it. In the end, the name should identify the purpose of the company or product, search engines should love it, and the domain ".com" should still be available.

When choosing a name for your business, the name should be easy to remember, easy to pronounce or spell, as well as compact and unique at the same time. You want a name that sets you apart from your competitors, is simple, and one that will be able to fit your business for years to come.

Your logo should be unique; imitating an established brand's logo should be avoided at all costs. Once your business evolves and areas such as your branding will evolve over time, updating a logo is a lot easier than updating a name. If you take the time to come up with the right business name to start with, you'll reap the dividends over the years.

The email signature you use is also important. A strong email name, logo design, and slogan will allow you to attract the best opportunities.

Business Name Commercial Tie-In Checklist

- ✓ Does the name accurately reflect the business image?
- ✓ Does the name identify your business – is it descriptive?
- ✓ Is your business name short, memorable, and easy to spell?
- ✓ Does your choice of business name stand out – is it unique?
- ✓ Does the name have a strong visual element – logo, colors?

On the other hand, some of the nation's most notable brands, such as Google, Apple, Amazon and Nike chose a non-descriptive name. You might ask, "How valuable was the name Google on the first day the search engine went live?" I'm willing to bet that this unique name meant absolutely nothing to the vast majority of people online at the time. However, as the company grew, this name began to grow in prestige and value.

Many small businesses are afraid of putting a name out there that says nothing about their offering and or a name that nobody knows. Make no mistake; it will be tough in the beginning. However, if you work hard at giving your name meaning, it may very well be the very thing that gives you an edge in the end.

Nonetheless, before choosing a commercial tie-in name or a name nobody has ever heard of before, you must consider legal requirements as well. For example, you should search the various indexes of company names to ensure your chosen name is not the same as an existing registered company. You may want to start with search engine searches using Google, Yahoo!, MSN, etc. You are also advised to check your name against trademark databases within and outside the U.S.

Inasmuch, there are a number of rules which apply to company names.

Business Name Legal Requirements Checklist

- ✓ Is the business name already in use?
- ✓ Is the business name trademarked by someone else?
- ✓ Is your business domain name available?
- ✓ Does your logo design exist?
- ✓ Is your slogan, catchphrase or jingle available?

The name of a business is not case sensitive. For example, the Articles of Incorporation or Certificate of Incorporation and USPTO will list the business name in capitals. But it is perfectly legal to use any combination of upper- and lower-case letters for the company name after formation, regardless of the format used in the charter documents and with the USPTO.

Once you have selected a business name, you should first register the name in the county or counties in which you choose "to do business in" with the County Clerk's office(s) therein. Then, if appropriate, you should also register the name in the state or states in which you choose "to do business in" with the Secretary of State's office(s) therein. You should also have a second-choice name ready in case the county or state confirms your first-choice name is unavailable.

Business Name County Filings

The purpose of registering a fictitious business name with the County Clerk is to ensure that consumers have access to the true names and addresses of the business owners. If conducting business as an individual, husband and wife, general partnership, co-partners, or other unincorporated association, a Fictitious Business Name Statement is not required as long as the business name contains the surname of all the owners, and does not indicate the existence of other owners. Similarly, if the business is conducted by a corporation, limited partnership (LP), limited liability partnership (LLP), or a limited liability company, a Fictitious Business Name Statement is required if the business name is not the same as the registered corporation, LP, LLP, or LLC name.

TRADE NAME

Filing Requirements

- ❖ Fictitious Business Name Statements must be filed before you begin your business or within forty days of your first transaction.

- ❖ A Fictitious Business Name Statement is effective for five years.

- ❖ Fictitious Business Name Statements must be filed in the county in which the principal place of business is based.

- ❖ An applicant may have more than one fictitious business name and there may be more than one registrant per fictitious business name.

- ❖ Registration of a Fictitious Business Name Statement does not guarantee exclusive use of that name; applicants are responsible for ensuring that the chosen fictitious business name does not duplicate a current registration or violate any trademark protocols.

- ❖ All information in the Fictitious Business Name Statement filed with the County Clerk is public record pursuant to the California Public Record Act including the residence address.

- ❖ Be certain the information in the statement is correct and complete before filing it. Once your statement has been filed, changes to that filing cannot be made, and no refunds will be issued.

TRADEMARK PROTECTION AND PROSECUTION

SAMPLE FICTITIOUS BUSINESS NAME STATEMENT FORM

TRADE NAME

Filing FBNS Checklist

- ✓ Research the name online or in-person at the County Clerk's office.
- ✓ Obtain an application online, in-person, or by mail.
- ✓ Complete the form in black ink. The second page of the form has specific instructions on how to complete the form.
- ✓ Check the current fee.
- ✓ Choose a payment method, online, in-person or by mail.
- ✓ Your copy and publication information (if needed) will be given to you at the County Clerk's office or returned to you by mail.

Publishing Requirement

After your statement has been filed, publishing is required under the following circumstances in the state of California (Business and Professions Code 17917): (a) new Fictitious Business Name Statement filing; (b) a renewal or re-filing of Fictitious Business Name Statement with changes; (c) a renewal or re-filing of Fictitious Business Name Statement occurring more than forty days after the expiration date; (d) the filing of a Statement of Abandonment of use of fictitious business name; or (e) the filing of a Statement of Withdrawal from partnership operating under fictitious business name. California law publishing requirements include:

- ❖ The legal notice must be published a total of four times (once a week for four consecutive weeks).
- ❖ The first publication must appear within thirty days of filing date.
- ❖ California Codes Business and Professions Code 17917(d) indicates an Affidavit showing the publication of the statement shall be filed with the County Clerk where Fictitious Business Name Statement was filed within thirty days after the completion of the publication.
- ❖ The newspaper may offer a service to file this Affidavit for you. You will want to check with the newspaper to receive information about the service and any associated charges.
- ❖ In other cases, the newspaper may give the Affidavit directly to you. You may bring the Affidavit to the County Clerk's office or mail it to them.
- ❖ All information on the Fictitious Business Name Statement including the residence address will be published.

If publishing is required, your statement must be published in a newspaper that has been adjudicated as one of general circulation as per California Government Code Section 6000. It is your responsibility to ascertain the current adjudication status of the newspaper you plan to use. Be sure to allow sufficient time for the newspaper to prepare your statement for publication. Failure to publish as required by law will cause your statement to expire, and will require a new statement to be filed, including the payment of another filing fee.

Business Name State Filings

Proposed names for sole proprietorships, partnerships, corporations, LLCs, as well as newly qualifying foreign (out-of-state) businesses and businesses of record preparing to change their name, should be pre-cleared through the name availability section of the Secretary of State's office of the appropriate state prior to the submittal of documents for filing. The pre-clearance and/or reservation of a business name is necessary to avoid the rejection of documents submitted to the Secretary of State for filing because of a name conflict.

Most secretaries of state maintain a consolidated list of the following: (i) names of all corporations, LLCs and limited partnerships organized under the laws of that state in good standing, (ii) names of all foreign corporations, LLCs and limited partnerships qualified to transact intrastate business in the state and in good standing, and (iii) names reserved for future issuance. Charter documents will not be accepted for filing if the stated name resembles closely, is confusingly similar to, or is the same as any name on the consolidated list.

For example, the California Secretary of State maintains a consolidated list of the following: (i) names of all California corporations in good standing, (ii) names of all foreign corporations qualified to transact intrastate business in California and in good standing, (iii) corporate names reserved under Section 201(c) of the California Corporations Code (the "Code"), (iv) names of nonqualified foreign corporations registered under Section 2101 of the Code, and (v) names that will become record names of domestic or qualified foreign corporations at some delayed effective date of a filed corporate instrument, such as a merger agreement. The Secretary of State will not accept Articles of Incorporation for filing if the stated corporate name resembles closely, is confusingly similar to, or is the same as any name on the consolidated list. Note that the Secretary of State deems the words "corporation", "incorporated" and "inc." to be one and the same word. See Code Section 201(b).

TRADE NAME

A further consideration in selecting a name is whether that name is available for use in other states where the organization will be conducting business. Most states have laws similar to that of California governing business names. State laws generally provide for the use of an "assumed" name in a foreign state when an organization's true name is not available in a state. The same considerations regarding name availability are applicable to limited partnerships and limited liability companies.

You should also give consideration at this time to trademark and trade name issues. You may also obtain trademark searches to determine if there are conflicting or similar trademark or trade names in use. In addition to searching the USPTO records, research firms, such as CORESEARCH and Thomson & Thomson, can perform these services for a fee. Giving careful consideration to these issues during the planning and organizational phase can save you considerable frustration and time and money in the future.

If a corporate, limited partnership or limited liability company name is not available because that name or a similar one is in use, it is possible to obtain the consent of the entity using the name. If you have received such consent, you file the consent with the Articles of Incorporation, Certificate of Limited Partnership, or Articles of Organization, respectively. You may obtain the address of the entity already in existence, and the name of its officers, from the Secretary of State's office.

When selecting a business name, it is advisable to check the business codes and other corporate statutes of the proposed state of incorporation for any special provisions relating to corporate names. In California, for instance, the words "bank," "trust," "trustee," or related words, may not be a part of the corporate name unless a Certificate of Approval of the Superintendent of Banks is attached to the Articles of Incorporation. The word "co-operative," or any abbreviation or derivation of that may not be part of a corporate name unless the corporation is incorporated pursuant to specified sections of the Code. For example, in some states the name of a person may not be used as a corporate name without the addition of a corporate ending or some other word or words, which show that the name is not that of the individual alone.

It should also be noted that the name of a California corporation formed as a close corporation must contain the word "corporation," "incorporated," "limited," or an abbreviation of one of such words. In addition, special rules apply for the names of professional corporations. Before selecting a name for a professional corporation, refer to the law expressly applicable to the particular professional corporation in the Business and Professions Code and to the rules and regulations of the particular state agency regulating the profession. There are also provisions governing the use of names by corporations that are organized for the furnishing of professional engineering services to be performed by licensed persons.

The availability of a name may be determined on a preliminary basis by calling the Secretary of State's office for corporations or for limited partnerships. Two names will be checked per each telephone call. (A name may not be reserved by a telephone call to the Secretary of State's office.) A telephone check is subject to later verification, and the Articles may be rejected if the telephone check was inaccurate. It is strongly recommended not to rely on verbal information obtained by telephone in proceeding to file Articles.

Filing Services

If you do not have a pre-paid account with sufficient funds already set up with the Secretary of State, it is recommended that the desired name immediately be reserved to ensure its availability through a filing service such as AmeriSearch, GKL Corporate/Search, CSC Networks/Prentice Hall Corporate Services, or CT Corporation. It is strongly advisable to obtain a minimum of three proposed names, ranked in order of preference, to facilitate reservation of a name in the event that the first-choice name is not available. The use of a filing service is more expensive than using a pre-paid account.

It is recommended that you have the filing service reserve the name as noted above, which is fast and relatively inexpensive. Alternatively, you may reserve a name by a written request directly to the Secretary of State; however, this is a much slower process. A written request for name reservation may include up to four names, listed in preferred order, with a request that the first available name be reserved. There is typically a nominal charge for each name reserved and the fee must accompany the request.

Name Reservation

In California, names are reserved for sixty days from the date of issuance of a Certificate of Reservation for Corporation Name. It is possible to reserve a name for a second sixty-day period after a one business day has elapsed following the expiration of the first sixty-day period, provided no other person has reserved the name during the one-day interim period.

In states other than California, the time period for which names will be reserved varies greatly. In Delaware, for instance, names are reserved for a period of thirty days. When a corporate name has been reserved in one or more states, it is advisable to calendar the expiration date.

It is important, but difficult, to understand the difference between the actions of a Secretary of State in allowing the use of a name and the issues involved in the use of a name or mark for purposes of identifying a good or service. The determination of a Secretary of State in approving the use of a name merely means that an entity has complied with state law that prohibits the Secretary of State from filing charter documents for a business with a name that so closely resembles the name of another business organized or qualified to do business in that state as to tend to deceive the public. Approval of a name by the Secretary of State does not imply anything other than that the proposed name has passed this statutory test.

A promising start-up business may find its business plan abruptly derailed when it receives a demand to change its name or face an injunction and penalties for trademark infringement. The business owner can avoid this problem by understanding the fundamentals of trademark law.

Trademarks vs. Trade Names

Trademark protection is based on a public policy determination that consumers will benefit if they can associate a particular name or mark with the person or entity that is the source of the good or service sold in connection with the name or mark. Registration or state reservation of a corporate trade name does not confer trademark rights in that mark, the first or "senior" user of a mark or name is considered the owner of that mark even if someone else has been the first to apply to register or actually register the mark.

According to basic state and federal trademark law, trademark rights are acquired by using a mark on a product and selling that product or by displaying a mark in connection with the advertisement of services. The scope of rights acquired by simple use of a mark will vary depending upon the extent to which the mark is used. For example, if a mark is used nationwide, the rights acquired in it (barring the existence if prior conflicting owners) will also be nationwide. On the other hand, use of a mark solely in a single state may result in rights only in that single state. It is possible, however, to reserve nationwide rights in a mark prior to its actual use by filing an "intent-to-use" application with the USPTO. Actual use of a reserved mark must follow in order to secure the ownership rights.

Therefore, the fact that the California Secretary of State does not object to the use of a particular name as the name of a corporation does not necessarily mean that other people or entities are not already using the proposed name in connection with goods or services. If this is true, it is possible that such party

TRADEMARK PROTECTION AND PROSECUTION

would be able to prevent the California corporation from causing "confusion" in the marketplace by using the proposed name. For that reason, if it is important that the corporate name also be used as a trademark or trade name, you should have a search conducted of the existing marks in your proposed area of activity in order to determine how protectable a particular name or mark will be prior to its adoption. Legal counsel can assist you in arranging such search.

Once it seems clear that no conflicts exist and the name or mark is adopted, there are various legal and administrative procedures that can be followed in order to maximize the level of protection that such name or mark will receive.

CHAPTER 8

TRADEMARK PROSECUTION PROCESS

To obtain a U.S. trademark, a trademark application must be filed in the United States Patent and Trademark Office (USPTO). The application which preferably is filed online (it's cheaper) contains a description of the goods or services, a drawing, and a specimen if the mark has already been used. The application must contain the date the applicant first used the mark anywhere in the world and the date the applicant first used the mark in interstate commerce in the United States for a "use" based application. The application does not require this if it is an "intent to use" based application. The application also includes the name of the applicant, the name and address to correspond, the identity of the goods or services that is the subject of the mark, the filing fee, and a basis for the application (either "use" based or "intent to use" based).

Trademark Manual of Examining Procedure

The Trademark Manual of Examining Procedure (TMEP) provides trademark examining attorneys in the USPTO, trademark applicants, and attorneys and representatives for trademark applicants with a reference work on the current law, practices, and procedures relative to prosecution of applications to register marks in the USPTO. The TMEP contains guidelines for examining attorneys and materials in the nature of information and interpretation, and outlines the procedures that examining attorneys are required or authorized to follow in the examination of trademark applications.

Identification of Goods and Services Manual

The acceptable Identification of Goods and Services Manual (ID Manual) lists identifications of goods and services and their respective classifications that the USPTO examining attorneys will accept without further inquiry if the specimens of record support the identification and classification, as explained earlier. Another resource is the International Schedule of Classes of Goods and Services, which lists, by class, of all of the headings for the international classes, which was also explained earlier.

Official Gazette

Every Tuesday, the USPTO issues the Official Gazette (OG), a publication that contains a depiction of the mark, the identification of goods and or services, and owner information for: (1) marks published for opposition on the Principal Register; (2) marks registered on the Principal Register; (3) marks registered on the Supplemental Register on the date of the particular issue in which the marks appear; and (4) updated registration certificates. The OG is presented in a .PDF format and is available for the fifty-two most recent issues.

Trademark Examination Guides

Between updates to the Trademark Manual of Examining Procedure (TMEP), the USPTO occasionally provides guidance about a particular issue through the issuance of an Examination Guide. Typically, as to that issue, the Examination Guide supersedes the current edition of the TMEP to the extent any inconsistency exists, and the guidance contained therein is usually incorporated into the next edition of the TMEP.

Design Search Code Manual

The USPTO assigns all marks containing design figurative elements six-digit numerical code(s) for searching purposes. This manual index' the categories, divisions, and sections that make up these codes. For example, a single five-pointed star would be coded in category 01 (celestial bodies, natural phenomena and geographical maps), division 01 (stars, comments) and section 03 (single star with five points), resulting in a complete design code of 01.01.03. The Design Search Code Manual also contains explanatory notes and specific guidelines that provide instructions for specific code sections, cross-reference notes that direct users to other code categories, sections and divisions, and notes describing elements that are included or excluded from a code section.

TRADEMARK PROSECUTION PROCESS

Trademark Prosecution Process Overview

The trademark prosecution process starts with your company's internal New Trademark Application Form. This form is typically completed by your marketing and sales or product development teams and submitted to management and or your Trademark Committee. The Trademark Committee should determine whether the trademark "candidate" would need trademark, patent, or copyright protection.

- ❖ A trademark is a word, phrase, symbol, and/or design that identifies and distinguishes the source of the goods of one party from those of others. A service mark is a word, phrase, symbol, and/or design that identifies and distinguishes the source of a service rather than goods. The term "trademark" is often used to refer to both trademarks and service marks.

    Must all marks be registered? No, but federal registration has several advantages, including a notice to the public of the registrant's claim of ownership of the mark, a legal presumption of ownership nationwide, and the exclusive right to use the mark on or in connection with the goods or services set forth in the registration.

- ❖ A patent is a limited duration property right relating to an invention, granted by the USPTO in exchange for public disclosure of the invention.

- ❖ A copyright protects works of authorship, such as writings, music, and works of art that have been tangibly expressed.

Trademark Attorney

If the Trademark Committee is not already staffed with a trademark attorney, you should determine whether you should hire such an attorney. Filing a trademark application at the USPTO starts a legal proceeding. Most applicants hire an attorney who specializes in trademark matters to represent them in the application process and provide legal advice. While a USPTO trademark examining attorney will try to help you through the process even if you do not hire a lawyer, no USPTO attorney may give you legal advice.

A private trademark attorney can help you before, during, and after the trademark application process; including policing and enforcing any trademark registration that may issue. While you are not required to have an attorney, an attorney may save you from future costly legal problems by conducting a comprehensive search of federal registrations, state registrations, and "common law" unregistered trademarks before you file your application. Comprehensive searches are important because other trademark owners may have protected legal rights in trademarks similar to yours that are not federally registered. Therefore, those trademarks will not appear in the USPTO's Trademark Electronic Search System (TESS) database but could still ultimately prevent your use of your mark.

In addition, trademark lawyers can help you during the application process with several things that could seriously impact your trademark rights, such as determining the best way to describe your goods and services and preparing responses to refusals to register that an examining attorney may issue. Finally, a private attorney can also assist in the policing and enforcement of your trademark rights. The USPTO only registers trademarks. You as the trademark owner are responsible for any enforcement.

Representation of the Mark

Next, the Trademark Committee and or trademark attorney should identify your mark format, that is, whether the trademark "candidate" is (1) a standard character mark, (2) a stylized or design mark, or (3) a sound mark. The standard character format should be used to register word(s), letter(s), number(s) or any combination thereof, without claim to any particular font style, size, or color, and absent any design element. Registration of a mark in the standard character format will provide broad rights, namely use in any manner of presentation. The stylized/design format, on the other hand, is appropriate if you wish to register a mark with a design element and/or word(s) and/or letter(s) having a particular stylized appearance that you wish to protect. Formats (1) and (2) may not be mixed in one mark, i.e., do not submit a representation of a mark that attempts to combine a standard character format and a stylized/design format.

Identify Goods and Services

The Trademark Committee should identify clearly the precise goods and or services to which the mark will apply. The acceptable Identification of Goods and Services Manual (ID Manual) contains a listing of acceptable identifications of goods and services. Any entry you choose must accurately describe your goods and services. A failure to correctly list the goods and services with which you use your mark, or intend to use your mark, may prevent you from registering your mark.

Trademark Clearance Search

The Trademark Committee should initiate trademark clearance searches by private sector and or search of the USPTO database to determine whether

TRADEMARK PROSECUTION PROCESS

anyone is already claiming trademark rights in a particular mark through a federal registration. That is, before submitting the trademark application, a trademark clearance search and opinion should be performed outside of the USPTO application process to determine whether any conflict with an existing mark exists and which the examiner might raise as an objection, and whether an outside party may object in opposition proceedings, or in litigation.

A trademark clearance search and opinion provide this determination. If a conflict does not exist, and your mark is not determined to be generic, descriptive, geographically descriptive, a surname, ornamental, or geographically mis-descriptive then application for federal registration is appropriate for filing with the USPTO to have the mark registered federally.

SAMPLE PRIVATE SECTOR TRADEMARK RESEARCH REPORT

THOMSON & THOMSON

Our File: 936-79411-55
Your File: _____

Trademark Research Report

Client Name: NATUS MEDICAL INC
Attention: SUSAN HANSEN
Date Received: July 2, 2002   Received by: Telephone
Date Completed: July 8, 2002

Mark Searched: BILIBLUE (OR) BILI BLUE

Type of Search: MCSS-LEVEL II

Goods/Services: MEDICAL SERVICES; MEDICAL INSTRUMENTS

TRADEMARK PROTECTION AND PROSECUTION

BILIBLUE (OR) BILI BLUE

Selected Databases
TRADEMARKSCAN: Canada, Austria, Benelux, Denmark, Finland, France, Germany, Italy, Liechtenstein, Monaco, Norway, Spain, Sweden, Switzerland, United Kingdom, Community Trademarks, Japan, International Register (selected countries only)

Full Text For Citations

BILOXI BLUES ref.1
T&T Trademark: BILOXI BLUES

TRADEMARKSCAN-- Canada

Application Number: 060316000
Registration Number: TMA359146
Mark Type: Trade-Mark
Status: Registered

Chronology
Filed: April 20, 1988
Advertised: November 16, 1988 Vol: 35 No: 1777
Allowed: May 1, 1989
Registered: August 4, 1989
Registration Type: TMA - Trademark Act

T&T International Class(es):
25   (Clothing)
Wares:
(1) Men's, ladies' and junior's jean wear, namely, jean jackets, shorts and pants.

BILIBLUE (OR) BILI BLUE

Reference: 26,117
Representative For Service:
LIBERMAN, SEGALL, FINKELBERG
4141 SHERBROOKE STREET WEST
SUITE 200
MONTREAL
QUEBEC H3Z 1B8
(514) 935-7783
Reference: 26,117

Declaration Of Use Information:
Declaration of use filed June 13, 1989 on wares marked (1)

Disclaims:
The right to the exclusive use of the word BLUES is disclaimed apart from the trade mark.
Subject Headings:
 BILOXI BLUES
BLUES, BILOXI

Action History
Registered on August 4, 1989
Allowed on May 1, 1989
Advertised on November 16, 1988
Correspondence Created on July 12, 1988
Search Recorded on July 4, 1988
Filed on April 20, 1988

TRADEMARK PROSECUTION PROCESS

BILIBLUE (OR) BILI BLUE

```
BILLY BLUES   ref.2
TRADEMARKSCAN-- France
Application Number:  44408592
Registration Number: 44408592
Status:   ENREGISTREMENT (REGISTRATION)
Application Date:    01 Decembre 1992 (December 1, 1992)
Expiration Date:     30 Novembre 2002 (November 30, 2002)
Duration:  10 years
Goods/Services:
   SAUCES POUR BARBECUE. RESTAURATION (ALIMENTATION) ET SERVICES DE BAR.
Goods/Services Translation:
   BARBECUE SAUCE. RESTAURANTS (FOOD) AND SERVICES OF BARS.

International Class(es):
30  (Epices, boulangerie/Staple foods)
42  (Services divers/Miscellaneous service marks)

Last Reported Owner:
BILLY BLUES FOOD CORPORATION, (Societe constituee sous les lois de l'Etat du Texas)
1250 NE Loop 410 - Suite 212, San Antonio, Texas 78209
US (ETATS-UNIS D'AMERIQUE/ UNITED STATES OF AMERICA)

Agent Information:
NOVAMARK INTERNATIONAL
63 bis, boulevard Bessieres, 75017 PARIS
   INPI File Number:  444085
Location:  I.N.P.I.
Last Full Publication:  15 Janvier 1993 (January 15, 1993)
In Journal:  BOPI NL 02 page 105
Notes:
   LIEU DE DEPOT (PLACE OF APPLICATION): I.N.P.I.

Historical Information:
PUBLICATION DU DEPOT (PUBLICATION OF APPLICATION):
BOPI NL Volume 02 page 105 dated 15 January 1993

AVIS D'ENREGISTREMENT (NOTIFICATION OF REGISTRATION):
BOPI NL Volume 19 page 283 dated 14 May 1993
```

BILIBLUE (OR) BILI BLUE

```
BILLY BLUES   ref.3
TRADEMARKSCAN-- Germany
Application Number:  B 96390 42WZ
Registration Number: 2045381
Status:   EINTRAGUNG (REGISTRATION)
Application Date:    18 August 1992 (August 18, 1992)
Registered:   21 September 1993 (September 21, 1993)
Expiration Date:     31 August 2002 (August 31, 2002)
Duration:  10 years
Goods/Services:
   SOSSEN (AUSGENOMMEN SALATSOSSEN), INSBESONDERE BARBECUE-SOSSEN; BEWIRTUNG VON GAESTEN
IN RESTAURANTS UND BARS, PARTY-SERVICE.
Goods/Services Translation:
   SAUCE (EXCEPT SALAD DRESSINGS), BARBECUE SAUCE; CATERING OF GUESTS IN RESTAURANTS AND
BARS, PARTY SERVICES.

International Class(es):
30  (Konditorwaren, Gewuerze/Staple foods)
42  (Verschiedene Dienstleistungen/Miscellaneous service marks)

Last Reported Owner:
Billy Blues Food Corporation, San Antonio
Tex
US (VEREINIGTE STAATEN/ UNITED STATES OF AMERICA)

Agent Information:
Stolberg, U., Graf, Dr.
1000 Hamburg
DE (DEUTSCHLAND (BRD))
Last Full Publication:  30 Oktober 1993 (October 30, 1993)
In Journal:  WBBL II 20 page 6483
```

TRADEMARK PROTECTION AND PROSECUTION

BILIBLUE (OR) BILI BLUE

BILBAO BLUE ref.7
TRADEMARKSCAN-- Spain
Application Number: 2231667M1
Registration Number: 2231667M1
Status: CONCESION (REGISTRATION)
Application Date: 03 Mayo 1999 (May 3, 1999)
Registered: 22 Mayo 2000 (May 22, 2000)
Expiration Date: 02 Mayo 2009 (May 2, 2009)
Duration: 10 years
Goods/Services:
 PAPEL, CARTON Y ARTICULOS DE ESTAS MATERIAS NO INCLUIDOS EN OTRAS CLASES; PRODUCTOS DE
 IMPRENTA; ARTICULOS DE ENCUADERNACION; FOTOGRAFIAS; PAPELERIA; ADHESIVOS (PEGAMENTOS)
 PARA LA PAPELERIA O LA CASA; MATERIAL PARA ARTISTAS;PINCELES; MAQUINAS DEESCRIBIR
 Y ARTICULOS DE OFICINA (EXCEPTO MUEBLES); MATERIAL DE INSTRUCCION O DE ENSENANZA
 (EXCEPTO APARATOS); MATERIAS PLASTICAS PARA EMBALAJE (NO INCLUIDAS EN OTRAS CLASES);
 CARACTERES DE IMPRENTA; BOLSAS O LAMINAS IMPRESAS O NO, PARA INVOLVER OEMBALAR.
 ETIQUETAS, ACUARELAS, DIBUJOS, FOTOGRABADOS.
Goods/Services Translation:
 PAPER, CARDBOARD AND ARTICLES MADE FROM THESE MATERIALS NOT INCLUDED IN OTHER CLASSES;
 PRINTED MATTER; BOOKBINDING ARTICLES; PHOTOGRAPHS; STATIONERY; ADHESIVES FOR STATIONERY
 (GLUES) OR HOUSEHOLD; MATERIALS FOR ARTISTS; BRUSHES; TYPEWRITERS ANDOFFICE REQUISITES
 (EXCEPT FURNITURE); TEACHING MATERIALS OR INSTRUCTION SERVICES (EXCEPT APPARATUS);
 PLASTICS FOR PACKAGING (NOT INCLUDED IN OTHER CLASSES); PRINTING TYPE; PURSES OR
 PRINTING PLATES OR NOT, FOR WRAPPING OR PACKAGING. LABELS, WATERCOLOURS, GRAPHIC PRINTS,
 PHOTO ENGRAVINGS.

International Class(es):
16 (Articulos de papel y productos de imprenta/Paper goods and printed matter)
Last Reported Owner:
SUASAGA MEABE JOSE LUIS
ES (ESPANA/ SPAIN)
Agent Information:
UNISAR ANASAGASTI, JESUS MARIA
Last Full Publication: 01 Julio 1999 (July 1, 1999)
In Journal: BOPI 2694 page 28466
Notes:
SUSPENDOS/EN SUSPENSO (SUSPENSION): DEFECTOS O MOTIVOS 01) FOR PARECIDO DETECTADO DE
OFICIO CON: CLASES M. COM. 0726059 BLUE 16 02) FOR OPOSICION BASADA EN: CLASES M. NAC.
2193151 BLUE 16
Historical Information:
SOLICITUD (APPLICATION):
BOPI Volume 2694 page 28466 dated 1 July 1999

SUSPENDOS/EN SUSPENSO (SUSPENSION):
BOPI Volume 2706 page 1098 dated 1 January 2000
 registered 22 November 1999

BILIBLUE (OR) BILI BLUE

BILLY BLUES ref.15
TRADEMARKSCAN-- Japan
Japanese Phonetics: BIRIIBURUUSU
Character Types: Roman
Application Number: H05-102861
Status: Lapsed (Expired)
Application Date: October 05, 1993
Duration: 10 YEARS
Law in Effect: 1991 Trademark Law
Final Disposition: Application Invalid
Final Disposition Date: October 25, 1996

International Class(es):
30 (Staple Foods)
National Class(es):
31A02 (Worcestershire sauce, Ketchup, Soy sauce, Vinegar, Essence of vinegar, Soba-
tsuyu (soup of soba), Salad dressing, White sauce, Mayonnaise, Sauce for barbecued meat)

Last Reported Owner:
BILLY BLOUSE FOOD CORP.

TEXAS
US(UNITED STATES)

Agent Information:
MARUYAMA TOSHIYUKI
Last Full Publication: January 10, 1996

Historical Information:
Date Published: January 10, 1996

TRADEMARK PROSECUTION PROCESS

You may conduct a search online for free via the USPTO database Trademark Electronic Search System (TESS) database. The search engine allows you to search the USPTO's database of registered trademarks and prior pending applications to find marks that may prevent registration due to a likelihood of confusion refusal. However, before conducting your search, you must understand the following: (1) what the database includes, (2) how to construct a complete search, and (3) how to interpret the search results.

- ❖ **What is in TESS?** TESS contains the records of active and inactive trademark registrations and applications, some of which could be found in the USPTO's examination of your application to be grounds for refusing to register your mark, i.e., if the examining attorney determines that a "likelihood of confusion" exists.

- ❖ **What is Not in TESS?** Some trademark owners with valid and protected trademark rights do not choose to register their marks with the USPTO, so those marks will not be found in this database. However, you should still consider these other marks when adopting a mark for your goods and or services. If a trademark is being used in the United States, the owner may have legally protected rights that are not the result of the USPTO registration process. You may therefore wish to consult a trademark attorney or professional trademark search firm for a more comprehensive search of, e.g., state registrations and common law marks.

- ❖ **Why should you perform a search?** The purpose of the search is to help determine whether a "likelihood of confusion" exists, i.e., whether any mark has already been registered or applied for at the USPTO that is (1) the same or similar to your mark; and (2) used on related products or for related services. Note that the identical mark could be registered to different parties if the goods or services are in no way related, e.g., for computers and soft drinks. Consequently, if your search reveals another mark that would definitely "block" your application based on the above standard, note that if you file anyway, the filing fee is a processing fee that the USPTO does not refund even if registration of your mark is refused.

- ❖ **Will your mark register if you do not find anything in TESS?** No, not necessarily. USPTO attorneys make decisions on whether marks may be registered. After you file your application, the USPTO will conduct its own search and other review, and might refuse your mark, based on several different possible grounds for refusal.

TRADEMARK PROTECTION AND PROSECUTION

❖ **How should you search?** The USPTO cannot provide guidance as to how you should search, beyond the linked HELP provided at the top of the first page of the TESS site. However, you must understand that a complete search is one that will uncover all similar marks, not just those that are identical. In addition to studying the marks, you must also closely study the listed goods and services to determine possible "relatedness." Searching for trademark availability is not the same as searching to register through a domain name registrar, for instances, a ".com" address, which focuses on exact or "dead on" hits, with no consideration given to similar names or use with related products and services. Also, if available, the domain name registrar may register a ".com" address on the same day as your search. The trademark registration process, on the other hand, is more complex. As part of the overall examination process, the USPTO will search its database to determine whether registration must be refused because a similar mark is already registered for related products or services. The USPTO does not offer advisory opinions on the availability of a mark prior to filing of an actual application.

❖ **Where can you find a table of color linings for older marks that were not filed in color but instead had drawings "lined" for color?** The Table of Color Linings is available at http://tess2.uspto.gov/tmdb/ dscm/dsc gl.htm#g15 (subsection G of Guideline #15).

If your mark includes a design element, you will need to search it by using a design code. To locate the proper design code(s), consult the Design Search Code Manual. Note: The USPTO is not able to conduct a search for you or provide legal advice concerning what would be a proper search.

If your search in TESS yields a mark that you think might conflict with your mark, make sure that the "Live/Dead Indicator" shows the mark to be "live." A "dead" mark could not be used to block your application.

TRADEMARK PROSECUTION PROCESS

SAMPLE USPTO TRADEMARK SEARCH

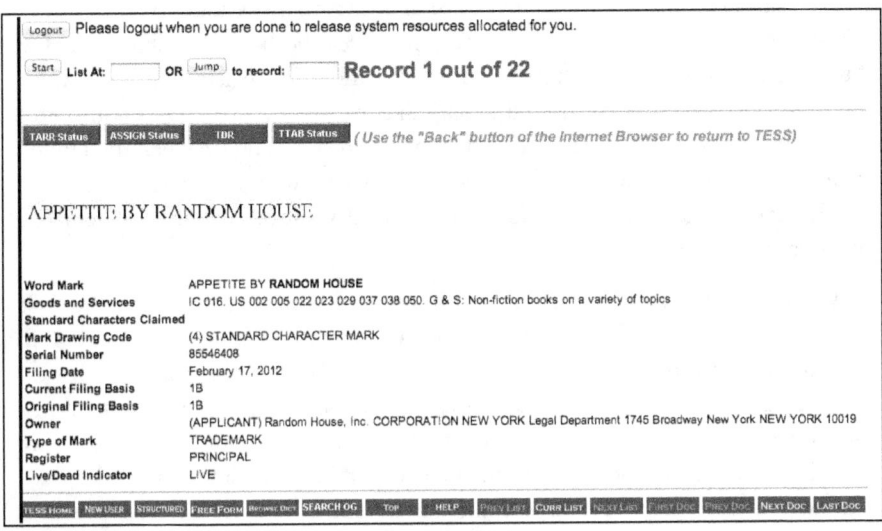

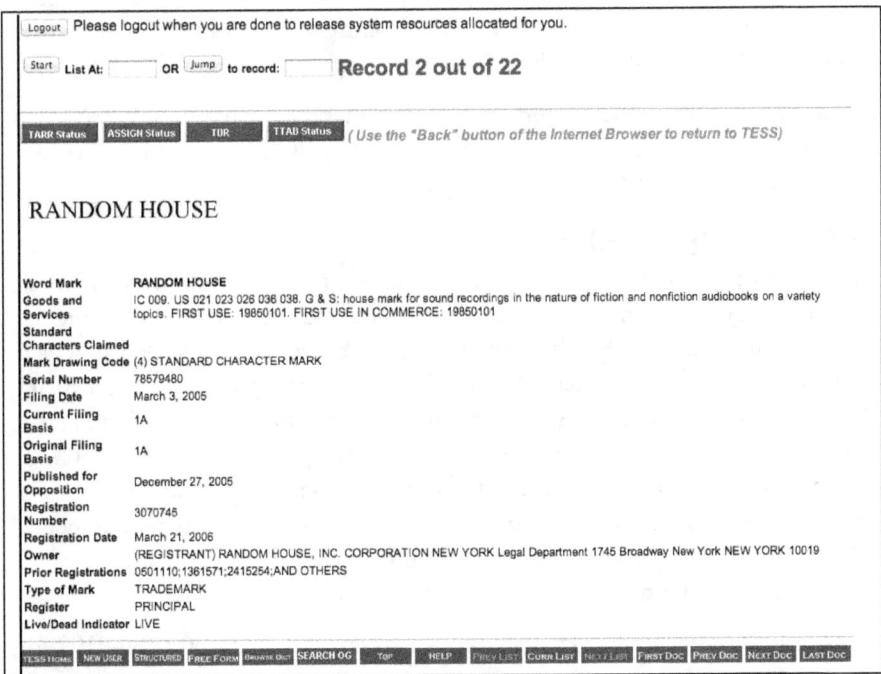

Proper "Basis" for Filing

Next, the Trademark Committee or management must identify the proper "basis" for filing a trademark application. Under the basis for filing of either "use in commerce" or "intent to use," prior to registration you must demonstrate that you have used the mark in commerce. The types of commerce encompassed in this definition are interstate, territorial, and between the United States and a foreign country. The basic difference between these two-filing basis is whether you have started to use the mark on all the goods or services identified in your application.

If you have already used your mark in commerce, you may file under the "use in commerce" basis. If you have not yet used your mark, but intend to use it in the future, you must file under the "intent to use" basis. This means you have a bona fide intent to use the mark in commerce; that is, you have more than just an idea but are less than market ready (for example, having a business plan, creating sample products, or performing other initial business activities). An "intent to use" basis requires filing an additional form and fee prior to registration that are not required if you file under "use in commerce" at the outset. Use is established by providing the date of first use of the mark anywhere and the date of first use of the mark in commerce, as well as submitting a specimen (example) showing how you use the mark in commerce.

Under certain international agreements, you may file in the U.S. based on a foreign application, foreign registration, or international registration. See the following chapter for specific requirements.

Filing the Application

The next step is to file the application. The online filing system allows you to fill out an application form and check it for completeness, and then submit the application directly to the USPTO over the Internet. You must decide which version of the form to file, namely, either a TEAS Plus application or a "regular" TEAS application. The TEAS Plus form has a lower filing fee of $275 per class of goods or services, but has stricter requirements, than the "regular" TEAS form. You must use the "regular" TEAS form, having a filing fee of $325 per class of goods or services, if you cannot satisfy the TEAS Plus requirements. Before accessing the electronic application form, you can preview the pages, to see what information will be required before starting the process.

You may also contact the Trademark Assistance Center at 1-800-786-9199 for a paper form. Paper forms are not processed as quickly as those submitted electronically, however.

TRADEMARK PROSECUTION PROCESS

Note that the application fee is a processing fee that is not refunded, even if ultimately no registration certificate issues; that is, not all applications result in registrations. Also note that all information you submit to the USPTO at any point in the application and or registration process will become public record, including your name, phone number, e-mail address, and street address.

The Application

- **The Mark.** Indicate the mark (for example, "THEORYTEC" or "PINSTRIPES AND DESIGN"). This should agree with the mark shown on the drawing page. If there is a discrepancy between the mark described in the written application and the mark displayed in the drawing, the drawing controls.

- **Classification.** It is not necessary to fill in this box. The USPTO will determine the proper International Classification based upon the identification of the goods and services in the application. However, if the applicant knows the International Class number(s) for the goods and services, the applicant may place the number(s) in this box. If the USPTO determines that the goods and services listed are in more than one class, the USPTO will notify the applicant during examination of the application, and the applicant will have the opportunity to pay the fees for any additional classes or to limit the goods and services to one or more classes.

- **The Owner of the Mark.** The name of the owner of the mark must be entered in this box. The application must be filed in the name of the owner of the mark, or the application will be void, and the applicant will forfeit the filing fee. The owner of the mark is the party who controls the nature and quality of the goods sold, or services rendered, under the mark. The owner may be an individual, a partnership, a corporation, or an association or similar firm. If the applicant is a corporation, the applicant's name is the name under which it is incorporated. If the applicant is a partnership, the applicant's name is the name under which it is organized.

- **The Owner's Address.** Enter the applicant's business address. If the applicant is an individual, enter either the applicant's business or home address.

- **Entity Type and Citizenship/Domicile.** The applicant must check the box, which indicates the type of entity applying. In addition, in the blank following the box, the applicant must specify the following information: (i) for an individual, the applicant's national citizenship; (ii) for a partnership, the names and national citizenship of the general partners and the state where the partnership is organized (if a U.S. partnership) or country (if a foreign partnership); (iii) for a corporation, the state of incorporation (if a U.S. corporation), or country (if a foreign corporation); or (iv) for another type of entity, specify the nature of the entity and the state where it is organized (if in the U.S.) or country where it is organized (if a foreign entity).

❖ **Identification of the Goods and or Services**. In this blank the applicant must state the specific goods and services for which registration is sought and with which the applicant has actually used the mark in commerce, or in the case of an "intent-to-use" application, has a bona fide intention to use the mark in commerce. Use clear and concise terms specifying the actual goods and services by their common commercial names. A mark can only be registered for specific goods and services. The goods and services listed will establish the scope of the applicant's rights in the relevant work.

The goods and services listed must be the applicant's actual "goods in trade" or the actual services the applicant renders for the benefit of others. Use language that would be readily understandable to the general public. For example, if the applicant uses or intends to use the mark to identify "candy," "word processors," "baseballs and baseball bats," "travel magazines," "dry cleaning services" or "restaurant services" the identification should clearly and concisely list each such item. If the applicant uses indefinite terms, such as "accessories," "components," "devices," "equipment," "food," "materials," "parts," "systems," "products," or the like, then those words must be followed by the word "namely" and the goods or services listed by their common commercial name(s). Note that the terms used in the classification listing are generally too broad. Do not use these terms by themselves.

The applicant must be very careful when identifying the goods and services. Because the filing of an application establishes certain presumptions of rights as of the filing date, the application may not be amended later to add any products or services not within the scope of the identification. For example, the identification of "clothing" could be amended to "shirts and jackets," which narrows the scope, but could not be amended to "retail clothing store services," which would change the scope. Similarly, "physical therapy services" could not be changed to "medical services" because this would broaden the scope of the identification. Also, if the identification includes a trade channel limitation, deleting that limitation would broaden the scope of the identification.

The identification of goods and services must not describe the mode of use of the mark, such as on labels, stationery, menus, signs, and containers or in advertising. There is another place on the application, called the "method-of-use clause," for this kind of information. For example, in the identification of goods and services, the term "advertising" usually is intended to identify a service rendered by advertising agencies. Moreover, "labels," "menus," "signs," and "containers" are specific goods. If the applicant identifies these goods or services by mistake, the applicant may not amend the identification to the actual goods or services of the applicant. Thus, if the identification indicates "menus," it could not be amended to "restaurant services." Similarly, if the goods are identified as "containers or labels for jam," the identification could not be amended to "jam."

Note: If nothing appears in this blank, or if the identification does not identify any recognizable goods or services, the application will be denied a filing date and returned to the applicant. For example, if the applicant specifies the mark itself or wording such as "company name," "corporate name," or "company logo," and nothing else, the application will be denied a filing date and returned to the applicant. If the applicant identifies the goods and services too broadly as, for example, "advertising and business," "miscellaneous goods and services," or just "products," or "services," the application will also be denied a filing date and returned to the applicant.

❖ **Basis for Filing.** The applicant must check at least one of the four boxes to specify a basis for filing the application. The applicant should also fill in all blanks which follow the checked box(es). Usually, an application is based upon either (1) use of the mark in commerce (the first box), or (2) a bona fide intention to use the mark in commerce (the second box). You may not check both the first and second box. If both the first and second boxes are checked, the USPTO will not accept the application and will return it. If an applicant wishes to apply to register a mark, for certain goods and services for which it is already using the mark in commerce, and also for other goods and services based on future use, separate applications must be filed to separate the relevant goods and services from each other.

Use of the Mark in Commerce. If the applicant is using the mark in commerce in relation to all of the goods and services listed in the application, check this first box and fill in the blanks. For example, in the first blank specify the date the trademark was first used to identify the goods and services in a type of commerce, which may be regulated by Congress. In the second blank specify the type of commerce, specifically a type of commerce, which may be related by Congress, in which the goods were sold or shipped, or the services were rendered. For example, indicate "interstate commerce" (commerce between two or more states) or commerce between the United States and a specific foreign country, for example, "commerce between the U.S. and Canada." In the third blank specify the dates that the mark was first used anywhere to identify the goods or services specified in the application. This date will be the same as the date of first use in commerce unless the applicant made some use, for example, within a single state, before the first use in commerce. In the fourth blank specify how the mark is placed on the goods or used with the services. This is referred to as the "method-of-use clause," and should not be confused with the identification of the goods and services described. For example, in relation to goods, state that "the mark is used on labels affixed to the goods," or "the mark is used on containers for the goods," whichever is accurate. In relation to services, state "the mark is used in advertisements for the services."

Bona Fide Intention to Use the Mark In Commerce. If the applicant has a bona fide intention to use the mark in commerce in relation to the goods or services specified in the application, check the second box and fill in the blank. The applicant should check this box if the mark has not been used at all or if the mark has been used on the specified goods or services only within a single state. For example, in the blank, state how the mark is intended to be placed on the goods or used with the services. For instance, for goods, state that "the mark will be used on labels affixed to the goods," or "the mark will be used on containers for the goods," whichever is accurate. For services, state "the mark will be used in advertisements for the services." The next spaces are usually used only by applicants from foreign countries who are filing in the United States under the international agreements. These applications are less common. For further information about treaty-based applications, contact the USPTO or private attorney.

❖ **Verification and Signature**. The applicant must verify the truth and accuracy of the information in the application and must sign the application. The declaration on the form is for this purpose. If the application is not signed, the application will not be granted a filing date and will be returned to the applicant. If the application is not signed by an appropriate person, the application will be found void and the filing

TRADEMARK PROSECUTION PROCESS

fee will be forfeited. Therefore, it is important that the proper person sign the application.

Who should sign? If the applicant is an individual, that individual must sign. If the applicant is a partnership, a general partner must sign. If the applicant is a corporation, association or similar organization, an officer of the corporation, association or organization must sign. An officer is a person who holds an office established in the articles of incorporation or the bylaws. Officers may not delegate this authority to non-officers. If the applicants are joint applicants, all joint applicants must sign.

The person who signs the application must indicate the date signed, provide a telephone number to be used if it is necessary to contact the applicant, and clearly print or type their name and position.

The Drawing Page

Every application must include a single drawing page. The word "drawing" merely refers to a "depiction of the mark" – there is no sketching involved. Moreover, if there is no drawing page, the application will be denied a filing date and returned to the applicant. The USPTO uses the drawing to file the mark in the USPTO search records and to print the mark in the Official Gazette and on the registration.

There are two forms of drawings: "special form drawings" and "standard character drawings." Additionally, the mark in the drawing must agree with the mark as used on the specimen in an application under Section 1 of the Trademark Act; as applied for or registered in a foreign country in an application under Section 44; or as it appears in the international registration in an application under Section 66(a).

- ❖ **Standard Character Mark.** A standard character mark is the most flexible of all mark depictions. It grants protection to the wording itself, without regard to the font style, size, or color. For example, the standard character format should be used to register word(s), letter(s), number(s) or any combination thereof, without claim to any particular font style, size, or color, and absent any design element. Although the mark looks like plain typed wording when registered, a standard character mark will provide broad rights, namely use in any manner of presentation, i.e., you can change how you display the wording over the life of the trademark.

TRADEMARK PROTECTION AND PROSECUTION

To register a mark consisting of only words, letters or numbers, without indicating any particular style or design, provide a typewritten drawing if preparing a paper application. In a typewritten drawing the mark must be typed entirely in CAPITAL LETTERS, even if the mark, as used, includes lower-case letters. Use a standard typewriter or keyboard or type of the same size and style as that on a standard typewriter or keyboard.

To indicate color, use the color linings. The appropriate lining should appear in the area where the relevant color would appear. If the drawing is lined for color, insert a statement in the written application to indicate so, for example, "The mark is lined for the colors red and green." A plain black-and-white drawing is acceptable even if the mark is used in color. Most drawings do not indicate specific colors.

- ❖ **Special Form Mark.** A special form mark, on the other hand, is a mark that comprises special characteristics, like fonts or designs or colors. Special form marks can be broken down into two categories: (1) stylized marks and (2) design marks. A stylized mark is a mark in which the wording appears in a particular font. A design mark can be a composite mark, in which you protect wording that is combined with a design. Or it can be a mark comprised of design elements alone.

To register a word mark in the form in which it is actually used or "intended to be used" in commerce, or any mark including a design, submit a special form drawing. In a special form drawing, the drawing must appear only in black-and-white, with every line and letter black and clear. No color or gray is allowed. Do not combine typed matter with special form in the same drawing.

You must also comply with additional requirements. For example, after uploading the mark image, you will see a field for entering the "literal element." This field is used to indicate all of the words that appear in the attached mark image. Do not use this field to add words, letters, or numbers that do not appear in the attached image. The drawing in special form must be a substantially exact representation of the mark as it appears on the specimens. Then, you must submit a complete description of the mark. It can be simple and very straightforward.

If the mark is in color, you must claim each of the colors in the mark and indicate the location of each of the colors within the mark. Be sure to be complete and precise. If you do not wish to claim any particular colors, simply submit a depiction of the mark in black and white and indicate that no colors are claimed.

TRADEMARK PROSECUTION PROCESS

Because of all of the additional requirements and limitations created by color special form marks, most applicants apply either for standard character marks or for special form marks that appear in black and white. This allows them the greatest flexibility in use of their marks as their businesses grow and change over the years.

Furthermore, applicant may apply to register any portion of a mark consisting of more than one element, provided the mark displayed in the drawing creates a separate impression apart from other elements it appears with on the specimens. For example, generally it is possible to register a word mark by itself even though the specimen shows the word mark used in combination with a design or as part of a logo. Do not include non-trademark matter in the drawing, such as informational matter that may appear on a label.

Ultimately, the applicant must decide exactly what to register and in what form. The USPTO considers the drawing controlling in determining exactly what mark the application covers.

The Fees

Fee increases, when necessary, usually take effect on October 1 of any given year. Contact the USPTO for current filing fee information. The USPTO receives no taxpayer funds. The USPTO's operations are supported entirely from fees paid by applicants and registrants.

In addition to the application filing fee, applicants filing based on a bona fide intention to use a mark in commerce must submit an additional fee for each class of goods or services in the application when filing any of the following: (i) an Amendment to Allege Use, (ii) a Statement of Use, and (iii) a Request for an Extension of Time to File a Statement of Use. Contact the USPTO for current fee information.

All payments must be made in United States currency, by check, post office money order, certified check, or electronic funds if filing the application online with the USPTO. Personal or business checks may be submitted. Make checks and money orders payable to: Commissioner for Trademarks.

The Specimens

The following information is designed to provide guidance regarding the specimens required to show use of the mark in commerce.

If the applicant has already used the mark in commerce and files based on this use in commerce, then the applicant must submit three specimens per class showing use of the mark in commerce with the application. If, instead, the application is based on a bona fide intention to use mark in commerce, the applicant must submit three specimens per class at the time the applicant files either an Amendment to Allege Use or a Statement of Use.

The specimens must be actual samples of how the mark is being used in commerce. The specimens may be identical, or they may be examples of three different uses showing the same mark.

If the mark is used on goods, examples of acceptable specimens are tags or labels, which are attached to the goods, containers for the goods, displays associated with the goods, or photographs of the goods showing use of the mark on the goods themselves. If it is impractical to send an actual specimen because of its size, photographs or other acceptable reproductions that show the mark on the goods, or packaging for the goods, must be furnished. Invoices, announcements, order forms, bills of lading, leaflets, brochures, catalogs, publicity releases, letterhead, and business cards generally are not acceptable specimens for goods.

If the mark is used for services, examples of acceptable specimens are signs, brochures about the services, advertisements for the services, business cards or stationery showing the mark in connection with the services, or photographs which show the mark either as it is used in the rendering or advertising of the services. In the case of a service mark, the specimens must either show the mark and include some clear reference to the type of services rendered under the mark in some form of advertising, or show the mark as it is used in the rendering of the service, for example on a store front or the side of a delivery or service truck.

Specimens may not be larger than 8-1/2 inches by 11 inches (21.59 cm by 27.94 cm) and must be flat. Smaller specimens, such as labels, may be stapled to a sheet of paper and labeled "Specimens." A separate sheet can be used for each class.

Additional Requirements for Intent-to-Use Applications

An applicant who files its application based on having a bona fide intention to use a mark in commerce must make use of the mark in commerce before the mark can be registered. After use in commerce begins, the applicant must submit: (i) three specimens evidencing use; (ii) an additional fee per class of goods or services in the application; and (iii) either (1) an Amendment to Allege Use if the application has not yet been approved for publication or (2) a Statement of Use if the mark has been published and the USPTO has issued a Notice of Allowance.

TRADEMARK PROSECUTION PROCESS

If the applicant will not make use of the mark in commerce within six-months of the Notice of Allowance, the applicant must file a Request for an Extension of Time to File a Statement of Use, or the application is abandoned.

SAMPLE TEAS PLUS APPLICATION FORM

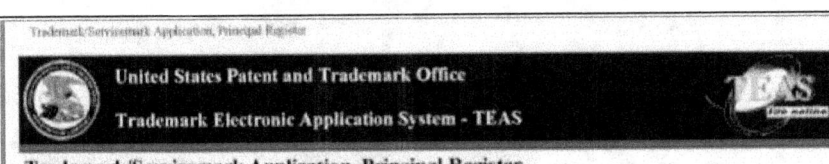

TRADEMARK PROTECTION AND PROSECUTION

> Trademark/Servicemark Application, Principal Register
>
> correspondence from the USPTO by e-mail during the pendency of the application.
>
> ○ **TEAS Form**
>
> Select this option, having a filing fee of $325 per class of goods and/or services, if you cannot satisfy the TEAS Plus requirements, as outlined above.
>
> [CONTINUE]
>
> | USPTO | Trademark Home | TEAS Home | INDEX | SEARCH | eBUSINESS | CONTACT US | Bug Report | Feedback | Help Desk | PRIVACY STATEMENT |

TRADEMARK PROSECUTION PROCESS

SAMPLE TEAS PLUS APPLICATION FORM

Navigation History: Instruction > Applicant > Mark > Goods/Services/Filing Basis > Attorney/Dom. Rep./Correspondence > Fee/Signature

PTO Form 1478 (Rev 9/2006)
OMB No. 0651-0009 (Exp 12/31/2011)

Trademark/Service Mark Application, Principal Register
TEAS Plus Application (Version 4.9)

NOTE: For an instructional video providing an overview of the most important issues you should be aware of when filing a trademark application, click here.

To file the application electronically, please complete the following steps:

1. Answer the first question below to create an application form showing only sections relevant to your specific filing.
2. For help at any point, click on any underlined word on any page.
3. After answering the first wizard question, click on the CONTINUE button at bottom of the page.
4. Once in the actual form, complete all fields with a * symbol, since they are mandatory fields for TEAS filing purposes.
5. Validate the form, using the "Validate" button at the end of the form. If there are errors, return to the form to make the correction. A "Warning" may be corrected or by-passed.
6. Double-check all entries through the links displayed on the Validation page.
7. You may save your work for submission at a later time by clicking on the Download Portable Data button at the bottom of the Validation page.
8. When ready to file, use the Pay/Submit button at the bottom of the Validation page. This will allow you to choose from three (3) different payment methods: credit card, automated deposit account, or electronic funds transfer.
9. After accessing the proper screen for payment, and making the appropriate entries, you will receive a confirmation screen if your transmission is successful. This screen will say SUCCESS! and will provide your assigned serial number.
10. You will receive an e-mail acknowledgement of your submission, which will repeat the assigned serial number and provide a summary of your submission.

TRADEMARK PROTECTION AND PROSECUTION

Trademark/Service Mark Application, Principal Register

Once you submit this application, we will not cancel the filing or refund your fee. The fee is a processing fee, which we do not refund even if we cannot issue a registration after our substantive review.

Important: ONCE YOU SUBMIT AN APPLICATION ELECTRONICALLY, THE USPTO WILL IMMEDIATELY ISSUE AN ELECTRONIC ACKNOWLEDGMENT OF RECEIPT. Please contact TEAS@uspto.gov if you do not receive this acknowledgment within 24 hours of transmission.

Contact Points:

- **General trademark information:** Please review the information posted at Where Do I Start. If you have remaining questions, e-mail TrademarkAssistanceCenter@uspto.gov, or telephone 1-800-786-9199.
- **Help:** For instructions on how to *use* the electronic forms, or help in resolving *technical* glitches, please e-mail TEAS@uspto.gov. Please include your telephone number in your e-mail, so we can talk to you directly, if necessary. Also, include the relevant serial number or registration number, if existing.
  NOTE: The TEAS Support Team focuses on problems related to the process of completing the electronic forms, not on what information would be correct for entry within a form, or other broader trademark issues. Please route those types of inquiries to the Trademark Assistance Center. However, please be aware that neither group can provide any sort of information in the nature of "legal advice." For legal advice, please consider contacting an attorney who specializes in intellectual property.
- **Bug Report:** If you think there is a "bug" within one of the electronic forms, please click Bug Report.
- **Status Information:** For an application with an assigned serial number, check Trademark Applications and Registrations Retrieval to view current status information, as well as the complete prosecution history. Do **not** attempt to check status until at least 7-10 days after submission of a filing, to allow sufficient time for all USPTO databases to be updated. You can view **all** items listed in the prosecution history section online at Trademark Document Retrieval, including all office actions sent by the USPTO.

TRADEMARK PROSECUTION PROCESS

Trademark/Service Mark Application, Principal Register

WARNING: This form has a session time limit of 60 minutes. Your "session" began as soon as you accessed this initial Form Wizard page. If you exceed the 60-minute time limit, the form will not validate and you must begin the entire process again; you can, however, extend the time limit. You should always try to have all information required to complete the form prior to starting any session.

1. Is an attorney filing this application?

⦿ Yes ○ No

2. [OPTIONAL] To access previously-saved data, use the "Browse/Choose File" button below to access the file from your local drive. **NOTE:** For specific instructions, please click here. **FAILURE TO FOLLOW THESE NEW INSTRUCTIONS WILL RESULT IN THE DISPLAY OF YOUR DATA IN AN XML FORMAT THAT CANNOT BE EDITED. NOTE:** Do NOT attempt to use the button below to upload an image file (for example, a specimen). You must use the button that will be presented for that purpose *within the proper section of the actual form.*

[_____] [Browse...]

[Continue]

Burden/Privacy Statement

The information collected on this form allows the PTO to determine whether a mark may be registered on the Principal or Supplemental register, and provides notice of an applicant's claim of ownership of the mark. Responses to the request for information are required to obtain the benefit of a registration on the Principal register. 15 U.S.C. §1051 et seq. and 37 C.F.R. Part 2. All information collected will be made public. Gathering and providing the information will require an estimated 15 to 23 minutes (depending if the application is based on an intent to use the mark in commerce, use of the mark in commerce, or a foreign application or registration). Please direct comments on the time needed to complete this form, and/or suggestions for reducing this burden to the Chief Information Officer, U.S. Patent and Trademark Office, U. S. Department of Commerce, P.O. Box 1450, Alexandria, VA 22313-1450. Please note that the PTO may not conduct or sponsor a collection of information using a form that does not display a valid OMB control number.

Help Desk | Bug Report | Feedback | TEAS Home | Trademark Home | USPTO

TRADEMARK PROTECTION AND PROSECUTION

SAMPLE TEAS PLUS APPLICATION FORM

United States Patent and Trademark Office
Trademark Electronic Application System - TEAS Application

Navigation History Instruction > Applicant > Mark > Goods/Services/Filing Basis > Attorney/Dom. Rep./Correspondence > Fee/Signature

PTO Form 1478 (Rev 9/2006)
OMB No. 0651-0009 (Exp 12/31/2011)

Trademark/Service Mark Application, Principal Register
TEAS Plus Application (Version 4.9)

NOTE: This identifies who owns the mark, not necessarily who is filing the application. For an instructional video focusing on what is meant by the term "applicant," click here.

Applicant Information

Note: This identifies who **owns** the mark, **not** necessarily who is **filing** the application.
Note: If there is more than one owner of the mark, complete the information for the first owner, and then click on the "Add Owner" button at the bottom of this page. Repeat, as necessary, for the appropriate listing of all owners. Warning: It is important to determine whether, in fact, the applicants are joint applicants, or some other entity type listed below.

| * Owner of Mark | (If an individual, use the following format: Last Name, First Name Middle Initial or Name, if applicable) |

☐ DBA (doing business as) ☐ AKA (also known as)
☐ TA (trading as) ☐ Formerly

* Entity Type

○ Individual
○ Corporation
○ Limited Liability Company
○ Partnership
○ Limited Partnership
○ Joint Venture
○ Sole Proprietorship
○ Trust
○ Estate
○ Other

⇐ Click the appropriate circle on the left to indicate the applicant's entity type. The form will then display the field(s) for entering information corresponding to that specific entity type. If your entity type is not one of the options displayed directly to the left, you must click on "Other" and then select the appropriate entry from the relevant pull-down box.

Internal Address

TRADEMARK PROSECUTION PROCESS

(Form image: Trademark/Service Mark Application, Principal Register — fields for Street Address, City, State (Required for U.S. applicants), Country or U.S. Territory, Zip/Postal Code (Required for U.S. applicants only), Phone Number, Fax Number, Internet E-mail Address, Website address, with buttons Go Back | Add Owner | Continue, followed by a Privacy Statement and footer links: Help Desk | Bug Report | Feedback | TEAS Home | Trademark Home | USPTO.)

TRADEMARK PROTECTION AND PROSECUTION

SAMPLE TEAS PLUS APPLICATION FORM

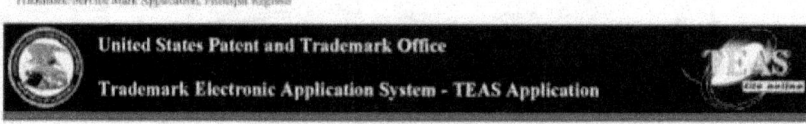

TRADEMARK PROSECUTION PROCESS

Trademark/Service Mark Application, Principal Register

* **Click the appropriate circle to indicate the Mark type:** ⦿ Standard Characters ○ Special Form (*Stylized and or Design*) ○ Sound mark

NOTE: For an instructional video on the importance of selecting the proper mark type, click here.

Enter the mark here: (**Note:** The entry can be in capital letters, lower case letters, or a combination thereof. Do **not** include the ™, ·, ®, or © symbols after the mark entry, because they are **not** part of the actual mark. If using Internet Explorer, the entry cannot exceed **2036** characters; otherwise, you must switch to another browser.)

[Preview USPTO-Generated Image]

NOTE: For how the USPTO determines what the display of the entered mark will be, click here.

NOTE: For information about mark display in USPTO databases, click here.

The "Additional Statement" section of this form is to enter various statement(s) that may pertain to the mark, for example, a disclaimer or translation. Because you are filing under **TEAS Plus**, you must enter the following, **if applicable within the facts of your application:** (1) claim of prior registration(s); (2) translation; (3) transliteration; (4) consent of individual identified in mark; and (5) concurrent use claim. You are not required to enter any other statement(s) at the time of filing; however, you may be required to add a statement(s) to the record during examination of the application. If you are unsure whether you should make such a statement, besides those specifically identified above, the examining attorney assigned to your application will issue a requirement, if appropriate.

☐ Check here to display the full listing of additional statements from which you may make your selection.

[Go Back] [Continue]

TRADEMARK PROTECTION AND PROSECUTION

SAMPLE TEAS PLUS APPLICATION FORM

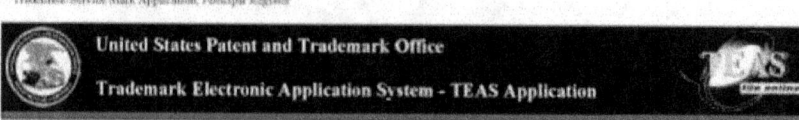

Trademark/Service Mark Application, Principal Register

United States Patent and Trademark Office
Trademark Electronic Application System - TEAS Application

Navigation History: Instruction > Applicant > Mark > Goods/Services/Filing Basis > Attorney/Dom. Rep./Correspondence > Fee/Signature

PTO Form 1478 (Rev 9/2006)
OMB No. 0651-0009 (Exp 12/31/2011)

Trademark/Service Mark Application, Principal Register
TEAS Plus Application (Version 4.9)

Goods and/or Services Information

Instructions:

Step 1: Click on the "Add Goods/Services by Searching IDManual" button below to select goods and/or services from the *Manual of Trademark Acceptable Identifications of Goods & Services* (IDManual).

Step 2: After creating the complete list of goods and/or services for this application, you will then be able in the next section of the form to designate the filing basis (or bases) appropriate for each listed item.

NOTE:

1. Your selection of goods/services must be precise and accurate. Do NOT simply select a listing that is "close" to your goods/services. If you do not find a listing that accurately identifies your goods/services, you may e-mail TMIDSUGGEST@uspto.gov to request that your identification be added to the IDManual, and then wait for the addition before filing using TEAS Plus. For more information on this process, click here. If your request is not approved or you wish to file immediately, you must use the regular TEAS form.
2. The TEAS Plus version of the IDManual intentionally does not include the following: (1) items classified in Classes A, B, or 200, because those marks are not eligible for filing under TEAS Plus; (2) any listings that appear in the "regular" manual under "000," because correct classification is required under TEAS Plus, and classification for these listings varies according to the additional information provided within the listing; and (3) the Class 25 listing of "Clothing, namely, ...", because this entry is too open-ended, and could result in items being listed that do not truly fall within this class. Since specific clothing items must be listed anyway, the TEAS Plus version of the form requires the *initial* selection of those specific

TRADEMARK PROSECUTION PROCESS

Trademark/Service Mark Application, Principal Register

items.

3. Some entries include instructional language beneath the actual entry, within < > symbols. This language is only to assist in the proper selection of an entry, and will NOT be included as part of the actual identification after the checked entry is inserted into the form. *New*

4. If you cannot access the IDManual through the "Add Goods/Services by Searching IDManual" button, try switching to another browser. If after changing browsers you still cannot access the IDManual through the "Add Goods/Services by Searching IDManual" button, please contact TEAS@uspto.gov.

WARNING: This form has a session time limit of 60 minutes. Your "session" began as soon as you accessed the initial Form Wizard page. If you exceed the 60-minute time limit, the form will not validate and you must begin the entire process again; you can, however, extend the time limit. You should always try to have all information required to complete the form prior to starting any session.

NOTE: For an instructional video on goods and services and the importance of making the proper selection, click here.

[Add Goods/Services]   [Remove Checked Goods/Services]

NOTE: Clicking "Go Back" will take you directly back to the MARK section of the form.

[Go Back]

Burden/Privacy Statement

The information collected on this form allows the PTO to determine whether a mark may be registered on the Principal or Supplemental register, and provides notice of an applicant's claim of ownership of the mark. Responses to the request for information are required to obtain the benefit of a registration on the Principal register: 15 U.S.C. §1051 et seq. and 37 C.F.R. Part 2. All information collected will be made public. Gathering and providing the information will require an estimated 15 to 21 minutes (depending if the application is based on an intent to use the mark in commerce, use of the mark in commerce, or a foreign application or registration). Please direct comments on the time needed to complete this form, and/or suggestions for reducing this burden to the Chief Information Officer, U.S. Patent and Trademark Office, U.S. Department of Commerce, P.O. Box 1450, Alexandria, VA 22313-1450. Please note that the PTO may not conduct or sponsor a collection of information using a form that does not display a valid OMB control number.

Help Desk | Bug Report | Feedback | TEAS Home | Trademark Home | USPTO

TRADEMARK PROTECTION AND PROSECUTION

SAMPLE TEAS PLUS APPLICATION FORM

Trademark Acceptable Identification of Goods & Services

 United States Patent and Trademark Office
Trademark Electronic Application System - Trademark ID Manual

WARNING: The ID manual has a session limit of 30 minutes. If you will be working within the IDManual for an extended period of time, it is critical that you keep your form session "alive." To do so, it is recommended that you select no more than 20 entries at a time, then click the "Insert Check Entries" button. On the next page that displays all of your selections, use the "Add Goods/Services by Searching IDManual" button to return to the Manual to continue the process; repeat this process until all of your items are displayed in the overall listing on the page for assigning a filing basis.

Search for: [_____] [Go]

Instructions:

Step 1: Enter a word or phrase to search for Goods and/or Services.

- Search requests can be for a single item (*e.g.*, pants), or multiple items (*e.g.*, pants shirts shoes). While also possible to search for goods and/or services in different classes at the same time (*e.g.*, pants baseballs), separate searches are recommended. The form will compile an "overall goods/services list," regardless of the search approach.
  NOTE: Most manual entries are displayed in the plural, *e.g.*, the entry is "soups," rather than "soup." While entering the search term "soup" will retrieve "soups," it would first be preceded by other listings, *e.g.*, "soup tureens" and "soup mixes."
- To search for an entry where the single entry consists of multiple words, enclose the complete entry within quotation marks; *e.g.*, enter "computer programs" rather than computer programs.
- To browse the complete listing of items in one or more classes, enter the following search criteria: class:NNN or class:(NNN NNN etc.), where NNN is the 3-digit International class number; *e.g.*, to search for all items in International Class 3, enter class:003; for all items in International Classes 25 and 42, enter class:(025 042).
- For a listing of all International class headings, including a summary of the types of items within each class, click here.
- For more information about using advanced query syntax (*e.g.*, using truncation), click here.

Step 2: Once the desired search criteria has been entered, click the "Go" button, and then all manual entries containing the requested term(s) will be displayed.
NOTE: Because the interfaces for TEAS and the *Trademark Acceptable Identification of Goods & Services Manual* differ, results for identical searches performed in each may vary slightly, even though both access the same data source.

TRADEMARK PROSECUTION PROCESS

SAMPLE TEAS PLUS APPLICATION FORM

Trademark/Service Mark Application, Principal Register
TEAS Plus Application (Version 4.9)

Basis for Filing

NOTE: For an instructional video on what is meant by "basis for filing," click here.

Applicant requests registration of the trademark/service mark identified previously with the United States Patent and Trademark Office on the Principal Register established by the Act of July 5, 1946 (15 U.S.C. §1051 *et seq.*) for the Class(es) and Goods and/or Services displayed below, and asserts herein the specific basis(es) that covers the listed Goods and/or Services.

Instructions for assigning filing basis(es):
For each of the items listed in the chart below, you can assign a specific filing basis, or if appropriate, multiple bases. If the list is incorrect, you can either add or delete items, using the appropriate buttons, *below*. For an explanation of the possible filing basis(es), as identified by the 4 buttons beneath the listing of goods/services, click here.

For complete step-by-step instructions on how correctly to assign the filing basis(es), click on the heading that corresponds to the factual scenario for this specific filing, *below*. For examples of filings corresponding to each of the heading descriptions, click on the link "*Examples*."

- **One class or multiple classes, with ONE filing basis for ALL listed items** *Examples*
  NOTE: This is the most common correct choice for any filing. The following are other options, but are much less likely to be appropriate:
- **One class or multiple classes, with same multiple filing bases for ALL listed items in class(es)** *Examples*
- **One class or multiple classes, with different filing basis(es) for different goods/services within the same class, and/or for different overall classes** *Examples*

TRADEMARK PROTECTION AND PROSECUTION

Trademark/Service Mark Application, Principal Register

NOTE: For an instructional video on goods and services and the importance of making the proper selection, click here.

[Add Goods/Services]
For instructions on how to add item(s) to the list displayed below, click *here*.

[Remove Checked Goods/Services]
For instructions on how to remove any item(s), click *here*.

☑ Select All	International Class	Goods and/or Services	Assigned Filing Basis(es)
☑			

NOTE: The 4 BUTTONS below identify the choices of filing basis to be assigned to the items listed in the table, *above*. For an explanation of each basis, click here. Because assignment of the correct basis to each item is critical, please read the explanations if you have *any* questions as to which basis(es) to select, before clicking the button(s), *below*, to begin the assignment of the basis(es).

WARNING: Registration Subject to Cancellation for Fraudulent Statements
You must ensure that statements made in filings to the USPTO are accurate, as inaccuracies may result in the cancellation of a trademark registration. The lack of a bona intention to use the mark with all goods and/or services included in an application, or the lack of use on all goods and/or services for which you claim use, could jeopardize the validity of the registration and result in its cancellation.

Section 1(a)	Section 1(b)	Section 44(d)	Section 44(e)
Actually using mark in commerce now	No use of mark yet, intending to use	Foreign application exists for same goods/services	Foreign registration exists for same goods/services

NOTE: Clicking "Go Back" will take you directly back to the MARK section of the form. Clicking "Continue" prior to assigning a filing basis will result in an error.

[Go Back] [Continue]

TRADEMARK PROSECUTION PROCESS

SAMPLE TEAS PLUS APPLICATION FORM

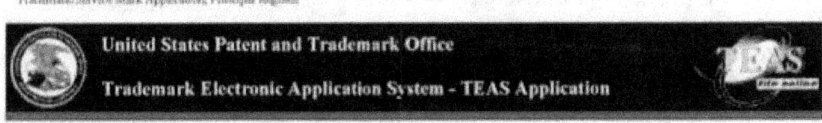

Navigation History: Instruction > Applicant > Mark > Goods/Services/Filing Basis > Attorney/Dom. Rep./Correspondence > Fee/Signature

PTO Form 1478 (Rev 9/2006)
OMB No. 0651-0009 (Exp 12/31/2011)

Trademark/Service Mark Application, Principal Register
TEAS Plus Application (Version 4.9)

Basis for Filing

NOTE: For an instructional video on what is meant by "basis for filing," click here.

Applicant requests registration of the trademark/service mark identified previously with the United States Patent and Trademark Office on the Principal Register established by the Act of July 5, 1946 (15 U.S.C. §1051 et seq.) for the Class(es) and Goods and/or Services displayed below, and asserts herein the specific basis(es) that covers the listed Goods and/or Services.

Instructions for assigning filing basis(es):

For each of the items listed in the chart below, you can assign a specific filing basis, or if appropriate, multiple bases. If the list is incorrect, you can either add or delete items, using the appropriate buttons, *below*. For an explanation of the possible filing basis(es), as identified by the 4 buttons beneath the listing of goods/services, click here.

For complete step-by-step instructions on how correctly to assign the filing basis(es), click on the heading that corresponds to the factual scenario for this specific filing, *below*. For examples of filings corresponding to each of the heading descriptions, click on the link *"Examples."*

- **One class or multiple classes, with ONE filing basis for ALL listed items** *Examples*
  NOTE: This is the most common correct choice for any filing. The following are other options, but are much less likely to be appropriate:
- **One class or multiple classes, with same multiple filing bases for ALL listed items in class(es)** *Examples*
- **One class or multiple classes, with different filing basis(es) for different goods/services within the same class, and/or for different overall classes** *Examples*

TRADEMARK PROTECTION AND PROSECUTION

Trademark/Service Mark Application, Principal Register

NOTE: For an instructional video on goods and services and the importance of making the proper selection, click here.

[Add Goods/Services]
For instructions on how to add item(s) to the list displayed below, click *here*.

[Remove Checked Goods/Services]
For instructions on how to remove any item(s), click *here*.

☑ Select All	International Class	Goods and/or Services	Assigned Filing Basis(es)
☑			

Section 1(a). Use in Commerce: The applicant is using the mark in commerce, or the applicant's related company or licensee is using the mark in commerce, or the applicant's predecessor in interest used the mark in commerce, on or in connection with the identified goods and/or services. 15 U.S.C. §1051(a), as amended. Applicant attaches, or will later submit, one specimen as a JPG/PDF image file showing the mark as used in commerce on or in connection with any item in the class of listed goods and/or services, regardless of whether the mark itself is in the standard character format or is a stylized or design mark. The specimen image file may be in color, and the image must be in color if color is being claimed as a feature of the mark

NOTE: For an instructional video on what is an appropriate specimen for a good or service, **click here**." NOTE: For attachment, the JPG/PDF image file (s) or sound/motion file(s) showing the specimen(s) must be on your local drive. The specimen file must show the *overall context* of how the mark is used, *e.g.*, on the packaging for the goods or in an advertisement for services, with the mark clearly displayed thereon or within. This file should NOT be either (1) the same file used in the mark section; or (2) a newly-created file that nonetheless shows *only* the mark by itself. (*Reminder*: Within the earlier mark section, if you attached an image file for a stylized/design mark or a sound/motion file, you must ensure that it only shows the mark by itself, and does not display anything that would not truly be considered part of the actual mark, *e.g.*, a scan of a complete business card would not be an acceptable mark image, although it may be an acceptable specimen).

[Remove this 1(a)]

* **Attach Specimen**	[Attach/Remove Specimen] ☐ Check this box if you are attaching a color specimen. NOTE: Check only if you believe your specimen is in color, yet you received after clicking the "CONTINUE" button a WARNING about lack of color within the specimen; otherwise, do not check this box, because the attached image was automatically accepted as color.

TRADEMARK PROSECUTION PROCESS

Trademark/Service Mark Application, Principal Register

Description of Specimen	
*Date of First Use of Mark Anywhere	By the applicant, or the applicant's related company, licensee, or predecessor in interest at least as early as (MM/DD/YYYY)
*Date of First Use of the Mark in Commerce	By the applicant, or the applicant's related company, licensee, or predecessor in interest at least as early as (MM/DD/YYYY)

Section 44(d) — Foreign application exists for same goods/services

Section 44(e) — Foreign registration exists for same goods/services

NOTE: To assign the selected filing basis, click on "Assign Filing Basis" button, below. If you selected the wrong basis, click on the "Remove this [basis]" button, above, and start over. To assign multiple bases, click on another basis button and complete the section (and repeat process again, if appropriate) before clicking on the "Assign Filing Basis" button.

[Assign Filing Basis] [Exit]

Burden/Privacy Statement

The information collected on this form allows the PTO to determine whether a mark may be registered on the Principal or Supplemental register, and provides notice of an applicant's claim of ownership of the mark. Responses to this request for information are required to obtain the benefit of a registration on the Principal register. 15 U.S.C. §1051 et seq. and 37 C.F.R. Part 2. All information collected will be made public. Gathering and providing the information will require an estimated 15 to 21 minutes (depending if the application is based on an intent to use the mark in commerce, use of the mark in commerce, or a foreign application or registration). Please direct comments on the time needed to complete this form, and/or suggestions for reducing this burden to the Chief Information Officer, U.S. Patent and Trademark Office, U. S. Department of Commerce, P.O. Box 1450, Alexandria, VA 22313-1450. Please note that the PTO may not conduct or sponsor a collection of information using a form that does not display a valid OMB control number.

Help Desk | Bug Report | Feedback | TEAS Home | Trademark Home | USPTO

TRADEMARK PROTECTION AND PROSECUTION

SAMPLE TEAS PLUS APPLICATION FORM

Trademark/Service Mark Application, Principal Register

United States Patent and Trademark Office
Trademark Electronic Application System - TEAS Application

Trademark/Service Mark Application, Principal Register

TEAS Plus Application

NOTE: You must "**Browse/Choose File**" AND "**Attach**" each file, as described in Steps 1 and 2 below. If you do NOT click on the "**Attach**" button after selecting the correct file via the "**Browse/Choose File**" button, the file will not be attached to the form.
WARNING: The file MUST be in the JPG/PDF format (not exceeding 5 megabytes per attachment) or .WAV, .WMV, .WMA, .MP3, .MPG, or .AVI format (not exceeding 5 megabytes for sound files or 30 megabytes for motion files).

To attach a file, please complete the following steps:
1. Click on "**Browse/Choose File**" button to select the file from your local drive.
2. Click on "**Attach**" button to attach the selected file.
3. To attach additional file(s), return to step 1.
4. To remove unwanted file(s), simply clicking "**Remove**" button/link right below the file(s).
5. Click on "**Return to Application**" and return back to the form, but ONLY once you see the file(s) loaded above.

WARNING: A submission must be complete within the "4 corners" of the actual transmitted document. Information only accessible through a link, but not part of the submission itself, will **NOT** be considered to be made of record. E.g., if you wish a catalogue to be considered as evidence, you must present the actual pages of the catalogue, and not merely reference that the catalogue is available for viewing at a particular url. The url will **NOT** be independently accessed as part of the examination process, and any materials presented only "by reference" will not constitute part of the actual file.

Click on the "Browse/Choose File" button to select a file you wish to upload:

[_____] [Browse] [Attach]

TRADEMARK PROSECUTION PROCESS

Trademark/Service Mark Application, Principal Register

Status:
File Uploaded:

To Upload Media Specimens:

Click on the "Browse/Choose File" button to select the sound/motion file (.WAV, .WMV, .WMA, .MP3, .MPG, or .AVI file) from your local drive.

[_____] [Browse] [Upload File]

[Return to Application]

Help Desk | Bug Report | Feedback | TEAS Home | Trademark Home | USPTO

TRADEMARK PROTECTION AND PROSECUTION

SAMPLE TEAS PLUS APPLICATION FORM

Trademark/Service Mark Application, Principal Register

United States Patent and Trademark Office
Trademark Electronic Application System - TEAS Application

Navigation History: Instruction > Applicant > Mark > Goods/Services/Filing Basis > Attorney/Dom. Rep./Correspondence > Fee/Signature

PTO Form 1478 (Rev 9/2006)
OMB No. 0651-0009 (Exp 12/31/2011)

Trademark/Service Mark Application, Principal Register
TEAS Plus Application (Version 4.9)

☑ Check here if an attorney is filing this form on behalf of applicant(s). If an attorney is not filing, simply click on the box if currently checked to "uncheck" that box.

☐ Check here if the applicant wishes to appoint a Domestic Representative. A Domestic Representative is OPTIONAL if the applicant's address is outside the United States. Once checked, a separate section of the form will appear to enter the Domestic Representative information.

	Attorney Information
* Correspondent Attorney Name	
Individual Attorney Docket/Reference Number	
Other Appointed Attorney(s)	
Firm Name	
Internal Address	
* Street Address	**NOTE:** You must limit your entry here, and for all remaining fields within this overall section (except City, see below), to no more than 40 characters (the storage limit for the USPTO database). You may need to abbreviate some words, e.g., St. instead of Street. Failure to do so may result in an undeliverable address, due to truncation at the 40 character limit.

TRADEMARK PROSECUTION PROCESS

Trademark/Service Mark Application, Principal Register

* **City**	NOTE: You must limit your entry here to no more than 22 characters.
* **State** (Required for U.S. applicants)	Select State — NOTE: You must include as part of the "city" entry any information related to geographical regions (e.g., provinces) not found in the dropdown lists for "States" or "Countries." Enter the city and then the geographical region, separated by a comma (e.g., Toronto, Ontario). In most instances, you will then also have to select the country within which the region is found, below.
* **Country or U.S. Territory**	Select Country or U.S. Territory
* **Zip/Postal Code** (Required for U.S. applicants only)	
Phone Number	
Fax Number	
* **Internet E-mail Address**	An e-mail address for communication with the appointed attorney must be provided. The attorney must keep this address current in the Office's records. Specific authorization for this communication may be made, below. ☐ Check here to authorize the USPTO to communicate with the appointed attorney via e-mail. (Informal communication is permissible without authorization.) NOTE: By checking this box, the appointed attorney acknowledges that it is solely responsible for receipt of USPTO documents sent via e-mail. The appointed attorney should periodically check the status of its application through the **Trademark Applications and Registrations Retrieval (TARR)** database, to see if the assigned examining attorney has e-mailed an Office Action. If an action has been sent to the provided e-mail address, the USPTO is not responsible for any e-mail not received due to the applicant's security or anti-spam software, or any problems within the applicant's e-mail system. All sent actions can be viewed on-line, from **Trademark Document Retrieval**.

[Go Back] [Continue]

TRADEMARK PROTECTION AND PROSECUTION

SAMPLE TEAS PLUS APPLICATION FORM

Trademark/Service Mark Application, Principal Register

United States Patent and Trademark Office
Trademark Electronic Application System - TEAS Application

Navigation History: Instruction > Applicant > Mark > Goods/Services/Filing Basis > Attorney/Dom. Rep./ Correspondence > Fee/Signature

PTO Form 1478 (Rev 9/2006)
OMB No. 0651-0009 (Exp 12/31/2011)

Trademark/Service Mark Application, Principal Register
TEAS Plus Application (Version 4.9)

Correspondence Information

Note: Where an attorney or domestic representative has been appointed, the USPTO will correspond ONLY with the listed appointment. Do NOT attempt to change the correspondence address to the owner's address.

*Name	a
Firm Name	
Internal Address	
*Street Address	a
	NOTE: You must limit your entry here, and for all remaining fields within this overall section (except City, see below), to no more than 40 characters (the storage limit for the USPTO database). You may need to abbreviate some words, e.g., St. instead of Street. Failure to do so may result in an undeliverable address, due to truncation at the 40 character limit.
*City	a
	NOTE: You must limit your entry here to no more than 22 characters.
*State (Required for U.S. applicants)	Missouri
	NOTE: You must include as part of the "city" entry any information related to geographical regions (e.g., provinces) not found in the dropdown lists for "States" or "Countries". Enter the city and then the geographical region, separated by a comma (e.g., Toronto, Ontario). In most instances, you will then also have to select the country within which the region is found, below.
*Country or U.S. Territory	United States

http://teasplus.uspto.gov/forms/teas_service (1 of 7)12/23/2011 8:29:39 PM

126

TRADEMARK PROSECUTION PROCESS

Trademark/Service Mark Application, Principal Register

* Zip/ Postal Code (Required for U.S. applicants only)	22202
Phone Number	555-555-5555
Fax Number	
* Internet E-mail Address	Primary Email Address: teas@uspto.gov Secondary Email Address(es) Enter up to 4 addresses, separated by either a **semicolon** or a **comma**. Only one e-mail address may be used for correspondence, in accordance with Office policy. The applicant must keep this address current in the Office's records. ☑ Check here to authorize the USPTO to communicate with the appointed attorney via e-mail. (Informal communication is permissible without authorization.) NOTE: By checking this box, the appointed attorney acknowledges that it is solely responsible for receipt of USPTO documents sent via e-mail. The appointed attorney should periodically check the status of its application through the Trademark Applications and Registrations Retrieval (TARR) database, to see if the assigned examining attorney has e-mailed an Office Action. If an action has been sent to the provided e-mail address, the USPTO is not responsible for any e-mail not received due to the applicant's security or anti-spam software, or any problems within the applicant's e-mail system. All best actions can be viewed on-line, from Trademark Document Retrieval.

[Go Back] [Continue]

Section/Privacy Statement

This information collected on this form allows the PTO to determine whether a mark may be registered on the Principal or Supplemental register, and provides notice of an applicant's claim of ownership of the mark. Responses to the request for information are required to obtain the benefit of a registration on the Principal register. 15 U.S.C. §1051 et seq. and 37 C.F.R. Part 2. All information collected will be made public. Gathering and providing the information will require an estimated 14 to 21 minutes (depending if the application is filed on an intent to use the mark in commerce, use of the mark in commerce, or a foreign application or registration). Please direct comments on the time needed to complete this form, and/or suggestions for reducing this burden to: the Chief Information Officer, U.S. Patent and Trademark Office, U.S. Department of Commerce, P.O. Box 1450, Alexandria, VA 22313-1450. Please note that the PTO may not conduct or sponsor a collection of information using a form that does not display a valid OMB control number.

Help Desk | Bug Report | Feedback | TEAS Home | Trademark Home | USPTO

Fri Dec 23 15:29:07 EST 2011

TRADEMARK PROTECTION AND PROSECUTION

SAMPLE TEAS PLUS APPLICATION FORM

Trademark/Service Mark Application, Principal Register

 United States Patent and Trademark Office
Trademark Electronic Application System - TEAS Application

Navigation History Instruction › Applicant › Mark › Goods/Services/Filing Basis › Attorney/Dom. Rep./Correspondence › Fee/Signature

PTO Form 1478 (Rev 9/2006)
OMB No. 0651-0009 (Exp 12/31/2011)

Trademark/Service Mark Application, Principal Register
TEAS Plus Application (Version 4.9)

Fee Information

Note: The total fee is computed based on the Number of Classes in which the goods and/or services associated with the mark are classified. If the free-text approach for the goods/services has been used, and different filing bases exist within the same class, neither the displayed Number of Classes nor Total Fee Due will be correct. You must manually adjust the Total Fee Paid amount, using the pull-down box to select the correct fee amount.

Note: Three payment options (credit card, automated deposit account, and Electronic Funds Transfer) will appear after clicking on the **Pay/Submit** button, which is available on the bottom of the Validation Page after completing and validating this form.

Number of Classes	1 (Class: 007)
Fee per class	$275
Total Fee Due	$275

Signature Information

Click to choose ONE signature method:
● Sign directly ○ E-mail Text Form to second party for signature ○ Handwritten pen-and-ink signature

Electronic Signature

The application will not be "signed" in the sense of a traditional paper document. To verify the contents of the application, the signatory must enter any alpha/numeric character(s) or combination thereof **of his or her choosing**, preceded and followed by the forward slash (/) symbol. The USPTO does not determine or pre-approve what the entry should be, but simply presumes that this specific entry has been adopted to serve the function of the signature. Most signatories simply enter their names between the two forward slashes, although acceptable "signatures" could include /john doe/; /jd/; or /123-4567/. The application may still be validated to check for missing information or errors even if the signature and date signed fields are left blank; however, you must specifically click the button for "Submit application unsigned," above.

DECLARATION

The undersigned, being hereby warned that willful false statements and the like so made are punishable by fine or imprisonment, or both, under 18 U.S.C. Section 1001, and that such willful false statements may jeopardize the validity of the form or any resulting registration, declares that he/she is properly authorized to execute this form on behalf of the applicant; he/she believes the applicant to be the owner of the trademark/service mark sought to be registered, or, if the form is being filed under 15 U.S.C. Section 1126(d) or (e), he/she believes applicant to be entitled to use such mark in commerce; to the best of his/her knowledge and belief no other person, firm, corporation, or association has the right to use the mark in commerce, either in the identical form thereof or in such near resemblance thereto as to be likely, when used on or in connection with the goods/services of such other person, to cause confusion, or to cause mistake, or to deceive; and that all statements made of his/her own knowledge are true; and that all statements made on information and belief are believed to be true.

TRADEMARK PROSECUTION PROCESS

TRADEMARK PROTECTION AND PROSECUTION

SAMPLE TEAS PLUS APPLICATION FORM

TRADEMARK PROSECUTION PROCESS

Trademark/Service Mark Application, Principal Register

■ STEP 2: If there are no errors and you are ready to file this application electronically, confirm the e-mail address for acknowledgment. Once you submit the form electronically, we will send an electronic acknowledgment of receipt to the e-mail address entered below. If no e-mail address appears, you must enter one. If we should send the acknowledgment to a different e-mail address, or to an additional address(es), please enter the proper address or additional address(es). For **multiple addresses/receipts**, please separate e-mail addresses by either a **semicolon** or a **comma**.

NOTE: This e-mail address is only for the purpose of receiving the acknowledgment that the transmission reached the USPTO, and is not related to the e-mail that will be used for correspondence purposes (although it could be the same address. The official e-mail address that the USPTO will use for any future communication is whatever appears in the specific correspondence section of the form.)

* **E-mail for acknowledgment**

    [teas@uspto.gov]

To ensure we can deliver your e-mail confirmation successfully, please re-enter your e-mail address(es) here:

* **E-mail for acknowledgment**

    [   ]

■ STEP 3: To download and save the form data, click on the **Download Portable Data** button at the bottom of this page. The information will be saved to your local drive. To begin the submission process with saved data, you must open a new form, and click on the "Browse/Choose File" button displayed on the initial form wizard page, at "**[OPTIONAL] To access previously-saved data, use the "Browse/Choose File" button below to access the file from your local drive.**" **REMINDER:** Do **NOT** try to open the saved .obj/.xml form directly. You must return to the very first page of the form, as if starting a brand new form, and then use the specific "Browse/Choose File" button on that page to import the saved file. Clicking on the "Continue" button at the bottom of that first page will then properly open the saved version of your form.

TRADEMARK PROTECTION AND PROSECUTION

Trademark/Service Mark Application, Principal Register

■ **STEP 4:** Read and check the following:

Important Notice:

Once you submit this application, we will not cancel the filing or refund your fee. The fee is a processing fee, which we do not refund even if we cannot issue a registration after our substantive review. This is true regardless of how soon after submission you might attempt to request cancellation of the filing. Therefore, please review **ALL** information carefully prior to transmission.

All information you submit to the USPTO at any point in the application and/or registration process will become public record, including your name, phone number, e-mail address, and street address. By filing this application, you acknowledge that **YOU HAVE NO RIGHT TO CONFIDENTIALITY** in the information disclosed. The public will be able to view this information in the USPTO's on-line databases and through internet search engines and other on-line databases. This information will remain public even if the application is later abandoned or any resulting registration is surrendered, cancelled, or expired. To maintain confidentiality of banking or credit card information, only enter payment information in the secure portion of the site after validating your form. For any information that may be subject to copyright protection, by submitting it to the USPTO, the filer is representing that he or she has the authority to grant, and is granting, the USPTO permission to make the information available in its on-line database and in copies of the application or registration record.

☐ If you have read and understand the above notice, please check the box before you click on the **Pay/Submit** button.

■ **STEP 5:** If you are ready to file electronically:
Click on the **Pay/Submit** button *below*, to access the site where you will select one of three possible payment methods. After successful entry of payment information, you can complete the submission to the USPTO. A valid transaction will result in a screen that says **SUCCESS!** Also, we will send an e-mail acknowledgment within 24 hours.
WARNING: Click on the Pay/Submit button **ONLY** if you are now entirely prepared to complete the Pay/Submit process. After clicking the button, you can **NOT** return to the form, since you will have left the TEAS site entirely. Once in the separate payment site, you **must** complete the Pay/Submit process within **30 minutes.** If you are not prepared to complete the process now, you should select the "Download Portable Data" option to save your form, and then complete the Pay/Submit process later. Or, if you have discovered any error, use the "Go Back to Modify" button to make a correction.
WARNING: Fee payments by credit card may **not** be made from 2 a.m. to 6 a.m. Sunday, Eastern Standard Time. If you are attempting to file during that specific period, you **must** use either (1) the deposit account or electronic funds transfer payment method; or (2) the "Download Portable Data" option to save your form, and then complete the Pay/Submit

TRADEMARK PROSECUTION PROCESS

Trademark/Service Mark Application, Principal Register

process later for a credit card payment.

[Go Back to Modify]   [Download Portable Data]   [Pay/Submit]

Burden/Privacy Statement

The information collected on this form allows the PTO to determine whether a mark may be registered on the Principal or Supplemental register, and provides notice of an applicant's claim of ownership of the mark. Responses to the request for information are required to obtain the benefit of a registration on the Principal register. 15 U.S.C. §1051 et seq. and 37 C.F.R. Part 2. All information collected will be made public. Gathering and providing the information will require an estimated 15 to 21 minutes (depending if the application is based on an intent to use the mark in commerce, use of the mark in commerce, or a foreign application or registration). Please direct comments on the time needed to complete this form, and/or suggestions for reducing this burden to the Chief Information Officer, U.S. Patent and Trademark Office, U.S. Department of Commerce, P.O. Box 1450, Alexandria, VA 22313-1450. Please note that the PTO may not conduct or sponsor a collection of information using a form that does not display a valid OMB control number.

Help Desk | Bug Report | Feedback | TEAS Home | Trademark Home | USPTO

Fri Dec 22 15:29:57 EST 2011

http://teasplus.uspto.gov/forms/teas.service (4 of 4)12/23/2011 3:30:09 PM

TRADEMARK PROTECTION AND PROSECUTION

SAMPLE TEAS PLUS APPLICATION FORM

PTO-Secure Payment Server SSL - Choose Payment Type

United States Patent and Trademark Office

Security enhancement for EFT payments and account maintenance
EFT payments and account maintenance requires multi-factor authentication. When attempting to pay with an EFT account or view/modify EFT account information, an e-mail is sent to the address associated with the account. Please follow the instructions in the e-mail to complete the transaction, and ensure your e-mail service is set up to accept e-mails from TRAMSupport@uspto.gov' and 'domavreply@uspto.gov'. (Note: Deposit account and credit card payment methods are not affected.)

The U.S. Patent and Trademark Office supports Secure Sockets Layer (SSL) for the security of all transactions. If you would like to read more about the security of your transaction click here.

Credit Card Payment

The USPTO accepts the following credit cards for payment.
Visa®, MasterCard®, Discover® and American Express®.

[Pay by Credit Card]

Deposit Account Payment

A USPTO Deposit Account is required to pay using this method.
For information about USPTO Deposit Accounts, click here.

[Pay by Deposit Account]

EFT Payment

An active EFT User Account is required to pay using this method.
For information about the EFT payment method, click here.
To sign up for an EFT User Account, click here.
Note: For a new EFT User Account, we must verify your banking information before you can pay by EFT.

[Pay by EFT]

TRADEMARK PROSECUTION PROCESS

USPTO Initial Review of Application

After the USPTO determines that you have met the minimum filing requirements, an application serial number is assigned, a filing receipt is issued, and the application is forwarded to an examining attorney. This may take a number of months. The examining attorney reviews the application to determine whether it complies with all applicable rules and statutes, and includes all required fees. Filing fees will not be refunded, even if the application is later refused registration on legal grounds.

Trademark Examining Attorney Reviews Application

A complete review includes a search for conflicting marks, and an examination of the electronic or written application, the drawing, and any specimen by the examining attorney. The examining attorney will search the USPTO records to determine if there is a conflict. The examiner reviews the records of the USPTO to determine if there is a conflict between your mark and another mark that is registered or is currently pending an application in the USPTO. The examining attorney looks at several factors such as similarity of the marks, the commercial impression between the goods or services listed in your application, and the existing mark or other third-party pending applications. The marks do not have to be identical, and the goods or services do not have to be exactly the same for a conflict to arise. It may be enough that the marks are similar, and the goods or services are related for the examining attorney to find a conflict and deny the registration of the application.

If the examining attorney finds a conflict exists, the examining attorney will refuse to register the mark on the grounds of likelihood of confusion. This is a major reason or factor why one should have an initial trademark clearance search and opinion performed before filing your trademark application. The examining attorney may refuse registration on other grounds too. The advantage of doing a trademark clearance search is so money is not wasted and a potential conflict with a third party is avoided. If the examining attorney determines the mark in the application is descriptive of the goods or service, or geographically descriptive of the goods or services, the trademark examiner will refuse registration.

Official Letters

If the examining attorney decides that a mark should not be registered, the examining attorney will issue an official letter (also known as an Office action) explaining any substantive reasons for refusal, and any technical or procedural deficiencies in the application. If only minor corrections are required, the examining attorney may contact the applicant by telephone or e-mail (if the applicant has authorized communication by telephone or e-mail). If the examining attorney sends an Office action, the applicant's response to the Office action must be received in the USPTO within six-months of the mailing date of the Office action, or the application will be declared abandoned.

TRADEMARK PROSECUTION PROCESS

Types of Official Letters

1. **Examiner's Amendment.** An examiner's amendment is a written confirmation of an amendment made to an application. Unless the applicant disagrees with the amendment, the applicant need not respond.

2. **Priority Action.** A priority action issues after the examining attorney consults with the applicant regarding problems with the application. This will include the reason why registration is being refused or how to satisfy certain application requirements. Unlike an examiner's amendment, the applicant must respond to a priority action within six-months from the date the priority action is issued, or the application will be abandoned.

3. **Office Action.** An Office Action issues to notify the applicant regarding problems with the application. This will include the reason why registration is being refused or what requirements must be satisfied. In most cases, the applicant must respond to an Office Action within six-months from the date the Office Action is issued, or the application will be abandoned.

    There are two types of Office Actions: non-final and final. A non-final Office Action raises an issue for the first time. A final Office Action issues when the applicant's response to the prior Office Action fails to address or overcome all issues. An applicant's only response to a final Office Action is either compliance with the requirements or appeal to the Trademark Trial and Appeal Board.

4. **Suspension Letter.** A suspension letter suspends the action on an application. An application may be suspended for a variety of reasons. These include waiting for the disposition of a cited prior pending application to be determined or waiting for an assignment of ownership to be recorded. Applicants do not have to respond to suspension letters.

Response Deadlines

Most responses to Office actions (official letters) must be received within six-months from the mailing date on the Office action. In certain circumstances, the Office action will specify a different response period. There are no extensions to the deadline specified in the letter. Examining attorneys have no discretion to extend the time period for filing a response. If applicants do not submit a timely response to an Office action, their applications will be declared abandoned.

Official Letter Responses

The USPTO strongly recommends filing a response electronically through the Trademark Electronic Application System (TEAS). All forms filed via TEAS are time/date stamped when received on the USPTO server, according to Eastern Standard Time (EST) and EST controls for purposes of determining the timeliness of a document. Any submission that arrives as of 11:59 p.m. EST will be given that day's filing date (i.e., regardless of the USPTO's "normal" hours).

However, responses may also be submitted by facsimile or regular mail. Applicants should address each issue raised by the examining attorney and include the applicant's name, mark, serial number, law office, and examining attorney in the body of the response. To ensure that a response is considered timely, an applicant may wish to add to the end of the response a properly completed "certificate of transmission" for responses submitted by facsimile or a properly completed "certificate of mailing" for responses submitted by mail. Applicants should retain a photocopy of the response with the signed certificate in the event that the response is lost or misplaced by the Office.

Timely Response

If the applicant's response does not overcome all objections, the examining attorney will issue a final refusal. To attempt to overcome a final refusal, the applicant may, for an additional fee, appeal to the Trademark Trial and Appeal Board, an administrative tribunal within the USPTO.

USPTO Publishes Mark

If the examining attorney raises no objections to registration, or if the applicant overcomes all objections, the examining attorney will approve the mark for publication in the Official Gazette, a weekly publication of the USPTO. The USPTO will send a Notice of Publication to the applicant stating the date published. After the mark is published in the Official Gazette, any party who believes it may be damaged by registration of the mark has thirty days from the publication date to file either an opposition to registration or a request to extend the time to oppose. An opposition is similar to a proceeding in a federal court, but is held before the Trademark Trial and Appeal Board. If no opposition is filed or if the opposition is unsuccessful, the application enters the next stage of the registration process.

TRADEMARK PROSECUTION PROCESS

Registration Certificate Issues for Applications Based on Use, Foreign Registrations, and International Registrations

A certificate of registration will issue for applications based on use, on a foreign registration under Section 44 of the Trademark Act, or an extension of protection of an international registration to the United States under Section 66(a). If the mark is published based upon the actual use of the mark in commerce, or on a foreign registration, and no party files an opposition or request to extend the time to oppose, the USPTO will normally register the mark and issue a Registration Certificate about twelve weeks after the date the mark was published. After the mark registers, the owner of the mark must file specific maintenance documents to keep the registration live.

Notice of Allowance Issues for Marks Based on an Intent-to-Use the Mark

If the mark is published based upon the applicant's bona fide intention to use the mark in commerce and no party files either an opposition or request to extend the time to oppose, the USPTO will issue a Notice of Allowance about twelve weeks after the date the mark was published. The applicant then has six-months from the date of the Notice of Allowance to either: (1) Use the mark in commerce and submit a Statement of Use; or (2) Request a six-month Extension of Time to File a Statement of Use (extension request).

A Notice of Allowance is a written notification from the USPTO that a specific mark has survived the opposition period following publication in the Official Gazette, and has consequently been allowed; it does not mean that the mark has registered yet. Receiving a Notice of Allowance is another step on the way to registration. Notices of Allowance are only issued for applications that have been filed based on an intent-to-use a mark in commerce under Trademark Act Section 1(b).

Statement of Use or Extension Request

The applicant has six-months from the mailing date of the Notice of Allowance in which to either file a Statement of Use or file an extension request. If the applicant is not using the mark in commerce on all of the goods or services listed in the Notice of Allowance, the applicant must file an extension request and the required fee(s) to avoid abandonment. Because extension requests are granted in six-month increments, applicant must continue to file extension requests every six-months. A total of five extension requests may be filed. The first extension request must be filed within six-months of the issuance date of the

TRADEMARK PROTECTION AND PROSECUTION

Notice of Allowance and subsequent requests before the expiration of a previously granted extension.

If the applicant is using the mark in commerce on all of the goods and services listed in the Notice of Allowance, the applicant must submit a Statement of Use and the required fee(s) within six-months from the date of the Notice of Allowance issued to avoid abandonment. Applicant cannot withdraw the Statement of Use; however, the applicant may file one extension request with the Statement of Use to provide more time to overcome deficiencies in the Statement of Use. No further extension requests may be filed.

If the applicant does not file a Statement of Use or extension request within six-months from the date the Notice of Allowance issued, the application is abandoned (no longer pending or under consideration for approval). To continue the application process, the applicant must file a Petition to Revive the Application within two-months of the abandonment date.

USPTO Reviews Statement of Use

If the minimum filing requirements are met, the Statement of Use is forwarded to the examining attorney. The examining attorney conducts a review of the Statement of Use to determine whether federal law permits registration. The applicant cannot withdraw the Statement of Use and the filing fee(s) will not be refunded, even if the application is later refused registration on legal grounds. If no refusals or additional requirements are identified, the examining attorney approves the Statement of Use.

If refusals or requirements must still be satisfied, the examining attorney assigned to the application issues a letter (Office Action) stating the refusals/requirements. This is the same process that occurs prior to publication of the mark if the examining attorney determines that legal requirements must be met. The process and timeframes remain the same, except that if issues are ultimately resolved and the Statement of Use is approved, the USPTO issues a Certificate of Registration within approximately two-months. If all issues are not resolved, the application will be abandoned.

Registration Certificate Issues

Within approximately two-months after the Statement of Use is approved, the USPTO issues a Certificate of Registration. To keep the registration "live," the registrant must file specific maintenance documents. Failure to make these required filings will result in cancellation and/or expiration of the registration.

TRADEMARK PROSECUTION PROCESS

Monitoring Status

Throughout the entire process, you should monitor the progress of your application through the Trademark Status and Document Retrieval (TSDR) system. It is important to check the status of your application every three- to four-months after the initial filing of the application, because otherwise you may miss a filing deadline.

Checking Status

Trademark applicants and registrants should monitor the status of their applications or registrations in cases where a notice of action from the USPTO is expected. An applicant is one that is filing or applying for a trademark and a registrant is one that has been granted a registration. Inquiries regarding the status of pending matters should be made during the following time periods:

- During the pendency of an application, an applicant should check the status of the application every six-months between the filing date of the application and the issuance of a registration; and

- After filing an Affidavit of Use or Excusable Nonuse under Section 8 or Section 71 of the Trademark Act, or a Renewal Application under Section 9 of the Act, a registrant should check the status of the registration every six-months until the registrant receives notice that the Affidavit or Renewal Application has been accepted.

If the status inquiry reveals that a filing is lost, that no action has been taken regarding correspondence that was submitted, or that some other problem exists, the applicant or registrant must promptly request corrective action. Failure to act diligently and follow up with appropriate action may result in denial of any later requested relief. The USPTO may deny petitions to reactivate abandoned applications and cancelled registrations when a party fails to inquire about the status of a pending matter within a reasonable time.

Protecting Your Rights

You are responsible for enforcing your rights if you receive a registration, because the USPTO does not "police" the use of marks. While the USPTO attempts to ensure that no other party receives a federal registration for an identical or similar mark for or as applied to related goods or services, the owner of the registration is responsible for bringing any legal action to stop a party from using an infringing mark.

CHAPTER 9

THE DRAWING PAGE

The drawing shows the mark sought to be registered. An applicant must submit a clear drawing with the original application in order to receive a filing date in any application for registration of a mark, except in applications for registration of sound, scent, and other non-visual marks. Submitting a specimen showing how the mark is or may be used (e.g., the overall packaging, a photograph of the goods, or an advertisement) does not satisfy the requirement for a clear drawing of the mark.

The drawing is used to reproduce the mark in the trademark Official Gazette and on the Registration Certificate. Thus, the main purpose of the drawing is to provide notice of the nature of the mark sought to be registered. The drawing of a mark is promptly entered into the automated records of the USPTO and is available to the public through the Trademark Electronic Search System (TESS) and the Trademark Applications and Registrations Retrieval (TARR) database on the USPTO website at http://tarr.uspto.gov/. Timely public notification of the filing of applications is important, because granting a filing date to an application potentially establishes a date of constructive use of the mark. Therefore, an application must include a clear drawing of the mark to receive a filing date.

Examining attorneys must require applicants to comply promptly with the drawing rules. Requests to defer drawing corrections until the application is approved for publication or registration should be denied.

Drawing Page Format

If processing a paper trademark application, the drawing must be on pure white, durable, non-shiny paper that is 8-1/2 (21.59 cm) inches wide by 11 (27.94 cm) inches long. There must be at least a one-inch (2.54 cm) margin on the sides, top and bottom of the page, and at least one inch between the heading and the display of the mark.

At the top of the drawing there must be a heading, listing on separate lines, the applicant's complete name, address, the goods and services specified in the application, and in the applications based on use in commerce, the date of first use of the mark and the date of first use of the mark in commerce. This heading should be typewritten. If the drawing is in special form, the heading should include a description of the essential elements of the mark.

The drawing of the mark should appear at the center of the page. The drawing of the mark may be in special character or it may be in special form. Remember, the depiction of the mark you submit now is what will appear on your registration certificate once the application process is completed. That is, you will not be able to add or subtract words and designs to the mark throughout the process, except in very rare circumstances. So, the mark you submit now is what will register later.

Drawing Must Show Only One Mark

An application must be limited to only one mark. Additionally, an applicant must submit "a clear drawing of the mark" to receive a filing date. An application that includes two or more drawings displaying materially different marks does not meet this requirement. Two marks are considered to be materially different if the substitution of one for the other would be a material alteration of the mark.

Accordingly, if an applicant submits two or more drawing pages, the application is denied a filing date, because the applicant has not met the requirement for a clear drawing of the mark. However, if an applicant submits a separate drawing page in a paper application showing a mark, and a different mark appears in the written application, the application will receive a filing date, and the drawing page will control for purposes of determining what the mark is. The USPTO will disregard the mark in the written application.

Similarly, if an applicant enters a standard character mark, or attaches a digitized image of a mark, in the "Mark" field of a TEAS application, and different mark appears in another field, the application will receive a filing date, and the mark entered in the "Mark" field will control for purposes of determining what the mark is.

The USPTO will not deny a filing date if the drawing shows spatially separate elements. If the applicant submits an application where the "drawing" is composed of multiple elements on a separate page, multiple elements on a single digitized image, or multiple elements in a separate area of the body of the application, the applicant has met the requirement for a clear drawing of the mark. The examining attorney must determine whether the matter presented for registration is a single mark projecting a unitary commercial impression.

If the examining attorney determines that spatially separate elements constitute two or more different marks, the examining attorney should refuse registration under Sections 1 and 45 of the Trademark Act on the ground that the applicant seeks registration of more than one mark. This refusal may apply in any application, regardless of the filing basis.

When registration is refused because the matter presented on the drawing does not constitute a single mark, the application filing fee will not be refunded. The applicant may amend the drawing if the amendment does not materially alter the mark, or may submit arguments that the matter on the drawing does in fact constitute a single mark.

Even if registration is sought for a three-dimensional mark, the applicant must submit a drawing depicting a single rendition of the mark. If the applicant submits a drawing that depicts a three-dimensional mark in multiple renditions, the examining attorney will require a substitute drawing depicting the mark in a single rendition. If the applicant believes that its mark cannot be adequately depicted in a single rendition, the applicant may file a petition requesting that the rule be waived.

If the mark is duplicated in some form on the drawing (e.g., a typed word and a stylized display of the same word), this is generally not considered to be two materially different marks, and deletion of one of the marks is permitted.

Drawing Must Be Limited to Mark

The drawing allows the USPTO to properly code and index the mark for search purposes, indicates what the mark is, and provides a means for reproducing the mark in the Official Gazette and on the Certificate of Registration. Therefore, matter must appear on the specimen that is not part of the mark should not be placed on the drawing. Purely informational matter, such as net weight, contents, or business addresses are generally not considered part of the mark.

Quotation marks and hyphens should not be included in the mark on a drawing, unless they are a part of the mark. Additionally, the drawing may not include extraneous matter, such as the letters "TM," "SM," the copyright notice ©, or the federal registration notice ®.

Standard Character Drawings

If submitting a standard character (typed) drawing, applicants who seek to register word(s), letter(s), number(s), or any combination thereof without claim to any particular font style, size, or color must submit a standard character drawing that shows the mark in black on white background. An applicant may submit a character drawing if:

- ❖ The application includes a statement that the mark is in standard characters and no claim is made to any particular font style, size, or color;
- ❖ The mark does not include a design element;
- ❖ All letters and words in the mark are depicted in Latin characters;
- ❖ All numerals in the mark are depicted in Roman or Arabic numerals; and
- ❖ The mark includes only common punctuation or diacritical marks.

Effective November 2, 2003, Trademark Rule 2.52, 37 C.F.R. Section 2.52, was amended to replace the term "typed" drawing with "standard character" drawing. Applicants who seek to register a mark without any claim as to the manner of display must submit a standard character drawing that complies with the requirements of 37 C.F.R. Section 2.52(a).

Requirements for Standard Character Drawings

A standard character drawing must show the mark in black on a white background. An applicant may submit a standard character drawing if the standard character drawing requirements above are met.

If the applicant files an application on paper, the applicant may depict the mark in any font style; may use bold or italicized letters; and may use both uppercase and lowercase letters, all uppercase letters, or all lowercase letters, since no claim is made to any particular font style, size, or color. The applicant does not have to display the art in all uppercase letters. If filing electronically via the Trademark Electronic Application System (TEAS), the applicant may neither depict the mark in any particular font style nor use bold or italicized letters. TEAS will automatically convert any wording typed into the standard-character field to a standardized typeface.

Superscripts, subscripts, exponents, or other characters that are not in the USPTO's standard character set are not permitted in standard character drawings. For example, a special form drawing is required for raised numerals. However, the degree symbol is permitted. Additionally, underlining is not permitted in a standard character drawing.

An applicant who submits a standard character drawing must also submit the following standard character claim: "The mark consists of standard characters without claim to any particular font style, size, or color." This statement will appear in the Official Gazette and on the certificate of registration.

List of Standard Characters

The USPTO has created a standard character set that lists letters, numerals, punctuation marks, and diacritical marks that may be used in a standard character drawing. The standard character set is available on the USPTO website. If the applicant has claimed standard character format and the drawing includes elements that are not in the set, then the examining attorney must treat the drawing as a special form drawing, ensure that the mark drawing code is changed, and require the applicant to delete the standard character claim.

In a Section 66(a) application, if the drawing includes elements that are not standard character set, the examining attorney must require deletion of the standard character claim even if the international registration indicates that the mark is in standard characters.

Drawing Contains Designs or Other Elements

If the application contains a standard character claim, but the mark includes a design element, or color, or a claim of a particular style or size of lettering, or other elements such that the mark does not meet requirements, then the examining attorney must: (1) treat the drawing as a special form drawing; (2) require that the application delete the standard character claim from the record; (3) ensure that the appropriate mark drawing code is entered into the Trademark Reporting and Monitoring (TRAM) database; and (4) if appropriate, add design search codes. Similarly, a standard character claim is not acceptable where the characters form shapes or designs, such as emoticons.

Material Alterations

A special form drawing containing a design element, color, a claim to a particular style or size of lettering, or other distinctive elements cannot be amended to a standard character drawing, unless the examining attorney determines that the amendment is not material. Conversely, a standard character drawing cannot be amended to be a special form drawing containing a design element, color, or a claim to a distinctive style or size of lettering, unless the examining attorney determines that the amendment is not material.

Standard Character Drawing and Specimen of Use

When the applicant submits a standard character, the mark shown in the drawing does not necessarily have to appear in the same font style, size, or color as the mark shown on the specimen of use. However, the examining attorney must review the mark depicted on the specimen to determine whether a standard character claim is appropriate, or whether a special form drawing is required.

If the examining attorney determines that the standard characters are displayed in a distinctive manner that changes the meaning or overall commercial impression of the mark, the examining attorney must process the drawing as a special form drawing, and require the applicant to delete the standard character claim. As with all drawings, the mark on the drawing must be a substantially exact representation of the mark used on the specimen in an application.

The examining attorney may delete the standard character claim by Examiner's Amendment after obtaining approval from the applicant or the applicant's qualified practitioner. When deleting a standard character claim, the examining attorney must ensure that the mark drawing code is changed.

Standard Character Drawing and Foreign Registration

In a Section 44 application, if the applicant claims standard characters, the examining attorney must ensure that the foreign registration also claims standard characters. If the foreign registration certificate does not indicate that the mark is in standard characters (or the equivalent), the examining attorney must inquire whether the foreign registration includes a claim that the mark is in standard characters (or the equivalent), or delete the standard character claim in the United States application. A statement that the foreign registration includes a claim that the mark is in standard characters may be entered through a note in the "Notes-to-the-File" section of the record, if there are no other outstanding issues.

Appendix E of the Trademark Manual of Examining Procedure (TMEP) lists countries that register marks in standard characters or the equivalent. For countries on this list, if all letters and words in the mark are in block capital or capital and lowercase Latin characters, all numerals are Roman or Arabic numbers, the mark includes only common punctuation or diacritical marks, and no stylization of lettering and/or numbers is claimed, the examining attorney need not inquire whether the registered mark in the foreign registration is in standard characters or the equivalent, unless the applicant has indicated that the mark is not standard characters or the equivalent. If the applicant has indicated that the mark is not in standard characters or the equivalent, but the foreign registration is from a country on the list and the mark meets the standards set forth above, the examining attorney must inquire about the discrepancy. In response to the inquiry, the applicant must either amend the application to claim standard characters, or confirm that the mark is not in standard characters or the equivalent. If a particular country is not on this list, the examiner must inquire as to whether the mark in the foreign registration is for a mark in standard characters or the equivalent.

The examining attorney may delete the standard character claim by Examiner's Amendment after obtaining approval from the applicant or applicant's qualified practitioner. When deleting a standard claim, the examining attorney must ensure that the mark drawing code is changed.

Drawings in "Typed" Format

If the application does not include a standard character claim, but the mark is shown in a format that would have been considered "typed" prior to November 2, 2003 (i.e., the mark is shown in capital letters, or the mark is specified as "typed" in the body of the application, on a separate drawing page, or on a cover letter filed with the application), the drawing will initially be coded and entered into the automated records of the USPTO as a special form drawing. However, the examining attorney must treat the drawing of the mark as a standard character drawing, and ensure that a standard character claim is entered into the record.

If the application is ready to be published for opposition, the examining attorney should enter the standard character claim by a no-call Examiner's Amendment. In this situation, no prior authorization from the applicant is required to add a claim by an Examiner's Amendment. If an Office action is necessary, it must include a requirement that the applicant submit a standard character claim. Once the applicant submits a standard character statement, the examining attorney should ensure that the mark drawing code is changed.

In a Section 44 application, the applicant cannot claim standard characters unless the foreign registration also claims standard characters.

In a Section 66(a) application, the request for extension of protection forwarded by the International Bureau (IB) normally indicates whether there is a standard character claim in the international registration. However, due to differences in requirements for standard character claims in different countries, there may be situations where the mark in the international registration meets the USPTO's requirements for a standard character claim, but no standard character claim is set forth in the international registration. If the international registration does not indicate that the mark is in standard characters, and the applicant seeks to amend the Section 66(a) application to add a standard character claim, the examining attorney must contact the supervisor of the Madrid Processing Unit via e-mail for instructions on how to proceed. The applicant may not add a standard character claim unless the mark meets the United States requirements for a standard character claim.

Drawings Where the Format Is Unclear

When it is unclear from the record whether the submitted drawing was intended to be a standard character drawing, the examining attorney must contact the applicant for clarification. For example, clarification is needed if the font style used in the mark on the drawing does not match the font style used on the specimen and there is no standard character claim in the application, or if the applicant files a paper application in which the mark is printed or written by hand. If the mark is intended to be in standard characters, then the examining attorney must require that the applicant amend the application to include the standard character claim. This may be done by Examiner's Amendment. Once the applicant submits this statement, the examining attorney should ensure that the mark drawing code is changed.

In a Section 44 application, the applicant cannot claim standard characters unless the foreign registration also claims standard characters.

In a Section 66(a) application, the request for extension of protection forwarded by the International Bureau (IB) normally indicates whether there is a standard character claim in the international registration. However, due to differences in requirements for standard character claims in different countries, there may be situations where the mark in the international registration meets the USPTO's requirements for a standard character claim, but no standard character claim is set forth in the international registration. If the international registration does not indicate the mark is in standard characters, and the applicant seeks to amend the Section 66(a) application to add a standard character claim, the examining attorney must contact the Madrid Processing Unit (MPU) for stated requirements for a standard character claim.

Alternatively, if the international registration indicates that the mark is in standard characters, but the drawing includes elements that are not in standard character set, the examining attorney must require deletion of the standard character claim even if the international registration indicates that the mark is in standard characters.

The Guide to the International Registration provides that if an Office "considers that the mark is not in standard characters, it may issue a refusal, for example, on the ground that the international registration covers two marks (one in standard characters and one in special characters) or that it is simply not clear for what protection is sought.

Typed Drawings

Prior to November 2, 2003, "standard character" drawings were known as "typed" drawings. The mark on a typed drawing had to be typed entirely in capital letters. A typed mark is the legal equivalent of a standard character mark.

Special Form Drawings

Applicants who seek to register a mark that includes a two or three-dimension design; color and/or word(s), letter(s), or number(s) or the combination thereof in a particular font style or size must submit a special form drawing. The drawing should show the mark in black on a white background, unless the mark includes color.

Characteristics of Special Form Drawings

A "special form drawing" is a drawing that presents a mark comprised, in whole or in part, of special characteristics such as elements of design or color, style(s) of lettering, or unusual form(s) of punctuation.

All special form drawings must be of a quality that will reproduce satisfactorily for scanning into the USPTO's database. If the drawing is not of a quality that will reproduce satisfactorily for scanning and printing in the Official Gazette and on the Certificate of Registration, the examining attorney must require a new drawing. If there is any doubt as to whether the drawing is acceptable, the examining attorney should contact the Office of Trademark Quality Review.

Pasted material, taped material, and correction fluid is not acceptable because it does not reproduce satisfactorily.

When Special Form Drawing is Required

A special form drawing is required if words, letters, or numerals are presented in a distinctive form that changes the meaning or overall commercial impression of the mark. Additionally, a special form drawing is required for marks that contain superscripts, subscripts, exponents, or other characters that are not in the USPTO's standard character set.

The USPTO encourages the use of standard character drawings. As a general rule, an applicant may submit a standard character drawing when a word, letter, numeral, or combination thereof creates a distinct commercial impression apart from the stylization or design element appearing on the specimen. If a mark remains the same in essence and is recognizable regardless of the form or manner of display that is presented, displaying the mark in standard character format affords a quick and efficient way of showing the essence of the mark.

For example, Trademark Trial and Appeal Board (TTAB) reversed refusal on the ground that the standard character mark on the drawing was not a substantially exact representation of the mark as actually used, finding that SPECTRAMET creates a distinct commercial impression apart from any stylization or design element appearing on the specimens, on which the letter "C" was displayed with an arrow design. In another example, TTAB ruled that the requirement that special form drawing be submitted to register OROWEAT displayed with wheat designs in the letter "O" was held improper. Yet another example, special form drawing not required when acronym makes an impression apart from design.

When an application is for a mark in standard characters, the examining attorney should consider the manner in which the mark is used on the specimen, and decide whether the mark includes an essential element or feature that cannot be produced by the use of standard characters. For example, if the mark comprises the prescription symbol Rx, a claim of standard characters would be inappropriate.

If the examining attorney determines that the mark in a standard character drawing should have been presented in special form, the applicant may submit a special form drawing if the amendment would not result in a material alteration of the mark. The applicant cannot substitute a special form drawing if the amendment would materially alter the mark. If a standard character drawing is amended to a special form drawing, the examining attorney must ensure that the mark drawing code is changed.

Electronically Submitted Drawings

The drawing in a Trademark Electronic Application System (TEAS) application must meet the requirements of 37 C.F.R. Sections 2.52 and 2.53. The USPTO has waived the requirement that drawings have a length and width of no less than 250 pixels and no more than 944 pixels. However, applicants are encouraged to continue to submit such drawings.

Standard Character Drawings Submitted Electronically

If an applicant is filing a standard character drawing, the applicant must enter the mark in the appropriate data field. The applicant must also submit a standard character claim, which is automatically generated once the applicant selects the standard character option. Consequently, when an application for a standard mark is filed through TEAS, the characters entered in the appropriate data field in the TEAS application or TEAS response form are automatically checked against the USPTO's standard character set.

If all the characters in the mark are in the standard character set, the USPTO will create a digitized image that meets requirements, and automatically generate the standard character statement. The application record will indicate that standard characters have been claimed and that the USPTO has created the image. The examining attorney need not check the standard character mark against the standard character set during examination.

Long Marks in Standard Character Drawings

When an applicant files an application for a standard mark through TEAS, the applicant must enter the mark in the appropriate data field.

A single line can consist of no more than twenty-six characters, including spaces. If the applicant enters a mark that exceeds twenty-six characters into the standard character word mark field, the USPTO's automated system will break the mark, so that it fits into the Official Gazette. After twenty-six characters, the mark will automatically continue onto the next line. The online TEAS instructions provide further information about breaks in long standard character marks. If a standard character mark exceeds twenty-six characters, and the applicant has a preference as to where the mark will be broken, the applicant should use the special form option, and attach a digitized image that meets requirements.

Special Form Drawings Submitted Electronically

If the mark is in special form, the applicant must attach a digitized image of the mark that meets the requirements of 37 C.F.R. Section 2.53(c) to the "Mark" field on the electronic application.

THE DRAWING PAGE

Requirements for Digitized Images

The mark image must be in .JPG format, and should be scanned at no less than 300 dots per inch and no more than 350 dots per inch, to produce the highest quality image. All lines must be clean, sharp and solid, must not be fine or crowded, and must produce a high-quality image. It is recommended that mark images have a length of no less than 250 pixels and no more than 944 pixels, and a width of no less than 250 pixels and no more than 944 pixels.

Mark images should have little or no white space appearing around the design of the mark. If scanning from a paper image of the mark, it may be necessary to cut out the mark and scan it with little or no surrounding white space. Failure to do this may cause the mark to appear very small in the USPTO's automated records, such that it may be difficult to recognize all words or design features of the mark. To ensure that there is a clear image of the mark in the automated records of the USPTO, examining attorneys and legal instruments examiners should view the mark on the Publication Review program available on the USPTO's internal computer network. If the mark is not clear, the examining attorney must require a new drawing that meets requirements.

When color is not claimed as a feature of the mark, the image must be depicted only in black and white. When scanning an image, the applicant should confirm that the settings on the scanner are set to create a black and white image file, not a color image file.

Mark images may not include extraneous matter such as the symbols "TM" or "SM" or the registration notice "®." The image should be limited to the mark.

Paper Drawings

A paper drawing must meet the requirements of sections 2.52 and 2.54. Paper drawings may be filed by mail or hand delivery. Drawings may not be submitted by facsimile transmission.

Type of Paper and Size of Mark

The mark on the drawing should be no larger than 3.15 inches high by 3.15 inches wide. The USPTO will create a digitized image of all drawings submitted on paper. The examining attorney must view the mark on the Publication Review program, available on the USPTO's internal computer network. If the display of the mark appears to be clear and accurate, the examining attorney will presume that the drawing meets the size requirements of the rule.

The drawing should:

- ❖ Be on non-shiny white paper that is separate from the application;

- ❖ Be on paper that is 8 to 8.5 inches wide and 11 to 11.69 inches long. One of the shorter sides of the sheet should be regarded as its top edge;

- ❖ Include the caption "DRAWING PAGE" at the top of the drawing beginning one inch from the top edge; and

- ❖ Depict the mark in black ink, or in color if color is claimed as a feature of the mark.

The drawing must be typed or made with ink or by a process that will provide high definition when scanned. A photolithographic, printer's proof copy, or other high-quality reproduction of the mark may be used. All lines must be clean, sharp and solid, and must not be fine or crowded.

Long Marks in Standard Character Drawings

Because all standard character drawings are stored in USPTO systems as an image, a standard character drawing must meet the 3.15 inch by 3.15-inch requirement. If the mark is too long to meet this requirement, applicant must submit an image on which the mark is broken in an appropriate place. It is suggested that the applicant use 14-point type to ensure that the mark will be legible in the Official Gazette and on the Certificate of Registration.

If an applicant submits an image on which the mark exceeds the size requirements, the USPTO will reduce the image so that it will meet these requirements. This could cause the mark to appear very small. To ensure that the mark will be legible in the Official Gazette and on the Certificate of Registration, the examining attorney should view the mark on the Publication Review program available on the USPTO's internal computer network. If the mark is not legible, the examining attorney must require a new drawing that meets such requirements.

Separate Drawing Page Preferred

The USPTO recommends that an applicant submit a drawing of the mark on a separate page from the written application. However, a separate drawing page is not mandatory. Instead of a drawing page, an applicant may include a drawing of the mark embedded in the application, in either the heading or the body of the application.

THE DRAWING PAGE

If the applicant identifies a separate page as a drawing (e.g., by labeling it as a drawing, or providing a heading with the applicant's name, address and the subject goods or services), this will be the only drawing considered.

A mark depicted on the specimen or in the foreign registration certificate will not be considered a drawing. Thus, if there is no separate drawing page, the examining attorney must review the application to determine what the mark is. If an embedded drawing, meets requirements, the examining attorney should accept it and not require a substitute drawing.

Effective October 30, 1999, a separate drawing page is considered part of the written application, not a separate element. Dates of use, disclaimers, descriptions of the mark, identifications of goods and services, and other information that appear on the drawing are also considered part of the written application. This applies to substitute drawings as well as original drawings. If there is an inconsistency between the information on the drawing page and the information in the body of the application, the examining attorney must require clarification.

If an applicant submits a separate drawing page showing a mark, and a different mark appears in the written application, the drawing page controls for purposes of determining what the mark is.

Color in the Mark

If the mark includes color, the drawing must show the mark in color, and the applicant must name the color(s), describe where the color(s) appear on the mark, and submit a claim that the color(s) is/are a feature of the mark.

If the applicant wishes to register the mark in color, the applicant must submit a color drawing and meet further requirements regarding the requirements for color drawings. If the applicant does not claim color as a feature of the mark, the applicant must submit a black and white drawing.

Generally, if the applicant has not made a color claim, the description of the mark should not mention color(s), because reference to color in the description of a non-color mark creates a misleading impression. However, in some cases, it may be appropriate to submit a black and white drawing and a description of the mark that refers to black, white, or gray, if the applicant states that color is not claimed as a feature of the mark. This occurs where the black, white, or gray is used as a means to indicate areas that are not part of the mark, such as background or transparent areas; to depict a certain aspect of the mark that is not a feature of the mark, such as dotted or broken line outlining to show placement of the mark; to represent shading or stippling; or to depict depth or three-dimensional shape.

Requirements for Color Drawings

For applications filed on or after November 2, 2003, the USPTO does not accept black and white drawings with a color claim, or drawings that show color by use of color lining patterns.

If the mark includes color, the drawing must show the mark in color. In addition, the application must include: (1) a claim that the color(s) is/are a feature of the mark; and (2) a color location statement in the "description of the mark" field naming the color(s) and describing where the color(s) appear(s) on the mark. A color drawing will not publish without both of these statements.

Color Must Be Claimed as a Feature of the Mark

If an applicant submits a color drawing, or a description of the mark that indicates the use of color on the mark, the applicant must claim color as a feature of the mark. If the color claim is unclear or ambiguous, the examining attorney must require clarification. If the color claim or mark description references changeable colors, the examining attorney must require an amended mark description that deletes the reference to the color in the mark varying or being changeable and restricts the description to only those colors shown on the drawing.

Alternatively, the applicant may amend to a black and white drawing, if the amendment would not constitute a material alteration. A properly worded color claim would read as follows:

> "The color(s) <name the color(s)> is/are claimed as a feature of the mark."

The color claim must include the generic name of the color(s) claimed. The color claim may also include a reference to a commercial color identification system. The USPTO does not endorse or recommend any one commercial color identification system.

In an application filed on or after November 2, 2003, an applicant cannot file a color drawing with a statement that "no claim is made to color" or "color is not a feature of the mark." If this occurs, the examining attorney must require the applicant to claim color as a feature of the mark. The applicant may not substitute a black and white drawing, unless the examining attorney determines that color is non-material.

THE DRAWING PAGE

Applicant Must Specify the Location of the Colors Claimed

If an applicant submits a color drawing, in addition to claiming the color(s), the applicant must include a separate statement specifying where the color(s) appear(s) on the mark. This statement is often referred to as a "color location statement." In a TEAS application, the color location statement should be set forth in the "description of the mark" field. A properly worded color location statement would read as follows:

> "The mark consists of <specify the color(s) and literal or design element(s) on which the color(s) appear, e.g., a red bird sitting on a green leaf. >

If the color location statement is unclear or ambiguous, the examining attorney must require clarification. If the statement references changeable colors, the examining attorney must require an amended mark description that deletes the reference to the color in the mark varying or being changeable and restricts the description to only those colors shown on the drawing. However, if the record contains an accurate and properly worded color claim listing all the colors, and an informal description of whether the colors appear, but one of the colors is omitted from the formal description of the colors in the mark, the examining attorney may enter an amendment of the color description that accurately reflects the location of all colors in the mark without prior approval by the applicant or the applicant's qualified practitioner.

For example, a TEAS applicant includes a statement in the "miscellaneous" field that refers to the mark as a blue, red, and yellow ball and includes an accurate and properly worded color claim listing all colors in the mark, but omits the color yellow from the description of the mark. The examining attorney may enter an amendment of the description to accurately reflect all colors in the mark.

The color location statement must include the generic name of the color claimed. The statement may also include a reference to a commercial color identification system. The USPTO does not endorse or recommend any one commercial color identification system. Additionally, it is usually not necessary to indicate shades of color, but the examining attorney has the discretion to require that the applicant indicate shades of a color, if necessary, to accurately describe the mark.

Color Drawings that Contain Black, White, or Gray

When color is claimed as a feature of the mark, the applicant must submit a color claim that identifies each color and a separate color location statement describing where each color appears in the mark. The applicant must claim all colors shown in the mark; the applicant cannot claim color for some elements of the mark and not others. For example, when the drawing includes solid black lettering as well as elements in other colors, the applicant must claim the color black as a feature of the mark and include reference to the black lettering in the color location statement. The applicant may not state that solid black lettering represents all colors, or that it represents the particular color of the label, product, packaging, advertisement, website, or other specimen on which the mark appears at any given time.

If color is claimed as a feature of the mark, the drawing may include black, white, and/or gray used in two ways: (1) as claimed features of the mark; and/or (2) as a means to depict a certain aspect of the mark that is not a feature of the mark, such as dotted or broken-line outlining to show placement of the mark on a product or package; to represent shading or stippling; to depict depth or three-dimensional shape; or to indicate areas that are not part of the mark, such as background or transparent areas.

The terms "background" and "transparent areas" refer to the white or black portions of the drawing which are not part of the mark, but appear or will appear in the particular color of the label, product, packaging, advertisement, website, or other acceptable specimen on which the mark is or will be displayed. The applicant may not claim that the background or transparent areas represent all colors or that they represent the particular color of the label, product, packaging, advertisement, website, or other specimen on which the mark appears at any given time.

If the applicant claims color as a feature of the mark, the examining attorney must require the applicant to:

- ❖ State that the color(s) black, white, and/or gray (and all other colors in the drawing) are claimed as a feature of the mark, and describe where the colors appear on the mark; or
- ❖ If appropriate, state that the black, white, and/or gray in the drawing represents background, outlining, shading, and/or transparent areas and is not part of the mark.

THE DRAWING PAGE

These statement(s) may be submitted in either a written amendment to the application or by an Examiner's Amendment. The examining attorney must ensure that the statement(s) is/are entered into the database. The statement(s) will be printed on the Registration Certificate.

The only exception to the requirement to claim or explain any black, white, and/or gray shown on the drawing is that, if the background of the drawing is white and it is clear that the white background is not part of the mark, no explanation of the white background is required. For example, if the drawing depicts the letters "ABC" in solid blue on a white background, or depicts a solid purple and green flower on a white background, no statement about the white background is required. On the other hand, if the shape of each of the letter's "ABC" is outlined in blue with an enclosed white interior, or if the purple and green flower is enclosed in a green or black rectangle, square, or circle with a white interior, the applicant must explain the purpose of the interior white areas on the drawing.

Broken Lines to Show Placement

If necessary, to adequately depict the commercial impression of the mark, the applicant may be required to submit a drawing that shows the placement of the mark by surrounding the mark with a proportionately accurate broken line representation of the particular goods, packaging, or advertising on which the mark appears. The applicant must also use broken lines to show any other matter not claimed as part of the mark. For any drawing using broken lines to indicate placement of the mark, or matter not claimed as part of the mark, the applicant must describe the mark and explain the purpose of the broken lines.

Occasionally, the position of the mark on the goods, or on a label or container, may be a feature of the mark. If necessary, to adequately depict the commercial impression of the mark, the examining attorney may require the applicant to submit a drawing that shows the placement of the mark by surrounding the mark with a proportionately accurate broken line representation of the particular goods, packaging, or advertising on which the mark appears. The applicant must also use broken lines to show any other matter not claimed as part of the mark. For any drawing using broken lines to indicate placement of the mark, or matter not claimed as part of the mark, the applicant must include a written description of the mark and explain the purpose of the broken lines, e.g., by indicating that the matter shown by the broken lines is not a part of the mark and that it serves only to show the position of the mark.

"Drawing" of Sound, Scent, or Non-Visual Mark

An applicant is not required to submit a drawing if the mark consists only of a sound, a scent, or other completely non-visual matter. For these types of marks, the applicant must submit a detailed description of the mark. Consequently, the applicant is not required to submit a drawing if the mark consists solely of a sound (e.g., music or words and music), a scent, or other completely non-visual matter.

In a paper application, the applicant should clearly indicate in the application that the mark is a "non-visual mark." If the applicant is submitting a TEAS application for a sound mark, the applicant should select "non-visual or multi-media mark" as the mark type. If the applicant is submitting a TEAS application for a scent mark, the applicant should indicate that the mark type is "standard character" and should type "scent mark" in the "standard character" field. The USPTO will enter the proper mark drawing code when the application is processed.

If the applicant selects "non-visual or multi-media mark" as the mark type, the applicant will be required to indicate whether it is attaching an audio or video file. The applicant should submit an audio or video reproduction of any sound mark. The purpose of this reproduction is to supplement and clarify the description of the mark. The reproduction should contain only the mark itself; it is not meant to be a specimen. The reproduction must be in an electronic file in .wav, .wmv, .wma, .mp3, .mpg, or .avi format and should not exceed five MB in size for audio files and thirty MB for video files because TEAS cannot accommodate larger files.

For paper filings, reproductions of sound marks must be submitted on compact discs (CDs), digital video discs (DVDs), videotapes, or audiotapes. The applicant should clearly and explicitly indicate that the reproduction of the mark contained on the disc or tape is meant to supplement the mark description and that it should be placed in the paper file jacket and not be discarded.

If the mark is a composite comprising both visual and non-visual matter, the applicant must submit a drawing depicting the visual matter, and include a description of the non-visual matter in the "description of the mark" field.

The applicant must also submit a detailed description of the mark for all non-visual marks. If the mark comprises music or words set to music, the applicant should generally submit the musical score sheet music to supplement or clarify the description of the mark. In a TEAS application or response, the score should be attached as a .JPEG or .PDF file in the "additional statements" section of the form, under "miscellaneous statements."

Three-Dimensional Marks

If the mark has three-dimensional features, the drawing must depict a single rendition of the mark, and the applicant must include a description of the mark indicating that the mark is three-dimensional. If the applicant believes that its mark cannot be adequately depicted in a single rendition, the applicant may file a petition requesting that the rule be waived.

Marks with Motion

If the mark has motion, the drawing may depict a single point in the movement, or the drawing may depict up to five freeze frames showing various points in the movement, whichever best depicts the commercial impression of the mark. The applicant must also describe the mark. Additionally, if the mark includes motion (i.e., a repetitive motion of short duration) as a feature, the applicant may submit a drawing that depicts a single point in the movement, or the applicant may submit a square drawing that contains up to five freeze frames showing various points in the movement, whichever best depicts the commercial impression of the mark. The applicant must also submit a detailed written description of the mark.

Mark on Drawing Must Agree with Mark on Specimen or Foreign Registration

In an application under Section 1(a) of the Trademark Act, the drawing of the mark must be a substantially exact representation of the mark as used on or in connection with the goods or services. In an application under Section 1(b) of the Trademark Act, the drawing of the mark must be a substantially exact representation of the mark as intended to be used on or in connection with the goods or services specified in the application, and once an Amendment to Allege Use or a Statement of Use has been filed, the drawing of the mark must be a substantially exact representation of the mark as used on or in connection with the goods or services.

In an application under Section 44 of the Trademark Act, the drawing of the mark must be a substantially exact representation of the mark as it appears in the drawing in the registration certificate of a mark duly registered in the applicant's country of origin. In an application under Section 66(a) of the Trademark Act, the drawing of the mark must be a substantially exact representation of the mark as it appears in the international registration.

Marks that Include Color and Other Elements

The extent to which color contributes to the commercial impression created by a mark is often determined by the type of mark in question (i.e., word mark, design mark, or trade dress). In some cases, color may play only an incidental or insignificant part in creating the commercial impression of a mark, such as color lettering of a word mark. In other cases, color is the only feature of the mark that creates a commercial impression, such as where the mark consists only of color(s) applied to goods or their packaging, or to articles used in the sale or advertising services.

Word Marks

In general, the addition, deletion, or amendment of color lettering in a word mark does not result in a material alteration of the mark. Word marks may appear as stylized marks in color lettering. With the possible exception of generic wording, the literal portions of word marks are likely to be the dominant portions that create the greatest commercial impression. In most cases, the color in the lettering is unlikely to have a significant impact on the commercial impression created by the mark.

Design Marks

In general, the addition, deletion, or amendment of color features in a design mark does not result in a material alteration of the mark. In a color design mark, the design portion is likely to be the most dominant portion of the mark in creating a commercial impression. Although the color portion is part of the mark, it only appears in the context of the design and is not a separable element. The color portion is, therefore, less likely than the design portion to play a significant role in likelihood of confusion or trademark selection considerations.

For example, the fact that two different designs, such as a red hat design and red boat design, may appear in identical colors is unlikely to result in a finding of likelihood of confusion. In contrast, if two boat designs are identical in stylization, it is likely that the designs would be held to be confusingly similar regardless of any differences in their respective colors.

Color Marks

The amendment of any color in a color mark is a prohibited material alteration. Color marks are marks that consist solely of one or more colors used on particular objects or substances as a source identified (as opposed to marks that include color in addition to other elements). Color marks generally appear in a drawing with the outline or configuration of the goods on which they appear to

THE DRAWING PAGE

show the placement of the color mark. However, the shape or configuration of the goods is not part of the mark. The mark is comprised solely of the color as applied to the object or substance, in the manner depicted and described, so that changing or amending the color of the mark would always change the entire commercial impression created by the mark.

For more information on drawings, the USPTO offers an online version of the Trademark Manual of Examining Procedures (TMEP) from their website.

CHAPTER 10

FOREIGN REGISTRATIONS

Trademark rights are acquired on a country-by-country basis. In many foreign jurisdictions, rights in a mark are established through registration, not through use in the United States. Therefore, it might be critical that your company (and your distributors or licensees) register rights in your marks in foreign countries.

Additional factors also need to be considered when using trademarks in foreign countries, as acts, which are legal in one country, may not be legal in another. For instances, some countries do not recognize the ® symbol. In others, an owner may forfeit its trademark rights through improper use of the ® symbol. In addition, use of third-party trademarks on packaging may be prohibited. Because of these concerns, for materials used in foreign countries, you should use a trademark legend to identify your company's trademark ownership, rather than a trademark symbol.

In addition, some countries prohibit the use of comparative advertising or use of another entity's trademarks on packaging. Thus, this is another reason why you should consult with a designated trademark law counsel for guidance concerning the correct use of marks in foreign countries.

Section 44 Applications

The United States has assumed certain obligations from agreements adopted at the Paris Convention for the Protection of Industrial Property and subsequent revisions to these agreements. The United States is also a member of the Inter-American Convention for Trademarks and Commercial Protection (also known as the "Pan-American Convention"), the Buenos Aires Convention for the Protection of Trade Marks and Commercial Names, the World Trade Organization, and certain other treaties and agreements.

Section 44 of the Trademark Act, 15 U.S.C. Section 1126, implements these agreements. Section 44 applications fall into two basic categories: (1) United States applications relying on foreign applications to secure a priority filing date in the United States under Section 44(d); and (2) United States applications relying on ownership of foreign registrations as a basis for registration in the United States under Section 44(e). Section 44(d) of the Act provides only a basis for receipt of a priority filing date, not a basis for publication or registration.

An applicant may file an application based solely on Section 44, or may claim Section 44 in addition to Section 1(a) or Section 1(b) as a filing basis. An applicant who claims more than one basis must comply with all application requirements for each basis asserted. Additionally, in an application based solely on Section 44, the applicant must submit a verified statement that the applicant has a bona fide intention to use the mark in commerce, but use in commerce is not required prior to registration. Thus, in limited circumstances, applicants domiciled in the United States may be entitled to file under Section 44, if they meet the requirements of the Act.

Eligible Applicants

To be eligible for registration under Section 44(e), an applicant must meet the following requirements:

- ❖ The applicant's country of origin must be a party to a treaty or agreement with the United States that provides for registration based on ownership of a foreign registration, or must extend reciprocal registration rights to nationals of the United States; and

- ❖ The applicant must be the owner of a valid registration in the applicant's country of origin.

If an applicant does not meet the requirements listed above, the examining attorney must refuse registration under Section 44(e). The applicant may amend the application to claim Section 1(a) or Section 1(b) as a basis. Therefore, an applicant domiciled in the United States cannot obtain registration under Section 44(e) unless the applicant is the owner of a registration from an eligible country other than the United States and the applicant can establish that the foreign country is the applicant's country of origin.

To be eligible for a priority filing date under Section 44(d), an applicant must meet the following requirements:

- ❖ The applicant's country of origin must be a party to an international treaty or agreement with the United States that provides a right of priority, or must extend reciprocal rights to priority to United States nationals; and

❖ The foreign application that is the basis for the priority claim must be filed in a country that either is a party to a treaty or agreement with the United States that provides a right of priority, or extends reciprocal rights to priority to United States nationals.

If an applicant does not meet the requirements listed above, the examining attorney must advise the applicant that it is not entitled to priority. If the applicant has not claimed another filing basis, the examining attorney must require the applicant to claim and perfect an acceptable basis before the application can be approved for publication or registration on the Supplemental Register. Thereafter, the examining attorney must ensure that the priority claim is deleted from the Trademark Reporting and Monitoring (TRAM) database, and conduct a new search of the records of the USPTO for conflicting marks.

In summary, to obtain a priority filing date under Section 44(d), the foreign application does not have to be filed in the applicant's country of origin. However, to obtain registration under Section 44(e) based on the foreign registration that will issue from the application on which the applicant relies for priority, the applicant must establish that the country in which the application was filed is its country of origin. Therefore, if the applicant files a Section 44(d) priority claim based on the application from a treaty country other than the country in which the applicant is domiciled, the examining attorney must advise the applicant that in order to rely on the registration issuing from the identified foreign application as its basis for registration, the applicant will be required to establish that the country where the foreign application was filed is its country of origin.

It is important to keep in mind that while Section 44(d) provides a basis for filing and priority filing date, it does not provide a basis for publication or registration. A party who files under Section 44(d) must establish a basis for registration. For example, a French corporation may rely on a first-filed application in Canada for its priority claim under Section 44(d), regardless of whether Canada is the applicant's country of origin. However, before the mark can be published for opposition in the United States, the French corporation must do one of the following: (1) establish Canada as its country of origin and rely on the prospective Canadian registration as its basis for registration in the United States; (2) assert use in commerce under Section 1(a) and or a bona fide intention to use in commerce under Section 1(b) as its basis for publication in the United States; or (3) rely on a registration from France as its basis for registration in the

FOREIGN REGISTRATIONS

United States. (An applicant domiciled or organized in the United States may claim priority under Section 44(d) based on ownership of an application in a treaty country other than the United States.)

Establishing Entitlement Under a Treaty

In a Section 44 application, the examining attorney must confirm that: (1) both the applicant's country of origin and the country where the applicant has filed the application or obtained registration are parties to a treaty or agreement with the United States (or that they extend reciprocal rights to United States nationals by law); and (2) the specific benefit that the applicant is claiming under Section 44 (i.e., the right to a priority filing date under Section 44(d) and or the right to registration under Section 44(e)) is provided for under the treaty or agreement.

To determine whether a particular country has a treaty with the United States that provides for the benefit that the applicant is claiming under Section 44, examining attorneys should consult Appendix B of the Trademark Manual of Examining Procedure. Appendix B lists the members of the Paris Convention, Inter-American Convention, Buenos Aires Convention, World Trade Organization, European Union ("EU"), and certain countries entitled to reciprocal treatment under other international agreements, as well as websites where examining attorneys can obtain updated information about these treaties and agreements.

In a Section 44 application or an amendment adding or substituting Section 44 as a basis, an eligible applicant may rely on an application filed in or registration issued by certain common offices of several states. A "common office of several states" refers to an entity serving as the issuing office for trademark registrations for an established group of countries. Examples include the Benelux Trademark Office, servicing Belgium, The Netherlands, and Luxemburg; and the African Intellectual Property Organization ("OAPI"), which issues registrations covering all member states (i.e., Benin, Burkina-Faso, Cameroon Central African Republic, Chad, Congo, Equatorial Guinea, Gabon, Guinea, Guinea-Bissau, Ivory Coast, Mali, Mauritania, Niger, Senegal, and Togo).

An applicant may also claim the benefits of Section 44 based on an application for a registration of a Community Trade Mark, if the applicant has a bona fide and effective industrial or commercial establishment in a country or state that is a member of the EU, formerly known as the European Community (EC) or European Economic Community (EEC).

If an eligible applicant filed an application or obtained a registration in a country that is a member of the Paris Convention, Inter-American Convention, World

Trade Organization, or European Union, the applicant can claim the benefits of either Section 44(d) or Section 44(e), if the applicant meets the requirements of those sections. An eligible applicant may also file under either Section 44(e) or Section 44(d) based on an application filed or registration obtained in Taiwan. On the other hand, if the applicant filed an application and obtained a registration in a country that is a member of the Buenos Aires Convention, the applicant may seek registration under Section 44(e), but may not obtain a priority filing date under Section 44(d).

In the case of agreements not covered, an applicant can establish its eligibility for the benefits of Section 44 by providing evidence of statutes or agreements establishing reciprocity between the United States and the relevant country. Examining attorneys may also consult sources such as Trademarks Throughout the World (Anne-Laure Covin, 5th ed. 2008) and World Trademark Law and Practice (Ethan Horwitz, 2nd ed. 2008), available to USPTO employees in the Trademark Law Library, for information about the trademark laws of foreign countries.

Establishing Country of Origin

To obtain registration under Section 44(e), the applicant must be the owner of a valid registration from the applicant's country of origin. To obtain a priority filing date under Section 44(d), the applicant's country of origin must be a treaty country, but the foreign application that is the basis for the priority claim does not have to be filed in the applicant's country of origin. An applicant domiciled or organized in the United States may be entitled to registration under Section 44(e) if the applicant can also claim a country of origin other than the United States.

Section 44(c) of the Trademark Act defines the applicant's country of origin as "the country in which the applicant has a bona fide and effective industrial or commercial establishment, or if applicant has not such an establishment, the country in which the applicant is domiciled, or if applicant has not a domicile in any of the countries described in paragraph (b) of this section, the country of which the applicant is a national." Under this definition, an applicant can have more than one country of origin.

If a Section 44 applicant is domiciled or incorporated in the relevant country, the examining attorney should presume that the country is the applicant's country of origin, and should not issue an inquiry about the applicant's country of origin.

FOREIGN REGISTRATIONS

If a Section 44(e) applicant is not domiciled or incorporated in the country that issued the foreign registration (or if a Section 44(d) applicant is not domiciled or incorporated in a treaty country), the examining attorney must require the applicant to establish that the country is its country of origin. Normally, a written statement by the applicant or the applicant's attorney that the applicant has a bona fide and effective industrial or commercial establishment in the relevant country will be sufficient to establish that the country is the applicant's country of origin. This statement does not have to be verified. If the application is otherwise eligible for approval for publication, or in condition to be allowed for registration on the Supplemental Register, the examining attorney may attempt to contact the applicant by phone or e-mail to obtain the statement. If the examining attorney is unable to reach the applicant by phone or e-mail, the examining attorney must issue an Office action. If the applicant responds by phone or e-mail, the examining attorney must issue an examiner's amendment to enter the statement into the record.

If any evidence in the record contradicts the applicant's assertion that the applicant has a bona fide and effective industrial or commercial establishment in the relevant country, the examining attorney should require the applicant to set forth the specific circumstances, which establish that the applicant maintains a bona fide and effective industrial or commercial establishment in the country. Relevant factors include the presence of production facilities, business offices, and personnel.

Note: The presence of an applicant's wholly owned subsidiary in a country does not, by itself, establish country of origin. The sale of goods or services outside the United States through related companies or licensees does not create a bona fide commercial establishment and thus does not establish country of origin. The United States, by definition, is not a country that has a treaty with the United States. Therefore, the term "country of origin" in Sections 44(b) and 44(c) means some country other than the United States.

United States Applicants

Section 44(b) of the Trademark Act provides that, "Any person whose country of origin is a party to any convention or treaty relating to trademarks, trade or commercial names, or the repression of unfair competition, to which the United States is also a party, or extends reciprocal rights to nationals of the United States by law, shall be entitled to the benefits of this section...."

Section 44(i) of the Act provides that "citizens or residents of the United States shall have the same benefits as are granted by this section to persons granted by this section to persons described in subsection 44(b)...." However, Section 44(i) does not provide an independent basis for a United States applicant to register a mark under Section 44(e).

The United States, by definition, is not a country that has a treaty with the United States. Therefore, the term "country of origin" in Section 44(b) means some country other than the United States, and the term "person" in Section 44(b) means a person who can claim a country of origin other than the United States.

An applicant domiciled in the United States may claim priority under Section 44(d) based on ownership of an application in a treaty country other than the United States, even if the other country is not the applicant's country of origin. However, an applicant domiciled in the United States may not obtain registration under Section 44(e) unless the applicant is the owner of a registration from an eligible country other than the United States and the applicant can establish that the foreign country is the applicant's country of origin.

For example, a Texas corporation may assert a priority claim under Section 44(d) based on ownership of an application in Mexico, regardless of whether Mexico is its country of origin. However, this applicant must also assert a valid basis for registration. The applicant may do so by asserting use in commerce under Section 1(a) and or a bona fide intention to use in commerce under Section 1(b) as its basis for publication. The applicant cannot obtain registration in the United States under Section 44(e) unless the applicant establishes that Mexico is one of its countries of origin.

Priority Filing Date Based on a Foreign Application

Section 44(d) of the Trademark Act, 15 U.S.C. Section 1126(d), provides for a priority filing date to eligible applicants who have filed an application in a treaty country as defined by Section 44(b). If an eligible applicant files the United States application claiming Section 44(d) priority within six-months of filing the first application to register the mark in a treaty country, the filing date of the first-filed foreign application is the effective filing date of the United States application.

The requirements for receipt of a priority filing date under Section 44(d) are:

- ❖ The eligible applicant must file a claim of priority within six-months of the filing date of the first-filed foreign application;

- ❖ The applicant must: (a) specify the filing date and country of the first regularly filed foreign application; or (b) state that the application is based upon a subsequent regularly filed application in the same foreign country, and that any prior-filed application has been withdrawn, abandoned, or otherwise disposed of, without having been laid open to the public inspection and without having any rights outstanding, and has not served as a basis for claiming a right of priority.

- ❖ The applicant must verify that the applicant has a bona fide intention to use the mark in commerce on or in connection with the goods or services listed in the application. If the verified statement is not filed with the initial application, the verified statement must also allege that the applicant has had a bona fide intention to use the mark in commerce since the filing date of the application.
- ❖ Both the non-United States applicant's country of origin and the country where the foreign application is filed must be a party to an international treaty or agreement with the United States that provides a right of priority, or must extend reciprocal rights to priority to United States nationals.
- ❖ The scope of the goods covered by the Section 44 basis cannot exceed the scope of the goods or services in the foreign application.
- ❖ The applicant must specify the serial number of the foreign application.

If the applicant is not domiciled in the United States, the applicant may designate a domestic representative, i.e., a person residing in the United States on who may be served notices or process in proceedings affecting the mark. This can be done through the Trademark Electronic Application System (TEAS).

The priority filing date also constitutes a constructive date of first use in the United States under 15 U.S.C. Section 1057(c), if the application matures into a registration. Therefore, the priority date cannot be later than the filing date of the U.S. application.

Section 44(d) of the Trademark Act provides only a basis for receipt of a priority filing date, not a basis for publication or registration. Consequently, in a Section 44(d) application, both the actual date the application was received in the USPTO and the priority date will appear in the Trademark Reporting and Monitoring (TRAM) database.

The "First-Filed" Requirement

The application relied upon under Section 44(d) must be the applicant's first application in a treaty country for the same mark and for the same goods or services. If the foreign country denominates an application in the foreign country as "An Application to Extend the Wares" or in some similar fashion, but the application is, in substance, the equivalent of a new application in the United States, the foreign application will be considered the first-filed for the purpose of meeting the requirements of Section 44(d) in the United States. However, the goods or services must be different from those covered by any previous application for the mark in a treaty country.

The Section 44(d) priority claim may be based upon a subsequently filed application in the same foreign country or common office of several states, if the first-filed application was withdrawn, abandoned, or otherwise disposed of without having any rights outstanding, and did not serve as a basis for claiming a right or priority.

The USPTO will presume that the application identified as the basis for the priority claim was the first filed, unless there is contradictory evidence in the record.

If the examining attorney determines that the application relied on was not the first filed, the examining attorney must advise the applicant that it is not entitled to priority. If the applicant has not claimed another filing basis, the examining attorney must require the applicant to claim and perfect a basis before the application can be approved for publication or for registration on the Supplemental Register. Additionally, the examining attorney should ensure that the priority claim is deleted from the TRAM database, and should conduct a new search of USPTO records for conflicting marks.

Priority Claim Must Be Filed Within Six Months of Foreign Filing

An applicant must file a claim of priority within six months after the filing date of the foreign application. The applicant can submit the priority claim after the filing date of the United States application, as long as the claim of priority is submitted within six months of the foreign filing and the claimed priority date is earlier than the filing date of the U.S. application.

For example, if an eligible applicant files in France on December 6, 2011, and in the United States on January 12, 2012, the applicant can add a priority claim to the United States application on or before June 6, 2012, if the applicant meets the requirements of Section 44(d). The applicant cannot add a priority claim to the United States application after June 6, 2012.

If an applicant claims priority under Section 44(d), but does not specify the filing date of the foreign application, the examining attorney must require that the applicant specify the date of the foreign filing.

If the applicant submits a claim of priority more than six months after the date of the foreign filing, the examining attorney must advise the applicant that it is not entitled to priority. IF the applicant has not claimed another filing basis, the examining attorney must require the applicant to claim and perfect an acceptable basis before the application can be approved for publication of for registration on the Supplemental Register. Additionally, the examining attorney should ensure that the priority claim is deleted from the TRAM database, and should conduct a new search of USPTO records for conflicting marks.

If the priority period ends on a Saturday, Sunday, or Federal holiday within the district of Columbia, the priority claim may be filed no later than the following day that is not a Saturday, Sunday, or a Federal holiday within the District of Columbia.

Basis for Registration Required

Section 44(d) of the Act provides a basis for receipt of a priority filing date, but not a basis for publication or registration. Before an application may be approved for publication, or allowed for registration on the Supplemental Register, the applicant must establish a basis for registration under Section 1(a), Section 1(b), or Section 44(e) of the Trademark Act.

An applicant may claim more than one basis for registration (i.e., Section 44(e) in addition to Section 1(a) or Section 1(b)). If the applicant claims a Section 1(b) basis, the applicant must file an allegation of use (i.e., either an Amendment to Allege Use or a Statement of Use before the mark can be registered.

A Section 44(d) applicant may not assert a basis under Section 66(a) of the Trademark Act, based on an extension of protection of an international registration to the United States.

Suspension Awaiting a Foreign Registration

In a Section 44(d) application filed via TEAS, the applicant is asked to specifically indicate that it does not intend to rely on Section 44(e) as a basis for registration, but wishes only to assert a valid claim of priority. If the applicant does not do so, an intent to rely on Section 44(e) is presumed and, when filed, the application will include a statement that the applicant intends to rely on Section 44(e) as a basis for registration.

If, on initial examination of the application, there are no refusals, requirements, or prior pending applications, the examining attorney will suspend action on the application pending receipt of the foreign registration. The Suspension Notice must include a search clause.

If, on initial examination, the examining attorney issues any refusals or other requirements, the Office action must also include a requirement that the applicant submit the foreign registration when it becomes available. Depending upon the applicant's response, the examining attorney will take appropriate action to place the application in condition for approval for publication, allowance for registration on the Supplemental Register, or final action on all other issues, and will then suspend further action pending receipt of the foreign registration. In the Notice of Suspension, the examining attorney must reference any continued refusals or requirements.

If, on initial examination, the only other issue is a prior pending application, the examining attorney will suspend action on the application pending receipt of the foreign registration and resolution of the prior pending application. The Suspension Notice must include a search clause. If the foreign registration is submitted while the prior pending application is pending, the application will be re-suspended, and the suspension letter will state that the foreign registration has been received but will not be examined until the prior pending application either abandons or registers. If the prior pending application abandons before the applicant submits the foreign registration, the examining attorney will re-suspend the application pending receipt of the foreign registration. The suspension letter must state that the prior application has abandoned and no longer poses a potential bar to registration. However, if the prior pending application registers before the foreign registration is submitted, the examining attorney will issue a non-final Office action with a Section 2(d) refusal and a requirement that the applicant submit the foreign registration when it becomes available. If the applicant responds, but the foreign registration cannot yet be provided, the application will be re-suspended. The Suspension Notice must indicate whether the Section 2(d) refusal is continued or withdrawn.

If the TEAS application indicates that that the applicant is not relying on Section 44(e) and no other basis for registration is claimed, the examining attorney must inquire since the application lacks a basis for registration. If, on initial examination, there are no refusals or requirements that would otherwise necessitate issuance of an Office action, this inquiry may be made via telephone or e-mail, if telephone or e-mail communication is authorized. The following actions should be taken based on the applicant's response to the inquiry:

- ❖ If the applicant responds that it intends to rely on Section 44(e) as the basis, the examining attorney must enter a Note to the File in the record and suspend the application pending receipt of the foreign registration. The Suspension Notice must include a search clause.

FOREIGN REGISTRATIONS

- ❖ If the applicant responds that it intends to rely solely on Section 1(b) as the basis, the examining attorney must issue an Examiner's Amendment so specifying.

- ❖ If the applicant responds that it intends to rely solely on Section 1(a) and the application does not include a specimen, dates of use, and/or the proper declaration, the examining attorney must issue a priority action specifying what actions the applicant must take.

If, however, there are other refusals or requirements, or the applicant cannot be reached by telephone or e-mail, the examining attorney must issue an Office action that includes the inquiry regarding whether the applicant intends to rely on Section 44(e) as a registration basis and note that, if so, the foreign registration is required when it becomes available.

If a Section 44(d) application filed on paper is silent as to whether the applicant intends to rely on Section 44(e), the USPTO will presume that the applicant intends to rely on Section 44(e) as a basis for registration and follow the same procedures as for TEAS applications.

Multiple-Basis Applications

If an applicant properly claims Section 44(d) as a basis for receipt of a priority filing date and asserts Section 1 as a second basis, the applicant may elect not to perfect the Section 44 basis and still retain the priority filing date. If the application is filed via TEAS and indicates that the applicant is relying on Section 44(e) as a basis for registration, the examining attorney must follow the procedures in the Trademark Manual of Examining Procedure (TMEP) with respect to the Section 44(e) basis. If the application indicates that the applicant is not relying on Section 44(e) as an additional basis for registration and is only asserting Section 44(d) to receive a priority filing date, the examining attorney must ensure that the TRAM database is updated accordingly.

When an application filed on paper is silent as to whether the applicant intends to rely on Section 44(e) as an additional basis for registration, the examining attorney must inquire as to whether the applicant intends to rely on the Section 44(e) basis. If, on initial examination, there are no refusals or requirements that would otherwise necessitate issuance of the Office action this inquiry may be made via telephone or e-mail, if telephone or e-mail communication is authorized. If the applicant intends to perfect the Section 44 basis, the examining attorney must make a Note to the File in the record and suspend the application pending receipt of the foreign registration. If the applicant does not wish to perfect the Section 44 basis, the examining attorney must issue an examiner's amendment to this effect. If the applicant cannot be reached by telephone or e-mail, the examining attorney must make a Note to the File in the record indicating the unsuccessful attempt to contact the applicant and suspend action on the application pending receipt of the foreign registration. The Suspension Notice must include a search clause.

If it is necessary to issue an Office action regarding any refusals or requirements, including a prior pending application, the examining attorney must inquire as to whether the applicant intends to perfect Section 44 as a second basis for registration and note that, if so, the foreign registration is required when it becomes available. After a response is received, if the application is in condition for approval for publication, allowance on the Supplemental Register, or final action, the examining attorney will suspend further action pending submission of the foreign registration and, if appropriate, resolution of the prior pending application. The examining attorney must suspend the application even if the response fails to indicate whether the applicant intends to perfect the Section 44 basis. In the Suspension Notice, the examining attorney must reference any refusals or requirements that are continued.

Periodic Inquiries Issued as to Status of Foreign Application

Examining attorneys must issue inquiries as to the status of the foreign application in applications that have been suspended for more than six-months. If the applicant does not respond to this inquiry within six-months of the issuance date, the application will be abandoned for failure to respond to an Office action.

If the applicant is unable to furnish a copy of the foreign registration before the expiration of time to respond to the inquiry, the applicant should advise the examining attorney of this fact. This may be done by telephone or e-mail. If the applicant states that the foreign registration has not yet issued, the examining attorney will issue a new Suspension Notice.

If the applicant states that the foreign registration has issued, but fails to send a copy, the examining attorney must issue an Office action requiring a copy.

Priority for Publication

To determine priority for publication, an application filed in the United States under Section 44(d) will be treated as if it were filed in the United States on the same date as the filing in the foreign country. The Section 44(d) application will receive priority over any application filed after the Section 44(d) applicant's priority filing date that might otherwise be a possible bar to registration under Section 2(d) of the Trademark Act due to a likelihood of confusion.

In some cases, another United States application filed after the Section 44(d) applicant's priority date may proceed to publication or registration because the Section 44(d) applicant had not yet filed in the United States when the examining attorney searched USPTO records for conflicting marks. If the USPTO learns that a Section 44(d) application is entitled to priority over another pending application before the other mark registers, the USPTO will take appropriate action to give the Section 44(d) application the priority to which it is entitled.

If an examining attorney discovers a conflicting application entitled to priority under Section 44(d) after taking action in a case, the examining attorney should issue a supplemental action correcting the situation. If the mark has been published, the examining attorney must request jurisdiction before issuing the action, unless a Notice of Allowance has issued.

However, if the conflicting mark has already registered, the USPTO does not have the authority to cancel the registration. The Section 44(d) applicant must take action to enforce its priority rights, e.g., by filing a petition to cancel the registration with the Trademark Trial and Appeal Board.

Filing Under Both Sections 44(d) and 44(e)

In some cases, a Section 44 applicant may have already received, before filing in the USPTO, a foreign registration as a result of the same foreign application upon which the applicant relies for priority under Section 44(d). This may occur in countries that do not examine applications prior to registration. In this situation, the applicant may file under both Sections 44(d) and 44(e).

An applicant may also claim priority under Section 44(d) based upon a foreign application, and proceed to registration under Section 44(e) based upon a different foreign registration. Both foreign countries must be parties to a treaty or agreement with the United States and the foreign registration must be from a country of origin of the applicant. If the applicant amends an application to rely on a different foreign registration, this is not considered a change in basis, but may require republication.

Application Based on More than One Foreign Application

An applicant may file an application in the United States based on more than one foreign application for different goods or services, or for different classes, if the applicant meets the requirements of Section 44(d) with respect to each foreign application on which the United States application is based. The applicant must specify which goods or services, or which classes, are covered by which foreign application. The mark in each foreign application must be the same mark for which registration is sought in the United States application.

Abandonment of the Foreign Application

If the foreign application relied on under Section 44(d) is abandoned during the prosecution of the United States application, the applicant may amend the application to rely on another basis. If the applicant met the requirements of Section 44(d) on the filing date of the United States application, the applicant would retain the priority filing date even if the foreign application is abandoned.

In this situation, the USPTO will presume that the applicant had a continuing valid basis, because the applicant had at least a bona fide intention to use the mark in commerce as of the application filing date, unless there is contradictory evidence in the record.

Applications Based on Foreign Registrations

If an eligible applicant owns a valid registration from the applicant's country of origin, the applicant may base its United States application on that foreign registration under Section 44(e).

A Section 44(e) application meet the following requirements:

- ❖ The applicant must be the owner of a valid registration in the applicant's country of origin.

- ❖ The applicant's country of origin must be a party to a treaty or agreement with the United States that provides for registration based on ownership of a foreign registration, or must extend reciprocal registration rights to nationals of the United States.

- ❖ The applicant must submit a true copy, a photocopy, a certification, or a certified copy of the registration in the applicant's country of origin.

- ❖ The applicant must verify that the applicant has a bona fide intention to use the mark in commerce on or in connection with the goods or services listed in the application. If the verified statement is not filed with the initial application, the verified statement must also allege that the applicant has had a bona fide intention to use the mark in commerce since the application filing date.

- ❖ The scope of the goods covered by the Section 44(e) basis cannot exceed the scope of the goods or services in the foreign registration.

FOREIGN REGISTRATIONS

If the applicant is not domiciled in the United States, the applicant is encouraged to designate a domestic representative, i.e., a person residing in the United States on who may be served notices or process in proceedings affecting the mark. This can be done through TEAS.

An applicant may not file an application under Section 44(e), or amend an application to add or substitute a Section 44(e) basis, before the registration in the applicant's country of origin has issued. An applicant can file under Section 44(d) within six-months after the filing date of an application in the applicant's country of origin. However, once this six-month priority period has passed, an applicant cannot file an application in the United States based on a pending foreign application.

Copy of Foreign Registration Required

Section 44(e) of the Trademark Act requires "a true copy, a photocopy, a certification, or a certified copy of the registration in the country of origin of the applicant." If a copy of the foreign registration is not included with the application as filed, the examining attorney must require submission of a copy of the foreign registration in the first Office action. The copy must show the name of the owner, the mark, and the goods or services for which the mark is registered.

If the applicant submits a copy of the foreign registration, it must be a copy of a document that has been issued to the applicant by or certified by the intellectual property office in the applicant's country of origin. A photocopy of the intellectual property office's publications or a printout from the intellectual property office's website is not sufficient to establish that the mark has been registered in that country and that the registration is in full force and effect, unless accompanied by a certification from the issuing office.

An English translation of a registration from the country of origin by itself is not an acceptable "copy" of the foreign registration. A certification or copy of the registration as issued by the intellectual property office of the country of origin is required, along with an English translation.

If an applicant files more than one application in the United States based on the same foreign registration, the applicant must file a copy of the foreign registration (and its English translation, if applicable), in each of the United States applications.

In a Section 44(e) application, the examining attorney will not suspend the application pending submission of a copy of the foreign registration, unless the applicant establishes that it cannot obtain a copy of the foreign registration due to extraordinary circumstances (e.g., war or natural disaster). However, the examining attorney may suspend the application pending receipt of proof of renewal of the foreign registration.

Status of the Foreign Registration

The foreign registration must be in force at the time the United States issues the registration based on that foreign registration.

If the record indicates that the foreign registration will expire before the United States registration will issue, the examining attorney must require that an applicant submit a certificate of renewal or other certification from the intellectual property office of the foreign country, or a copy of the foreign registration that shows that the foreign registration has been renewed and will be in force at the time the registration issues in the United States, along with an English translation. Generally, the examining attorney should require proof of renewal if it appears that the foreign registration will expire within six-months after the date of approval for publication.

If the applicant states that renewal is pending in the foreign country, the examining attorney should suspend the application pending receipt of proof of renewal. A photocopy of the intellectual property office's publications or a printout from the intellectual property office's website is not sufficient to establish that the registration has been renewed in that country and is in full force and effect, unless accompanied by a certification from the issuing office.

If an applicant submits a certified copy or certification of the foreign registration that is certified by the foreign government agency who issued the foreign registration, the examining attorney should inquire concerning renewal only if the certified copy of the foreign registration indicates that the registration will expire after the date on which the foreign government agency issued the certified copy or certification of the foreign registration. For example, if a certified copy of a foreign registration was issued by the trademark agency in the foreign country on January 5, 2009, and the certified copy indicates that the registration expired on June 1, 2008, no inquiry is necessary. The USPTO presumes that the foreign country would not have issued a certified copy of the registration unless the registration had been renewed. This applies only to a certified copy or certification issued by the foreign trademark agency. If the copy of the registration is not certified by the foreign trademark agency, and the record indicates that the foreign registration will expire before the United States registration will issue, the examining attorney must require that the applicant submit a copy of the foreign registration showing that the registration has been renewed.

If the examining attorney determines that the foreign registration is not in force, the examining attorney will refuse registration under Section 44(e). The applicant may amend the application to claim another basis.

Translation of the Foreign Registration or Renewal Document

If the foreign registration, certificate of renewal, or other certification of renewal from the intellectual property office of the foreign country is not in English, the applicant must provide a translation. The translator should sign the translation, but does not have to swear to the translation.

Application May be Based on More than One Foreign Registration

A United States application may be based on more than one foreign registration. The applicant must meet all requirements of the Trademark Act and rules for each foreign registration upon which the United States application is based, and must specify which goods or services are covered by which foreign registration.

If a Section 44 applicant amends an application to rely on a different foreign registration after publication, this is not considered a change in basis. However, if the amendment is acceptable, the application must be republished.

Ownership of the Foreign Application or Registration

If an applicant claims Section 44 as the filing basis in the original United States application, or if the applicant omits the basis from the original United States application and subsequently claims Section 44 as the basis, the applicant must be the owner of the foreign application or registration on the filing date of the United States application.

Proof of ownership may consist of a copy of an assignment document recorded in the foreign country, or a statement from the agency administering the trademark register in the foreign country establishing that the applicant was the owner of the foreign application or registration as of the United States application filing date. Other forms of proof may also be acceptable. If the transfer of ownership took place before the United States application filing date, the Section 44 basis will be considered valid, even if the change in ownership was not yet recorded in the foreign country on the United States application filing date.

If the applicant was not the owner of the foreign application or registration on the United States application filing date, the examining attorney must refuse registration under Section 44. The applicant may amend the application to claim Section 1(a) or Section1 (b) as a basis.

If a Section 44(d) applicant was not the owner of the foreign application on the United States application filing date, the examining attorney should advise the applicant that it is not entitled to priority, ensure that the priority claim is deleted from the Trademark Reporting and Monitoring (TRAM) database, and conduct a new search of USPTO records for conflicting marks.

Section 44 Added to or Substituted for Valid Section 1 Basis

If an application is properly filed based on Section 1(a) or Section 1(b), and the applicant later amends the application to add or substitute Section 44 as a basis, the applicant must be the owner of the foreign application or registration as of the filing date of the amendment adding or substituting Section 44 as a basis for registration.

If the applicant owned the foreign application or registration on the filing date of the amendment, but did not own the foreign application or registration on the filing date of the United States application, the applicant will retain the original filing date in the United States, as long as there was a continuing valid basis since the application filing date.

If the foreign application or registration identifies a party other than the Section 44 applicant as the owner, the examining attorney will require the applicant to establish that the applicant was the owner of the foreign application or registration of the filing date of the amendment adding or substituting Section 44 as a basis. If the applicant was not the owner of the foreign application or registration on the filing date of the amendment, the examining attorney must refuse registration under Section 44.

Assignment of Section 44 Applications

A Section 44 applicant may assign the foreign application or registration and/or the United States application from the original applicant to another party.

In order to continue to claim the benefits of Section 44 after such an assignment, the assignee of the United States application must be eligible for the benefits of Section 44. To be eligible for registration under Section 44(e), the assignee must establish that the country that issued the relevant registration is the assignee's country of origin. To be eligible for a priority filing date under Section 44(d), any non-United States assignee must establish that the assignee's country of origin is a party to an international treaty or agreement with the United States that provides a right of priority, or extends reciprocal rights of priority to United States nationals.

In an application based solely on Section 44, if the assignee is not entitled to registration under Section 44(e), the examining attorney must refuse registration under that basis. The applicant may amend the application to claim Section 1(a) or Section 1(b) as a basis.

In a Section 44(d) application, if the assignee is not eligible for a priority filing date (i.e., a non-United States applicant whose country of origin is not a party to any convention or treaty as outlined in Section 44(b)), the examining attorney must advise the assignee that it is not entitled to priority, ensure that the priority claim is deleted from the TRAM database, and conduct a new search of USPTO records for conflicting marks.

The Trademark Act requires that an applicant own the underlying application or registration at the time of filing in the United States (or as of the filing date of the amendment adding or substituting Section 44 as a basis, for an application originally based on Section 1(a) or Section 1(b), and later amended to add or substitute Section 44 as a basis). However, if the applicant was the owner of the foreign application or registration on the filing date of the United States application (or amendment adding or substituting Section 44 as a basis), the applicant may assign the United States application to another party without assigning the underlying foreign application or registration to that party. Therefore, examining attorneys should not require proof of assignment of the underlying foreign application or registration when an applicant assigns the United States application.

If the United States application is assigned to a party who is not domiciled in the United States, the assignee may file an appointment of a domestic representative with the assignment of the United States application. The USPTO encourages parties who do not reside in the United States to designate domestic representatives. This can be done through TEAS.

Standards for Registration

Although Section 44 exempts eligible applicants from the use requirements of Section 1 of the Trademark Act, Section 44 applicants must meet all other requirements for registration set forth in the Trademark Act and relevant rules. Registration in a foreign country does not automatically ensure eligibility for registration in the United States. That is, it is impossible to read Section 44(e) to require the registration of foreign marks that fail to meet United States requirements for eligibility. Section 44 applicants are subject to the section 2 bars to registration.

The foreign registration that is the basis for the United States application may include disclaimers or may be a secondary register, equivalent to the Supplemental Register. The United States application will be reviewed according to the standards for registrability in the United States, and the examining attorney will not require a disclaimer, amendment to the Supplemental Register, or any other amendment unless it is required under United States law and USPTO policy.

Bona Fide Intention to Use the Mark in Commerce

Any application filed under Section 44(d) or Section 44(e) on either the Principal or the Supplemental Register must include a verified statement that the applicant has a bona fide intention to use the mark in commerce. If the verified statement is not filed with the initial application, the verified statement must also allege that the applicant has had a bona fide intention to use the mark in commerce as of the application filing date.

Thus, the allegation of the applicant's bona fide intention to use the mark in commerce is required even if use in commerce is asserted in the application.

Allegation of Use and Specimen of Use

Although Section 44 applicants must assert a bona fide intention to use the mark in commerce, Section 44 applicants do not have to allege use or provide specimens or dates of use prior to registration on either the Principal or Supplemental Register in an application based solely on Section 44. However, if a Section 44 applicant wishes to assert use in commerce under Section 1(a) or a bona fide intention to use the mark in commerce under Section 1(b) as an additional basis, then the applicant must comply with all applicable requirements related to the second basis asserted.

If the applicant provides specimens gratuitously in a Section 44 application, the examining attorney may refer to the specimens to determine issues unrelated to use, such as whether the mark is merely descriptive.

When the Section 44 application, as submitted, raises questions concerning the registrability of the mark, the examining attorney may request an explanation, information, literature, or other materials to assist in consideration of the application.

Proof of Acquired Distinctiveness

A Section 44 applicant may assert that a mark has acquired distinctiveness if the applicant establishes that the mark has become distinctive of its goods or services in commerce in the same manner that any other applicant must. For these purposes, the applicant may not rely on use other than use in commerce that may be regulated by the United States Congress, that is, the applicant may not rely on use solely in a foreign country or between two foreign countries.

Drawings

Applicants filing under Section 44 must comply with the drawing requirements.

Drawing of the Mark in Foreign Registration

The drawing of the mark must be a "substantially exact representation of the mark as it appears in the drawing in the registration certificate of a mark duly registered in the country of origin of the applicant.

The "substantially exact representation" standard is construed narrowly. Only slight, inconsequential variations between the mark in the United States application and the mark shown in the foreign registration are permitted. For example, non-material informational matter such as net weight or contents may be deleted. Beyond such limited exceptions, however, any difference between the mark on the drawing and the mark in the foreign registration requires the examining attorney to refuse registration.

The standard for determining whether the mark in the drawing agrees with the mark in the foreign registration is stricter than the standard used to determine whether specimens support use of a mark in an application under Section 1 of the Trademark Act. The Trademark Trial and Appeal Board reasoned that a stricter standard is appropriate in Section 44 cases because Section 44 applications represent an exception to the use requirements of the Trademark Act, and that this exception should be construed narrowly to ensure that a foreign applicant cannot obtain a registration in the United States of matter that could not have been registered in the foreign country.

If the mark in the foreign registration is in standard characters, the mark in the United States application must also be in standard characters. If the foreign registration certificate does not indicate that the mark is in standard characters (or the legal equivalent), the examining attorney must inquire whether the foreign registration includes a claim that the mark is in standard characters. The applicant must either submit an affirmative statement that the foreign registration includes a claim that the mark is in standard characters (or the legal equivalent), or delete the standard character claim in the United States application.

Likewise, if the mark in the foreign registration is in special form, the drawing of the mark in the United States application must appear in the same special form. If the mark in the foreign registration shows color, the applicant must submit a color photocopy of the foreign registration. All claims of color made in the foreign registration must also be made in the United States application. The applicant must also comply with all requirements for a color drawing of the mark.

If the foreign registration is not issued in color, the examining attorney may require evidence to establish that a colored mark in a United States application is a substantially exact representation of the mark in the foreign registration.

If a Section 44 application is based on a foreign registration that depicts the mark in color, but no claim of color is made in the registration document, the examining attorney must inquire whether the foreign registration includes a claim of color(s) as a feature of the mark. The applicant must either: (1) submit an affirmative statement that color is claimed as a feature of the mark in the foreign registration; or (2) submit a statement that although the mark is registered in its country of origin featuring a color depiction of the mark, no claim of color is made in that registration. If the examining attorney determines that the color is a non-material element of the drawing, the applicant may be given the option of submitting a black-and-white drawing.

The mark on the drawing in the United States application may not be a translation or transliteration of the mark in the foreign registration.

If the United States application is based on both a foreign registration and use in commerce, the mark on the drawing in the United States application must not only be a substantially exact representation of the mark in the foreign registration, but also may not differ in a material way from the mark shown on the specimen(s) of record.

One Mark Per Application

If the foreign application or registration covers a series of distinct marks, the applicant must file separate applications in the United States to register each of the marks the applicant wishes to register in the United States. For example, some countries permit registration of several versions of a mark in a single application. In the United States, separate applications are required. The drawing in the United States application must show only one mark.

FOREIGN REGISTRATIONS

Amendment of Drawing

Section 44 applicants often try to amend the mark in the United States application to overcome an objection that the mark in the drawing does not agree with the mark in the foreign registration. An applicant cannot amend the drawing in the United States application to conform to the mark in the foreign registration if the amendment would result in a material alteration of the mark on the drawing submitted with the original application in the United States. Thus, when a Section 44 applicant proposes to amend its drawing, the examining attorney must consider: (1) whether the proposed amendment of the drawing would result in a material alteration of the mark on the original drawing; and (2) whether the proposed amendment would result in a mark that is a substantially exact representation of the mark in the foreign registration.

Three-Dimensional and Non-Visual Marks

If the foreign application or registration depicts several views of a three-dimensional mark, the examining attorney must require the applicant to submit an acceptable drawing that depicts a single rendition of the mark. In the alternative, the applicant may petition the Director to waive the requirement and accept a drawing featuring multiple views of the mark.

In all such cases, the applicant must indicate that the mark is three-dimensional. If necessary, to adequately depict the commercial impression of the mark, the applicant may be required to submit a drawing that shows the placement of the mark by surrounding the mark with a proportionately accurate broken line representation of the particular goods, packaging, or advertising on which the mark appears. The applicant must also use broken lines to show matter not claimed as part of the mark. For any drawing using broken lines to indicate placement of the mark, or matter not claimed as part of the mark, the applicant must include a written description of the mark and explain the purpose of the broken lines, e.g., by indicating that the matter shown by the broken lines is not a part of the mark and that it serves only to show the position of the mark.

With respect to sound, scent, and other non-visual marks, an applicant is not required to submit a drawing, but must submit a detailed description of the mark. If the foreign registration includes a drawing, such as a musical staff depicting the notes of which a sound mark is comprised, the United States application need not include such a drawing. As the drawing of the mark must be a substantially exact representation of the mark in the foreign registration, and the description of the mark defines the mark sought to be registered in a non-visual mark, the description of the mark in the United States application must be substantially comparable to any description of the mark in the foreign application or registration.

Identification of Goods and Services

The identification of goods and services in a Section 44 application must comply with the same standards that govern other applications. If the United States application is Section 44, the identification of goods and services covered by the Section 44 basis may not exceed the scope of the goods and services identified in the foreign registration.

Designation of Domestic Representative

An applicant not domiciled in the United States may file a document designating the name and address of a person residing in the United States upon who notices or process in proceedings affecting the mark may be served. The USPTO encourages parties who do not reside in the United States to designate domestic representatives. This can be done through TEAS.

Applications for the Supplemental Register

A Section 44 applicant may apply to register a mark on the Supplemental Register, and a Section 44 applicant may amend an application from the Principal Register to the Supplemental Register without filing any allegation of use. It is not necessary to change the application filing date after an amendment to the Supplemental Register in a Section 44 application.

Registration Independent of Foreign Registration

Once issued, the United States registration issuing from a Section 44 application exists independent of the underlying foreign registration and is subject to all provisions of the Trademark Act that apply to all other registrations, such as affidavits of use, renewals amendments, assignments, and similar matters.

International Registration As Basis

An international registration issued by the International Bureau of the World Intellectual Property Organization can be the basis for a Section 44(e) application only if the international registration shows that there is an extension of protection of the international registration to applicant's country of origin. A request for an extension of protection of the international registration to applicant's country of origin is not sufficient.

An applicant should submit a copy of the registration (or certificate of extension of protection) issued by the national trademark office in the applicant's country of origin. If the application's country of origin does not issue registration or certificates of extension of protection, the applicant may submit a copy of the international registration, showing that protection of the international registration has been extended to applicant's country of origin. A copy of a request for an extension of protection of the international registration to applicant's country of origin is not sufficient.

If the applicant is not domiciled or incorporated in the relevant country, examining attorney must require the applicant to establish that the country is its country of origin.

The applicant must meet all the requirements of the Trademark Act and the Trademark Rules of Practice for Section 44(e) applications. The requirements of Section 66(a) applications are not applicable.

The identification of goods and services covered by the Section 44(e) basis may not exceed the scope of the goods and services identified in the registered extension of protection in the applicant's country of origin.

An extension of protection of an international registration cannot be the basis for a Section 44(d) application, because neither the international application nor the request for extension of protection is the first application filed in a treaty country for the same mark for the same goods or services. The basic application or basic registration upon which the international registration is based was the first-filed application.

If the applicant wants to base a Section 44(e) application on the basic registration that was the basis for the international registration, the applicant must submit a copy of the basic registration issued by the Office of Origin, i.e., the country or intergovernmental organization who issued the registration which provided the basis for the international registration. The applicant cannot submit the international registration, because an international registration does not provide protection in the territory of the Contracting Party whose office is the Office of Origin. Madrid Protocol.

Registration Under the Madrid Protocol

The Protocol Relating to the Madrid Agreement Concerning the International Registration of Marks (Madrid Protocol) is an international treaty that allows a trademark owner to seek registration in any of the countries or intergovernmental organizations that have joined the Madrid Protocol by submitting a single application, called an international application. The International Bureau (IB) of the World Intellectual Property Organization

(WIPO) in Geneva, Switzerland administers the international registration system.

The Madrid Protocol became effective in the United States on November 2, 2003. The Madrid Protocol Implementation Act of 2002 (MPIA) amended the Trademark Act to provide that: (1) the owner of a United States application and/or registration may seek protection of its mark in any of the countries or intergovernmental organizations party to the Madrid Protocol by submitting a single international application to the IB through the United States Patent and Trademark Office (USPTO); and (2) the holder of an international registration may request an extension of protection of the international registration to the United States. A notice of final rulemaking amending the Trademark Rules of Practice to incorporate the MPIA was published September 26, 2003.

Overview of the Madrid System of International Registration

The Madrid system of international registration is governed by two treaties: the Madrid Agreement Concerning the International Registration of Marks, which dates from 1891, and the Protocol Relating to the Madrid Agreement, which was adopted in 1989, entered into force on December 1, 1995, and came into operation on April 1, 1996. The United States is party only to the Protocol, not to the Agreement.

The Madrid system is administered by the IB. To apply for an international registration under the Madrid Protocol, an applicant must be a national of, be domiciled in, or have a real and effective industrial or commercial establishment in one of the countries or intergovernmental organizations that are members of the Protocol (Contracting Parties). The application must be based on one or more trademark application(s) filed in, or registration(s) issued by, the trademark office of one of the Contracting Parties ("basic application(s)" or "basic registration(s)"). The international application must be for the same mark and include a list of goods or services that is identical to or narrower than the list of goods or services in the basic application or registration. The international application must designate one or more Contracting Parties in which an extension of protection of the international registration is sought.

The applicant must submit the international application through the trademark office of the Contracting Party in which the basic application or registration is held (Office of Origin). The Office of Origin must certify that the information in the international application corresponds with the information in the basic application or registration, and then forward the international application to the

FOREIGN REGISTRATIONS

IB. If the IB receives the international application within two-months of the date of receipt in the Office of Origin, the date of the international registration is the date of receipt in the Office of Origin. If the IB does not receive the international application within two-months of the date it was received by the Office of Origin, the date of the international registration is the date on which the international application is received by the IB.

The international registration is depended on the basic application or registration for five years from the international registration date. If the basic application or registration is abandoned, cancelled, or expired, in whole or in part, during this five-year period, the IB will cancel the international registration accordingly.

The holder of an international registration may request protection in additional Contracting Parties by submitting a subsequent designation. A subsequent designation is a request by the holder of an international registration for an extension of protection of the registration to additional Contracting Parties.

Each Contracting Party designated in an international application or subsequent designation will examine the request for extension of protection as a national trademark application under its domestic laws. Under Article 5 and Common Regs. 16 and 17, there are strict time limits (a maximum of eighteen-months) for the trademark office of a Contracting Party to refuse a request for extension of protection. If the Contracting Party does not notify the IB of a refusal within this time period, the mark is automatically protected. However, the extension of protection may be invalidated in accordance with the same procedures for invalidating a national registration, e.g., by cancellation.

The Madrid Protocol may apply to the USPTO in three ways:

- ❖ **Office of Origin.** The USPTO is the Office of Origin if an international application or registration is based on an application pending in or a registration issued by the USPTO.

- ❖ **Office of a Designated Contracting Party.** The USPTO is the office of a designated Contracting Party if the holder of an international registration requests an extension of protection of that registration to the United States.

- ❖ **Office of the Contracting Party of the Holder.** If the holder of an international registration is a national of, is domiciled in, or has a real and effective industrial or commercial establishment in the United States, the holder can file certain requests with the IB through the

USPTO, such as requests to record changes of ownership and restrictions on the holder's right to dispose of an international registration. The expression "Contracting Party of the Holder" includes the "Office of Origin," as well as any other Contracting Party in which a holder is a national, is domiciled, or has a real and effective industrial or commercial establishment.

For more information on foreign registrations, the USPTO offers an online version of the Trademark Manual of Examining Procedures (TMEP) from their website.

CHAPTER 11

TRADEMARK MAINTENANCE

Trademark rights can last forever, but in order to keep your federal trademark registration you must continue to use the mark in commerce and file the required maintenance documents at regular intervals. The first maintenance document must be filed between the fifth and sixth years after registration and the remaining documents must be filed between the ninth and tenth years after registration, and then every ten years thereafter. Failure to file these documents will result in the cancellation or loss of your federal registration.

Post Registration Timeline – Non-Madrid Protocol

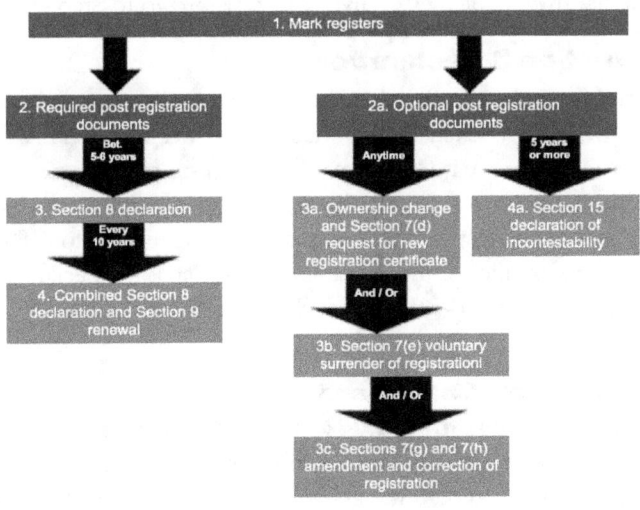

TRADEMARK PROTECTION AND PROSECUTION

The above-referenced post registration timeline is for all registrations except Madrid Protocol-based registrations. However, it does not cover every post-registration scenario. The following is an overview of the process steps and time frames for maintaining a trademark registration. After a registration issues, to keep the registration "alive" or valid, the registration owner must file specific documents and pay fees at regular intervals. Failure to file these documents will result in the cancellation of your registration.

Step 1. Mark Registers

After a registration issues, to keep the registration "alive" or valid, the registration owner must file specific documents and pay fees at regular intervals. The deadlines for filing these documents are calculated from the registration date shown on the registration certificate. Failure to file these documents will result in the cancellation and/or expiration of your registration. The USPTO does not issue reminders of these deadlines. Go to Step 2 for required post registration documents and go to Step 2a for optional post registration documents.

Step 2. Required Post Registration Documents

The following documents must be timely filed to maintain a registration. Go to Step 3.

Step 2a. Optional Post Registration Documents

The following documents are not mandatory to maintain a registration. For optional documents that may be filed anytime go to Step 3a and for optional documents that may be filed every five years or more go to Step 4a.

Step 3. Section 8 Declaration

Between the fifth and sixth year after the registration date the owner must file a Declaration of Use or Excusable Nonuse under Section 8. This declaration requires a fee. The filing may also be made within a six-month grace period after the expiration of the sixth year with the payment of an additional fee. Failure to file this declaration will result in the cancellation of the registration. The USPTO does not issue a reminder of these deadlines. The Section 8 declaration may be combined with an optional Section 15 declaration of incontestability. Go to Step 4.

Step 3a. Ownership Change and Section 7(d) Request for New Registration Certificate

An owner may transfer or assign a registered mark to a new owner. The new owner is encouraged to record the assignment with the USPTO. If the owner would like a new registration certificate, the owner must submit a separate request showing that the assignment has been recorded with the USPTO. A fee is required. Go to Step 3b.

Step 3b. Section 7(e) Voluntary Surrender of Registration

The owner of a registration may voluntarily surrender the registration, in its entirety or for a portion of the goods and/or services. No fee is required. Go to Step 3c.

Step 3c. Section 7(g) and 7(h) Amendment and Correction of Registration

A registration owner may file a Section 7 request to amend or correct the registration at any time. The amendment may not materially alter the mark or broaden the goods and/or services. A fee is required, except for corrections due to USPTO error.

Step 4. Combined Section 8 Declaration and Section 9 Renewal

Between the ninth and tenth year after the registration date and every ten years thereafter, the owner must file a Combined Declaration of Use or Excusable Nonuse and Application for Renewal under Sections 8 and 9. This filing requires a fee. The filing may also be made within a six-month grace period after the tenth year with the payment of an additional fee. Failure to file this declaration will result in the cancellation and/or expiration of the registration. The USPTO does not issue a reminder of these deadlines.

Step 4a. Section 15 Declaration of Incontestability

A Section 15 declaration may only be filed for a mark on the Principal Register that has been in continuous use in commerce for a period of five years after the date of the registration and there is no adverse decision(s) or pending proceeding(s) involving rights in the mark. "Incontestability" enhances the legal presumptions the registration receives. This declaration requires a fee.

Post Registration Timeline – Madrid Protocol

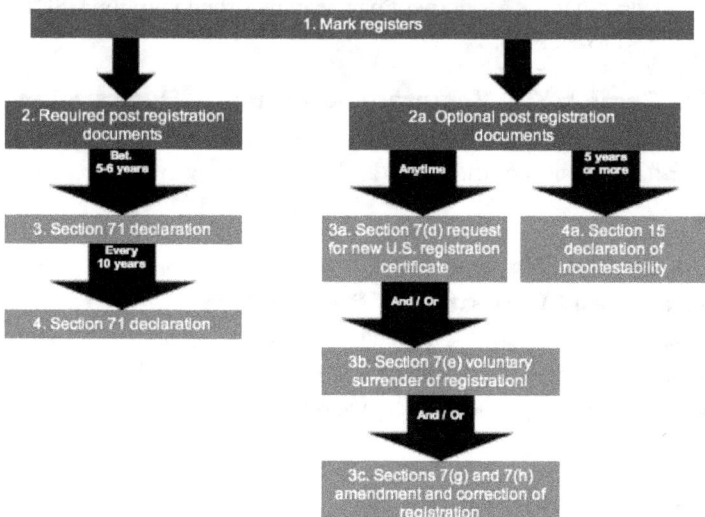

The above-referenced post registration timeline is for Madrid Protocol-based registrations. However, it does not cover every post-registration scenario. The following is an overview of the process steps and time frames for maintaining a Madrid Protocol-based registration. After protection is granted to the international registration and a United States registration issues, to keep protection in the United States, the United States registration owner must file specific documents and pay fees at regular intervals. Failure to file these documents will result in the cancellation of your United States registration and the invalidation of protection of the international registration by the USPTO.

Step 1. Mark Registers

After a United States registration issues, to keep the registration "alive" or valid, the United States registration owner must file specific documents and pay fees at regular intervals. The deadline for filing Section 71 Declarations of Use and Excusable Nonuse are calculated from the registration date shown on the United States Registration Certificate. However, the deadlines for renewing the international registration with the International Bureau of the World Intellectual Property Organization are calculated from the international registration date. Failure to file both of these documents will result in cancellation of your United States registration. The USPTO does not issue reminders of these deadlines. Go to Step 2 for required post registration documents and go to Step 2a for optional post registration documents.

Step 2. Required Post Registration Documents
The following documents must be timely filed to maintain a registration. Go to Step 3.

Step 2a. Optional Post Registration Documents
The following documents are not mandatory to maintain a registration. For optional documents that may be filed anytime go to Step 3a and for optional documents that may be filed every five years or more go to Step 4a.

Step 3. Owner Files Section 71 Declaration
Between the fifth and sixth year after the USPTO issues the United States registration, the United States registration owner must file directly with the USPTO a Declaration of Use or Excusable Nonuse. This declaration requires a fee and specimens of use. The filing may also be made within a six-month grace period after the expiration of the sixth year with the payment of an additional fee. Failure to file this declaration will result in the cancellation of the United States registration and invalidation of the extension of protection of the international registration to the United States. The USPTO does not issue a reminder of this deadline. Go to Step 4.

Step 3a. Section 7(d) Request
The owner of a registered extension of protection to the United States may only request a new United States Registration Certificate for the unexpired part of the registration period after filing the appropriate change request with the International Bureau (IB) of the World Intellectual Property Organization. Any change in ownership, such as by assignment, transfer, or change of name, must first be recorded at the IB. The IB will notify the USPTO of any changes of ownership that affect the extension of protection to the United States, including partial changes of ownership of less than all of the goods and or services. The USPTO will update its electronic records to reflect the change. If the owner would like a new United States Registration Certificate, the owner must submit a separate request and pay the required fee. Go to Step 3b.

Step 3b. Section 7(e) Voluntary Surrender
A United States registration owner may voluntarily surrender the United States registration, in its entirety or for a portion of the goods and or services. No fee is required. Go to Step 3c.

Step 3c. Sections 7(g) and 7(h) Amendment or Correction

A United States registration owner may file a request to amend or correct the United States registration at any time, but only in limited circumstances where the change will affect only the extension of protection of the United States. No amendments to the mark or to broaden the goods and or services are allowed. A fee is required, except for corrections due to USPTO error.

Step 4. Owner Files Section 71 Declaration

Between the ninth and tenth year after the registration date and every ten years thereafter, the United States registration owner must file directly with the USPTO a Declaration of Use or Excusable Nonuse. This declaration requires a fee and specimens of use. The filing may also be made within a six-month grace period after the tenth year with the payment of an additional fee.

Failure to file this declaration will result in the cancellation of the United States registration and invalidation of the extension of protection of the international registration to the United States. In addition, the international registration must be renewed with the International Bureau every ten years from the date of international registration. Failure to file this renewal will result in the cancellation of the United States registration. The UPSTO does not issue a reminder of these deadlines.

Step 4a. Section 15 Declaration of Incontestability

A Section 15 declaration may be filed for a mark on the Principal Register that has been in continuous use in commerce for a period of five years after the date of the United States registration and there is no adverse decision(s) or pending proceeding(s) involving rights in the mark. "Incontestability" enhances the legal presumptions the United States registration receives. This declaration requires a fee.

Declaration of Continued Use

A Section 8 declaration of continued use is a sworn statement, filed by the owner of a registration that the mark is in use in commerce. (Section 8 of the Trademark Act, 15 U.S.C. Section 1058.) If the owner is claiming excusable nonuse of the mark, a Section 8 Declaration of Excusable Nonuse may be filed. The purpose of the Section 8 declaration is to remove marks no longer in use from the register.

The USPTO will cancel any registration on either the Principal Register or the Supplemental Register if the current owner of the registration does not file a

TRADEMARK MAINTENANCE

timely Section 8 declaration during the prescribed time periods. The USPTO has no authority to waive or extend the deadline for filing a property Section 8 declaration. Registrations cancelled due to the failure to file a Section 8 declaration cannot be reinstated or "revived." A new application to pursue registration of the mark again must be filed.

The owner of the registration must file a Section 8 declaration during the following time periods:

- **First Filing Deadline.** File a Declaration of Use (or excusable nonuse) between the fifth and sixth years after the registration date. If the declaration is accepted, the registration will continue in force for the remainder of the ten-year period from the registration date, unless cancelled by an order of the Commissioner for Trademark or a federal court.

- **Subsequent Filing Deadline.** File a Declaration of Use (or excusable nonuse) and an Application for Renewal between the ninth and tenth years after the registration date, and between every ninth and tenth years after the registration date thereafter.

The above documents will be accepted as timely if filed within six-months after the deadlines listed above with the payment of an additional fee. The current fee for filing a Section 8 declaration is $100 per class of goods or services. The additional grace period surcharge is also $100 per class of goods or services for filing during the six-month grace period.

A Section 8 declaration must include:

- The registration number;
- The name and address of the current owner;
- The fee for filing the declaration;
- If the mark is in use: a statement that the registered mark is in use in commerce; a list of the goods or services recited in the registration on or in connection with which the mark is in use; and one specimen per class of goods or services. Examples of acceptable specimens are tags/labels for goods, and advertisements for services; and
- A signed and dated affidavit or declaration.

The owner or a person who is properly authorized to sign on behalf of the owner may sign the Section 8 declaration. That is: (1) a person with legal authority to bind the owner; (2) a person with firsthand knowledge of the facts and actual or implied authority to act on behalf of the owner; or (3) an attorney who has actual written or verbal power of attorney or an implied power of attorney from the owner.

Trademark specialists in the post-registration division review section 8 declarations. If the Section 8 declaration is accepted, the USPTO will send a Notice of Acceptance. If the Section 8 declaration is refused, the USPTO will send an Office Action stating the reasons for refusal and any remedies available.

Declaration of Excusable Non-Use

A Section 8 declaration of excusable nonuse is a sworn statement, filed by the owner of a registration, that the mark is not in use in commerce due to special circumstances that excuse such nonuse and is not due to any intention to abandon the mark.

If the owner of the registration is claiming excusable nonuse of the mark, the Section 8 declaration must include:

- The registration number;
- The name and address of the current owner;
- The fee for filing the declaration;
- A list of the goods or services in the registration on or in connection with which the mark is not in use in commerce; the date of the last use of the mark in commerce; the approximate date when use in commerce is expected to resume; details regarding the reason for nonuse; and specific steps being taken to resume use; and
- A signed and dated affidavit or declaration.

In general, nonuse must be temporary, and the owner must clearly demonstrate how the circumstances prevent use of the mark in commerce and what efforts are being made to resume use. Please note that nonuse due to the decreased demand for a product does not by itself constitute "excusable nonuse."

Once the USPTO accepts the Section 8 declaration of excusable nonuse, the owner of the registration is not required to file another Section 8 declaration until the next statutory filing period.

Declaration of Incontestability of a Mark

A Section 15 declaration is a sworn statement, filed by the owner of a mark registered on the Principal Register, claiming "incontestable" rights in the mark for the goods or services specified. Marks registered on the Supplemental Register are not eligible for claims of incontestable rights under Section 15.

An "incontestable" registration is conclusive evidence of the validity of the registered mark, of the registration of the mark, of the owner's ownership of the mark and of the owner's exclusive right to use the mark with the goods or services. The claim of incontestability is subject to certain limited exceptions set forth in Sections 15 and 33(b) of the Trademark Act. Also, the filing of a Section 15 declaration is optional. An owner may choose to claim the benefits of incontestability by filing a Section 15 declaration or may elect to retain the registration without those benefits. The term of the registration, for purpose of renewal, is not affected in either event.

A Section 15 declaration may not be filed until the mark has been in continuous use in commerce for at least five consecutive years subsequent to the date of registration for marks registered under the Trademark Act of 1946 (and subsequent to the date of publication under Section 12(c) of the Trademark Act, for marks registered under the Trademark Acts of 1905 and 1881 for which the benefits of the Trademark Act of 1946 have been claimed). The Section 15 declaration must be executed and filed within one year following a five-year period of continuous use of the mark in commerce.

The current fee for filing a Section 15 declaration is ~$200 per class of goods or services and the filing fee for a Sections 7 and 15 combined declaration is ~$300 per class.

A Section 15 declaration must include:

- ❖ The registration number and the date of registration;
- ❖ The fee for each class of goods or services in the registration to which the declaration pertains;

TRADEMARK PROTECTION AND PROSECUTION

- ❖ A statement that: (1) the mark has been in continuous use in commerce for a period of five years subsequent to the date of registration, or the date of publication, on or in connection with the goods or services recited in the registration and is still in use in commerce; (2) there has been no final decision adverse to the owner's claim of ownership of the mark for the goods or services, or to the owner's right to register the mark or to keep the same on the register; and (3) there is no proceeding involving the claimed rights pending in the USPTO or in a court of law and not finally disposed of; and
- ❖ A signed and dated affidavit or declaration.

The USPTO neither examines the merits of Section 15 declarations nor "accepts" Section 15 declarations. However, the USPTO will review a Section 15 declaration to determine whether it complies with statutory requirements. The USPTO will acknowledge receipt of only those Section 15 declarations that meet all statutory requirements.

TRADEMARK MAINTENANCE

SAMPLE COMBINED DECLARTION OF USE AND INCONTESTABILITY UNDER SECTION 8 AND 15 FORM

Combined Declaration of Use and Incontestability under Sections 8 & 15

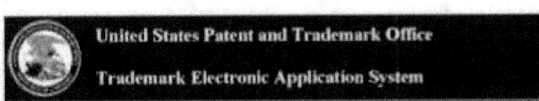 

United States Patent and Trademark Office
Trademark Electronic Application System

PTO Form PTO Form 1583 (Rev 5/2009)
OMB No. 0651-0055 (Exp. 06/30/2012)

Combined Declaration of Use and Incontestability Under Section 8 and 15
(15 U.S.C. §§ 1058 & 1065)

TEAS - Version 4.8 : 01/22/2011

You may file a Combined Declaration of Use & Incontestability under Sections 8 & 15 only if you have continuously used a mark registered on the Principal (not Supplemental) Register in commerce for five (5) consecutive years after the date of registration. You must file the Combined Declaration, specimen, and fee on a date that falls on or between the fifth (5th) and sixth (6th) anniversaries of the registration (or, for an extra fee of $100.00 per class, you may file within the six-month grace period following the sixth anniversary date). If you have NOT continuously used the mark in commerce for five (5) consecutive years, you must *still* file a Section 8 Declaration. You must subsequently file a Section 8 declaration, specimen, and fee on a date that falls on or between the ninth (9th) and tenth (10th) anniversaries of the registration, and each successive ten-year period thereafter (or, for an extra fee of $100.00 per class, you may file within the six-month grace period). FAILURE TO FILE THE SECTION 8 DECLARATION WILL RESULT IN CANCELLATION OF THE REGISTRATION. Note: Because the time for filing a ten-year Section 8 declaration coincides with the time for filing a Section 9 renewal application, a combined §§ 8 & 9 form exists.

NOTE: You must complete any field preceded by the symbol "*".

WARNING: This form has a session time limit of 60 minutes. Your "session" began as soon as you accessed this initial Form Wizard page. If you exceed the 60-minute time limit, the form will not validate and you must begin the entire process again; you can, however, extend the time limit. You should always try to have all information required to complete the form prior to starting any session.

TRADEMARK PROTECTION AND PROSECUTION

Combined Declaration of Use and Incontestability under Sections 8 & 15

* Enter a Registration Number: _____ *(required only if completing the form for the first time)*
WARNING: Be sure you are entering a registration number and NOT a serial number.

OR

Access previously-saved data using the "Browse/Choose File" button below to access the file from your local drive. NOTE: For specific instructions, please click here. **FAILURE TO FOLLOW THESE INSTRUCTIONS WILL RESULT IN THE DISPLAY OF YOUR DATA IN AN XML FORMAT THAT CANNOT BE EDITED.** NOTE: Do NOT attempt to use the button below to upload an image file (for example, a specimen). You must use the button that will be presented for that purpose *within the proper section of the actual form.*

[_____] [Browse...]

WARNING: You are filing a Section 8 affidavit of use and a Section 15 affidavit of incontestability. If a Section 9 renewal application is also due, it is not included here. If necessary, please see the Combined declaration of use in commerce application for renewal of registration of mark under Sections 8 & 9. If a **Section 9 renewal application** is due and is not timely filed, your registration will be cancelled. Please make sure you file all the required forms, and that the owner name identified on the form(s) is correct.

[Continue] [Clear]

Privacy Policy

The information collected on this form allows the applicant to demonstrate that it has commenced use of the mark in commerce. With respect to applications filed on the basis of an intent to use the mark, responses to the request for information are required to obtain the benefit of a registration on the Principal or Supplemental register. 15 U.S.C. §§ 1058 and 1065 and 37 CFR Part 2, 2.167 and 2.168. All information collected will be made public. Gathering and providing the information will require an estimated 3 minutes. Please direct comments on the time needed to complete this form, and/or suggestions for reducing this burden to the Chief Information Officer, U.S. Patent and Trademark Office, U.S. Department of Commerce, P.O. Box 1450, Alexandria, VA 22313-1450. Please note that the USPTO may not conduct or sponsor a collection of information using a form that does not display a valid OMB control number.

Help Desk | Bug Report | Feedback | TEAS Home | Trademark Home | USPTO

TRADEMARK MAINTENANCE

SAMPLE COMBINED DECLARTION OF USE AND INCONTESTABILITY UNDER
SECTION 8 AND 15 FORM

Combined Declaration of Use and Incontestability under Sections 8 & 15

United States Patent and Trademark Office
Trademark Electronic Application System

Navigation History: **Wizard** > Mark Info > Owner > Miscellaneous Statement > Goods/Services > Correspondence > Fee > Signature

PTO Form PTO Form 1583 (Rev 5/2006)
OMB No. 0651-0055 (Exp. 06/30/2012)

Combined Declaration of Use and Incontestability Under Section 8 and 15

(15 U.S.C. § § 1058 & 1065)

TEAS - Version 4.8 : 01/22/2011

Each field name links to the relevant section of the "HELP" instructions that will appear at the bottom of the screen. Fields containing the symbol "*" **must** be completed; all other relevant fields should be completed if the information is known. If there are multiple signatories, click on the Form Wizard.

Important: ONCE THIS FORM IS SUBMITTED ELECTRONICALLY, THE OFFICE WILL IMMEDIATELY PROVIDE THE SENDER WITH AN ELECTRONIC ACKNOWLEDGMENT OF RECEIPT. Please contact TEAS@uspto.gov if you do not receive this acknowledgment within 24 hours of transmission (or by the next business day).

Contact Points:
For **general** trademark information, please e-mail TrademarkAssistanceCenter@uspto.gov, or telephone 1-800-786-9199. If you need help in resolving **technical** glitches, please e-mail TEAS@uspto.gov. Please include your telephone number in your e-mail, so we can talk to you directly, if necessary. For **status** information, use http://tarr.uspto.gov.

NOTE: Do NOT attempt to check status until at least 72 hours after submission of a filing, to allow sufficient time for our databases to be updated.

TRADEMARK PROTECTION AND PROSECUTION

Combined Declaration of Use and Incontestability under Sections 8 & 15

Instructions

To file this form, please complete the following steps:
1. Fill out all fields for which information is known. Fields with a * symbol are mandatory for filing purposes and must be completed.
2. Validate the form, using the "button" at the end of the form. If there are errors, go back to step 1.
3. Use the Pay/Submit button at the bottom of the Validation Screen. This will allow you to choose from 3 different payment methods: credit card, automated deposit account, or electronic funds transfer. After accessing the proper screen for payment, and making the appropriate entries, you will receive a confirmation screen if your transmission is successful. Or, use the "Download Portable Data" Button to save your work for submission at a later time.
4. You will receive an e-mail acknowledgement of your submission.

TRADEMARK MAINTENANCE

Combined Declaration of Use and Incontestability under Sections 8 & 15

Registration Number:	
Mark:	
Registration Date	
Currently Authorized Correspondence E-mail Address	

NOTE: If the e-mail address listed above is either no longer correct for receiving USPTO correspondence or contains a typographical error, please go to the Correspondence Address form to update or correct the e-mail address AND reauthorize the USPTO to communicate with you by e-mail. It is critical that you maintain a current e-mail address with the USPTO. For any technical issues with this process, please contact TEAS@uspto.gov.

WARNING: For an application filed under TEAS Plus, the failure to maintain a correct e-mail address for ongoing e-mail communication will result in the loss of TEAS Plus status and a requirement to pay $50 per class.

1. Is an attorney filing this form?

NOTE: The USPTO considers powers of attorney to end upon either (1) the date of registration, or (2) the final acceptance or denial of a required post-registration filing. Therefore, if you answer YES to this question and file this form, the USPTO will presume that you are the registrant's attorney. This filing will automatically update the "Attorney of Record" and the "Correspondence Address" data fields in the USPTO's TARR database. After submission of this form, it is not necessary to file a separate Appointment of Attorney form or Change of Correspondence Address form. Once the USPTO recognizes an attorney with respect to the submission of a required post-registration filing, such as an affidavit under Section 8, an application for renewal under Section 9, etc., the USPTO will recognize only that attorney for all submissions related to that filing, such as responses to Office actions, petitions, etc., unless and until the registrant revokes and appoints a new power of attorney or the filing is completely resolved (e.g., by acceptance, renewal, or abandonment).

○ Yes ⦿ No

2. Do you want to appoint a Domestic Representative?

TRADEMARK PROTECTION AND PROSECUTION

Combined Declaration of Use and Incontestability under Sections 8 & 15

○ Yes ◉ No

[Go Back] [Continue]

Privacy Policy

The information collected on this form allows the applicant to demonstrate that it has commenced use of the mark in commerce. With respect to applications filed on the basis of an intent to use the mark, responses to the request for information are required to obtain the benefit of a registration on the Principal or Supplemental register. 15 U.S.C. §§ 1058 and 1065 and 37 CFR Part 2, 2.167 and 2.168. All information collected will be made public. Gathering and providing the information will require an estimated 3 minutes. Please direct comments on the time needed to complete this form, and/or suggestions for reducing this burden to the Chief Information Officer, U.S. Patent and Trademark Office, U.S. Department of Commerce, P.O. Box 1450, Alexandria, VA 22313-1450. Please note that the USPTO may not conduct or sponsor a collection of information using a form that does not display a valid OMB control number.

Help Desk | Bug Report | Feedback | TEAS Home | Trademark Home | USPTO

TRADEMARK MAINTENANCE

SAMPLE COMBINED DECLARTION OF USE AND INCONTESTABILITY UNDER SECTION 8 AND 15 FORM

United States Patent and Trademark Office
Trademark Electronic Application System

Combined Declaration of Use and Incontestability Under Section 8 and 15
(15 U.S.C. §§ 1058 & 1065)

TEAS - Version 4.8 : 01/22/2011

Owner Information

☐ Check this box to modify the owner name that appears below if the name does not identify the current owner of the registration.
Note: If this change relates to a change in the correspondence address or e-mail, please use the Change of Correspondence Address Form.

*Name

WARNING: If the entity or person whose name appears immediately above is **not** the current owner of the registration, you **must** ensure that the current owner data is correct *on this form* prior to transmission. Furthermore, the document cannot be accepted and USPTO records will not be updated unless you file a change of name document/assignment and recordation form.

If the correct name does not appear in the box above, before filing you must:
(1) submit a change of name document/assignment and recordation form if you have not previously done so;
(2) check the box above (top) that appears to the left of the words "Check this box to modify the owner name;"
(3) delete the name that appears immediately above; and
(4) type in the name of the *current* owner of the registration.
Note: If an individual, use the following format: Last Name, First Name Middle Initial or Name, if applicable.

☐ DBA (doing business as) ☐ AKA (also known as)
☐ TA (trading as) ☐ Formerly

TRADEMARK PROTECTION AND PROSECUTION

Combined Declaration of Use and Incontestability under Sections 8 & 15

Entity Type		
○ Individual		
● Corporation		
○ Limited Liability Company		
○ Partnership	**State or Country of Incorporation**	If U.S. Corporation [ ] OR If non-U.S. Corporation [Country] Note: You may correct an error or omission in the original listing. However, if the State/Country of Incorporation has actually changed, you should file an assignment document form PTO-1594.
○ Limited Partnership		
○ Joint Venture		
○ Sole Proprietorship		
○ Trust		
○ Estate		
○ Other		
Internal Address	[ ]
* Street Address	[ ] NOTE: You must limit your entry here, and for all remaining fields within this overall section (except City, see below), to no more than 40 characters (the storage limit for the USPTO database). You may need to abbreviate some words, e.g., St. instead of Street. Failure to do so may result in an undeliverable address, due to truncation at the 40 character limit.
* City	[ ] NOTE: You must limit your entry here to no more than 22 characters.
* State (Required for U.S. applicants)	[ ] NOTE: You must include as part of the "city" entry any information related to geographical regions (e.g., provinces) not found in the dropdown lists for "States" or "Countries." Enter the city and then the geographical region, separated by a comma (e.g., Toronto, Ontario). In most instances, you will then also have to select the country within which the region is found, below.
* Country or U.S. Territory	[ ]
* Zip/Postal Code (Required for U.S. applicants only)	[ ]
Phone Number	[ ]
Fax Number	[ ]

TRADEMARK MAINTENANCE

Combined Declaration of Use and Incontestability under Sections 8 & 15

Internet E-mail Address

While the application may list an e-mail address for the owner, owner's attorney, and/or owner's domestic representative, **only** one e-mail address may be used for correspondence, in accordance with Office policy. The owner must keep this address current in the Office's records.

☐ Check here to authorize the USPTO to communicate with the owner via e-mail.

NOTE: By checking this box, the owner acknowledges that it is solely responsible for receipt of USPTO documents sent via e-mail. The owner should periodically check the status of its application through the Trademark Applications and Registrations Retrieval (TARR) database, to see if the assigned examining attorney has e-mailed an Office Action. If an action has been sent to the provided e-mail address, the USPTO is not responsible for any e-mail not received due to the owner's security or anti-spam software, or any problems within the owner's e-mail system. All sent actions can be viewed on-line, from Trademark Document Retrieval.

[Go Back] [Continue]

Privacy Policy

The information collected on this form allows the applicant to demonstrate that it has commenced use of the mark in commerce. With respect to applications filed on the basis of an intent to use the mark, responses to the request for information are required to obtain the benefit of a registration on the Principal or Supplemental register. 15 U.S.C. § § 1058 and 1065 and 17 CFR Part 2, 2.167 and 2.168. All information collected will be made public. Gathering and providing the information will require an estimated 3 minutes. Please direct comments on the time needed to complete this form, and/or suggestions for reducing this burden to the Chief Information Officer, U.S. Patent and Trademark Office, U.S. Department of Commerce, P.O. Box 1450, Alexandria, VA 22313-1450. Please note that the USPTO may not conduct or sponsor a collection of information using a form that does not display a valid OMB control number.

Help Desk | Bug Report | Feedback | TEAS Home | Trademark Home | USPTO

TRADEMARK PROTECTION AND PROSECUTION

SAMPLE COMBINED DECLARTION OF USE AND INCONTESTABILITY UNDER SECTION 8 AND 15 FORM

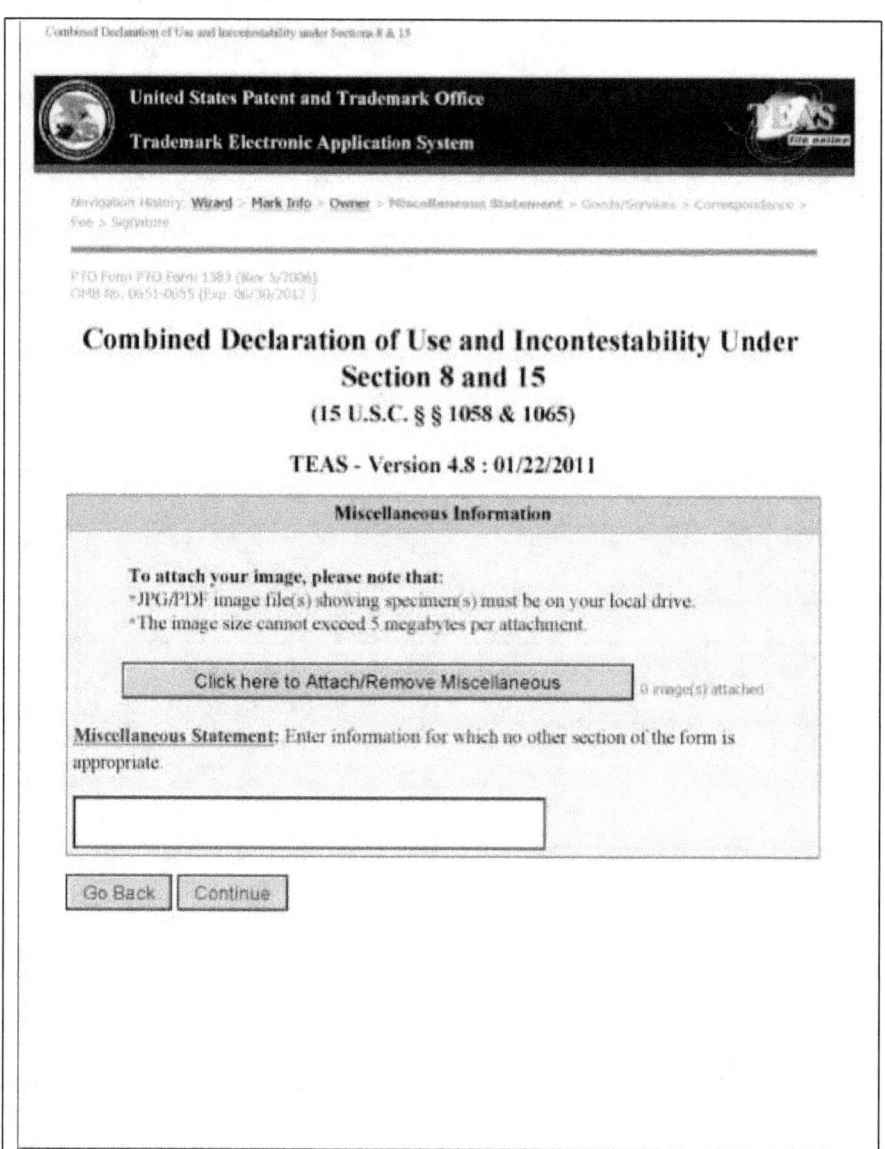

TRADEMARK MAINTENANCE

SAMPLE COMBINED DECLARTION OF USE AND INCONTESTABILITY UNDER SECTION 8 AND 15 FORM

Combined Declaration of Use and Incontestability under Sections 8 & 15

United States Patent and Trademark Office
Trademark Electronic Application System

Navigation History: Wizard > Mark Info > Owner > Miscellaneous Statement > Goods/Services > Correspondence > Fee > Signature

PTO Form PTO Form 1583 (Rev 5/2006)
OMB No. 0651-0055 (Exp. 06/30/2012)

Combined Declaration of Use and Incontestability Under Section 8 and 15
(15 U.S.C. § § 1058 & 1065)

TEAS - Version 4.8 : 01/22/2011

Goods and/or Services Information

WARNING: Registration Subject to Cancellation for Fraudulent Statements
You must ensure that statements made in filings to the USPTO are accurate, as inaccuracies may result in the cancellation of a trademark registration. The lack of use on all goods and/or services for which you claim use in a post-registration filing with the USPTO could jeopardize the validity of the registration and result in its cancellation.

Enter information for the Class

* International Class:
Current listing of goods/services:

[   ]

○ The mark is in use in commerce on or in connection with **all** of the goods or services listed in the existing registration for this specific class; **and** the mark has been continuously used in commerce for five (5) consecutive years after the date of registration, or the date of publication under Section 12(c), and is still in use in commerce on or in connection with **all** goods or services listed in the existing registration for this class. Also, no final decision adverse to the owner's claim of ownership of such mark for those goods or services exists, or to the owner's right to register the same or to keep the same on the register; and, no proceeding involving said rights pending and not disposed of in either the U.S. Patent and Trademark Office or the courts exists. **WARNING:** Any item listed below will be permanently deleted from the registration and at that point may NOT be reinserted.

213

TRADEMARK PROTECTION AND PROSECUTION

Combined Declaration of Use and Incontestability under Sections 8 & 15

○ The filing does **not** cover this specific class. This entire class is to be **deleted** from the registration.

○ **Deleted Goods or Services:** The mark is in use in commerce on or in connection with **all** of the goods or services listed in the existing registration for this specific class; **and** the mark has been continuously used in commerce for five (5) consecutive years after the date of registration, or the date of publication under Section 12(c), and is still in use in commerce on or in connection with all goods or services listed in the existing registration for this class. Also, no final decision adverse to the owner's claim of ownership of such mark for those goods or services exists, or to the owner's right to register the same or to keep the same on the register; and, no proceeding involving said rights pending and not disposed of in either the U.S. Patent and Trademark Office or the courts exists.

The above statements are all entirely true, **EXCEPT** for the goods or services listed below. In the following space, list only those goods or services appearing in the registration that this filing does **NOT** cover and that should be permanently deleted.

[   ]

LEAVE THIS SPACE BLANK IF THIS FILING COVERS **ALL** GOODS OR SERVICES IN THE EXISTING REGISTRATION FOR THIS SPECIFIC CLASS.

Remaining Goods or Services: The mark is in use in commerce on or in connection with the following goods or services listed in the existing registration for this specific class:

[   ]

ENTER HOW THE **COMPLETE** "FINAL" LISTING SHOULD READ THAT WILL IDENTIFY THE GOODS/SERVICES IN USE IN COMMERCE FOR THIS SPECIFIC REGISTRATION (*I.E., REMOVE* THOSE GOODS OR SERVICES IDENTIFIED IN THE PRECEDING BOX). DO NOT ATTEMPT TO ADD OR MODIFY ANY OTHER WORDING, SINCE SUCH CHANGES ARE NOT ALLOWED.

Use Information
NOTE: If deleting an entire class, you can by-pass any fields listed therein as being "mandatory."

TRADEMARK MAINTENANCE

Combined Declaration of Use and Incontestability under Sections 8 & 15

*Specimen Image File
NOTE: For an **instructional video** on what is an appropriate specimen for a good or service, click here. (To view video, you must have Windows Media Player installed. For information about downloading Windows Media Player, click here.)

To attach your image, please note that:
- *JPG/PDF image file(s) showing specimen(s) must be on your local drive.
- *The image size cannot exceed 5 megabytes per attachment.

[Click here to Attach Specimen(s)]   0 image(s) attached

*Describe what the specimen submitted consists of:

[   ]

[Go Back] [Continue]

Privacy Policy

The information collected on this form allows the applicant to demonstrate that it has commenced use of the mark in commerce. With respect to applications filed on the basis of an intent to use the mark, responses to the request for information are required to obtain the benefit of a registration on the Principal or Supplemental register. 15 U.S.C. § § 1058 and 1065 and 37 CFR Part 2, 2.167 and 2.168. All information collected will be made public. Gathering and providing the information will require an estimated 3 minutes. Please direct comments on the time needed to complete this form, and/or suggestions for reducing this burden to the Chief Information Officer, U.S. Patent and Trademark Office, U.S. Department of Commerce, P.O. Box 1450, Alexandria, VA 22313-1450. Please note that the USPTO may not conduct or sponsor a collection of information using a form that does not display a valid OMB control number.

Help Desk | Bug Report | Feedback | TEAS Home | Trademark Home | USPTO

TRADEMARK PROTECTION AND PROSECUTION

SAMPLE COMBINED DECLARTION OF USE AND INCONTESTABILITY UNDER SECTION 8 AND 15 FORM

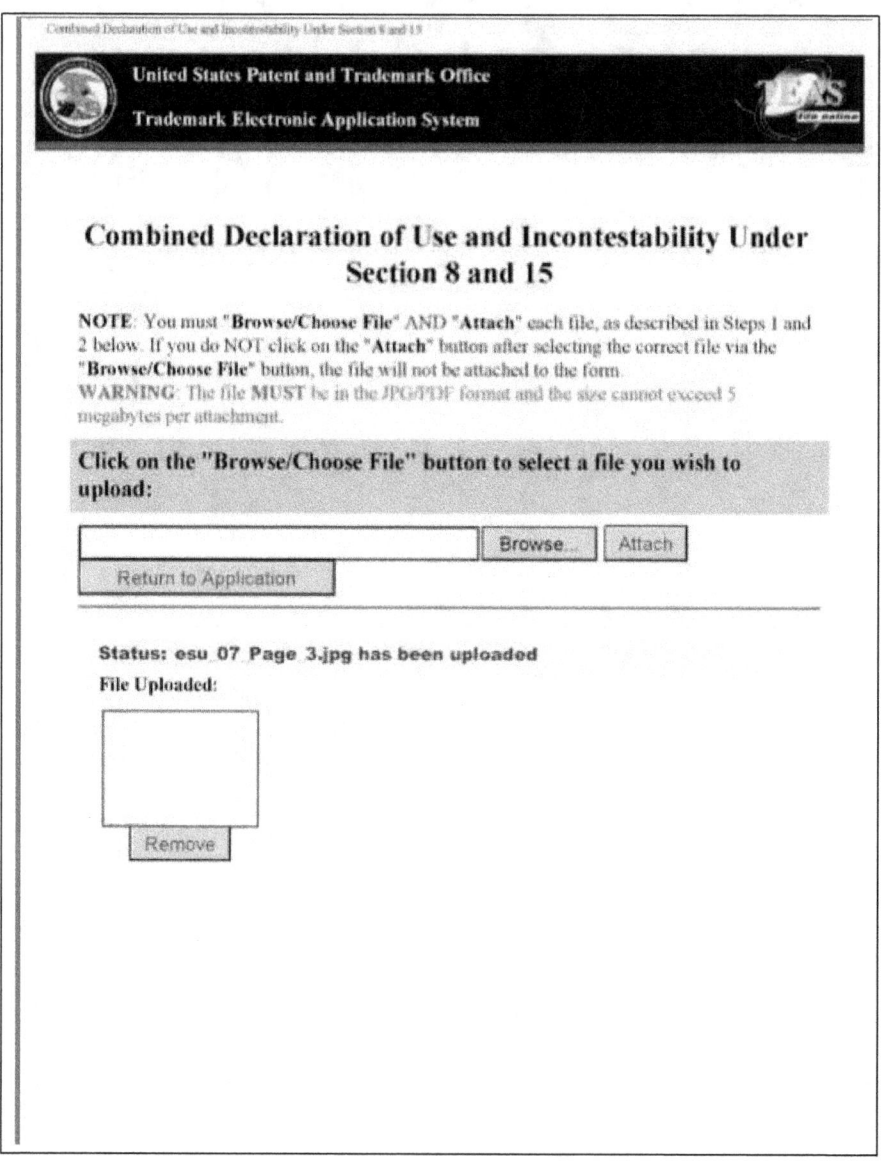

TRADEMARK MAINTENANCE

Combined Declaration of Use and Incontestability Under Section 8 and 15

To attach an image, please complete the following steps:
1. Click on **"Browse/Choose File"** button to select the scanned file (JPG/PDF format only) from your local drive.
2. Click on **"Attach"** button to attach the selected file.
3. To attach additional file(s), return to step 1.
4. To remove unwanted file(s), simply clicking **"Remove"** button right below the file(s).
5. Click on **"Return to Application"** and return back to the form, but ONLY once you see the file(s) loaded above.

WARNING: A submission must be complete within the "4 corners" of the actual transmitted document. Information only accessible through a link, but not part of the submission itself, will **NOT** be considered to be made of record. E.g., if you wish a catalogue to be considered as evidence, you must present the actual pages of the catalogue, and not merely reference that the catalogue is available for viewing at a particular url. The url will **NOT** be independently accessed as part of the examination process, and any materials presented only "by reference" will not constitute part of the actual file.

Help Desk | Bug Report | Feedback | TEAS Home | Trademark Home | USPTO

TRADEMARK PROTECTION AND PROSECUTION

SAMPLE COMBINED DECLARTION OF USE AND INCONTESTABILITY UNDER SECTION 8 AND 15 FORM

Combined Declaration of Use and Incontestability under Sections 8 & 15

United States Patent and Trademark Office
Trademark Electronic Application System

Navigation History: Wizard > Mark Info > Owner > Miscellaneous Statement > Goods/Services > Correspondence > Fee > Signature

PTO Form PTO Form 1583 (Rev 5/2008)
OMB No. 0651-0055 (Exp. 06/30/2012)

Combined Declaration of Use and Incontestability Under Section 8 and 15

(15 U.S.C. §§ 1058 & 1065)

TEAS - Version 4.8 : 01/22/2011

Correspondence Information	
Current Correspondence Information	
* Correspondent Name	
Firm Name	
Docket/Reference Number	
Internal Address	
* Street Address	NOTE: You must limit your entry here, and for all remaining fields within this overall section (except City, see *below*), to no more than 40 characters (the storage limit for the USPTO database). You may need to abbreviate some words, *e.g.*, St. instead of Street. Failure to do so may result in an undeliverable address, due to truncation at the 40 character limit.
* City	NOTE: You must limit your entry here to no more than 22 characters.

TRADEMARK MAINTENANCE

Combined Declaration of Use and Incontestability under Sections 8 & 15

*State (Required for U.S. applicants only)	NOTE: You must include as part of the "city" entry any information related to geographical regions (e.g., provinces) not found in the dropdown lists for "States" or "Countries." Enter the city and then the geographical region, separated by a comma (e.g., Toronto, Ontario). In most instances, you will then also have to select the country within which the region is found, below.
*Country or U.S. Territories	
*Zip/Postal Code (Required for U.S. applicants only)	
Phone Number	
Fax Number	
Internet E-mail Address	☐ Check here to authorize the USPTO to communicate with the registrant or its representative via e-mail. NOTE: While you may list an e-mail address for the registrant, registrant's attorney, and/or registrant's domestic representative, **only** one e-mail address may be used for correspondence, in accordance with Office policy. You must keep this address current in the Office's records. NOTE: By checking this box, you acknowledge sole responsibility for receipt of USPTO documents sent via e-mail. You should periodically check the status of your filing through the Trademark Applications and Registrations Retrieval (TARR) database, to see if the Post Registration Division has e-mailed an Office Action. If an action has been sent to the provided e-mail address, the USPTO is not responsible for any e-mail not received due to e-mail security or anti-spam software, or any other problems with your e-mail system.

[Go Back] [Continue]

Privacy Policy

The information collected on this form allows the applicant to demonstrate that it has commenced use of the mark in commerce. With respect to applications filed on the basis of an intent to use the mark, responses to the request for information are required to obtain the benefit of a registration on the Principal or Supplemental register. 15 U.S.C. § § 1056 and 1065 and 37 CFR Part 2, 2.167 and 2.168. All information collected will be made public. Gathering and providing the information will require an estimated 5 minutes. Please direct comments on the time needed to complete this form, and/or suggestions for reducing this burden to the Chief Information Officer, U.S. Patent and Trademark Office, U.S. Department of Commerce, P.O. Box 1450, Alexandria, VA 22313-1450. Please note that the USPTO may not conduct or sponsor a collection of information using a form that does not display a valid OMB control number.

Help Desk | Bug Report | Feedback | TEAS Home | Trademark Home | USPTO

TRADEMARK PROTECTION AND PROSECUTION

SAMPLE COMBINED DECLARTION OF USE AND INCONTESTABILITY UNDER SECTION 8 AND 15 FORM

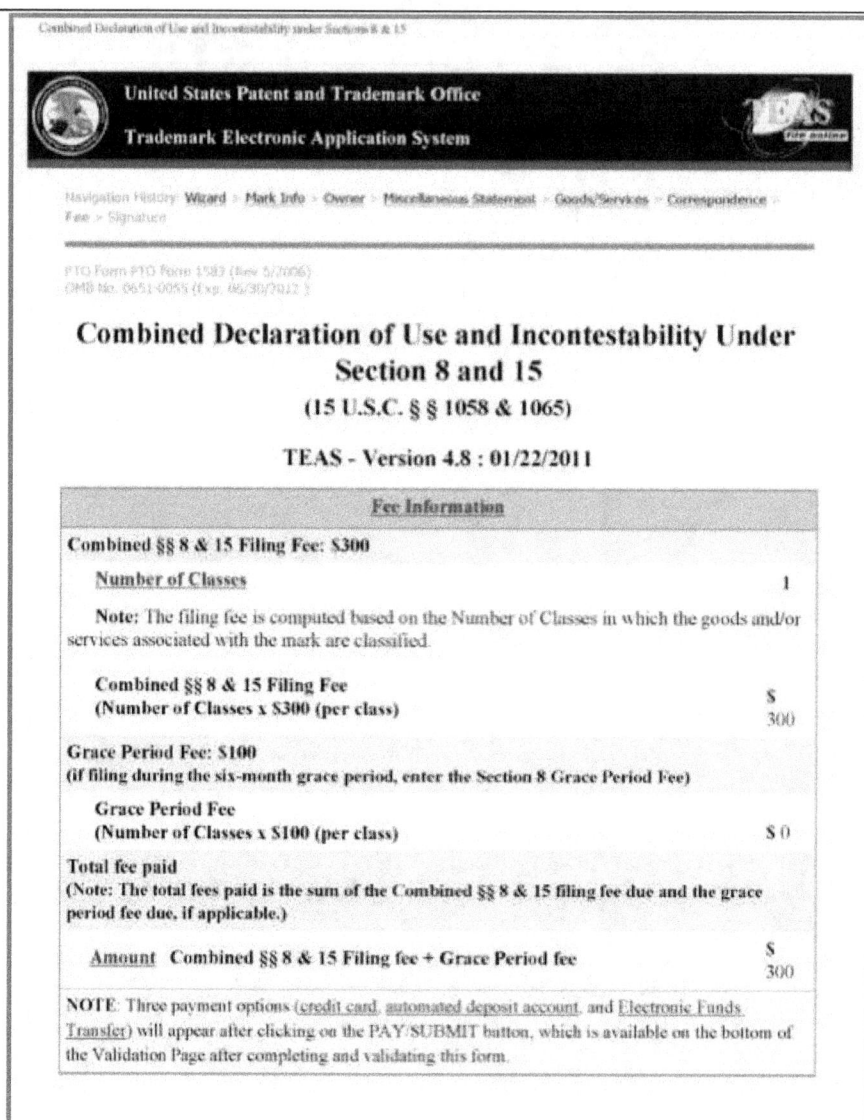

TRADEMARK MAINTENANCE

Combined Declaration of Use and Incontestability under Sections 8 & 15

[Go Back] [Continue]

Privacy Policy

The information collected on this form allows the applicant to demonstrate that it has commenced use of the mark in commerce. With respect to applications filed on the basis of an intent to use the mark, responses to the request for information are required to obtain the benefit of a registration on the Principal or Supplemental register. 15 U.S.C. §§ 1058 and 1065 and 37 CFR Part 2, 2.167 and 2.168. All information collected will be made public. Gathering and providing the information will require an estimated 3 minutes. Please direct comments on the time needed to complete this form, and/or suggestions for reducing this burden to the Chief Information Officer, U.S. Patent and Trademark Office, U.S. Department of Commerce, P.O. Box 1450, Alexandria, VA 22313-1450. Please note that the USPTO may not conduct or sponsor a collection of information using a form that does not display a valid OMB control number.

Help Desk | Bug Report | Feedback | TEAS Home | Trademark Home | USPTO

TRADEMARK PROTECTION AND PROSECUTION

SAMPLE COMBINED DECLARTION OF USE AND INCONTESTABILITY UNDER SECTION 8 AND 15 FORM

TRADEMARK MAINTENANCE

Combined Declaration of Use and Incontestability under Sections 8 & 15

* Signature		* Date Signed	
	NOTE: Only one signature is required, regardless of the number of applicants. The person signing for each section may be different, depending on who has the required knowledge to sign.		(MM/DD/YYYY)
* Signatory's Name			
* Signatory's Position	NOTE: Enter the appropriate title or the relationship to the applicant - if an individual, enter "Owner;" if an attorney, enter "Attorney of record, [specify at least one state] bar member;" if an authorized signatory of a business entity enter, e.g., "President," "Vice President," "General Partner" (if a partnership), or "Principal" (if a limited liability company).		

[Go Back] [Validate]

Privacy Policy

This information collected on this form allows the applicant to demonstrate that it has commenced use of the mark in commerce, with respect to applications filed on the basis of an intent to use the mark, responses to the required information are required to obtain the benefit of a registration on the Principal or Supplemental register. 15 U.S.C. § § 1058 and 1065 and 37 CFR Parts 2, 2.161 and 2.162. All information collected will be made public. Gathering and providing the information will require an estimated 5 minutes. Please direct comments on the time required to complete this form, and/or suggestions for reducing the burden to the Chief Information Officer, U.S. Patent and Trademark Office, U.S. Department of Commerce, P.O. Box 1450, Alexandria, VA 22313-1450. Please note that the USPTO may not conduct or sponsor a collection of information using a form that does not display a valid OMB control number.

Help Desk | Bug Report | Feedback | TEAS Home | Trademark Home | USPTO

TRADEMARK PROTECTION AND PROSECUTION

SAMPLE COMBINED DECLARTION OF USE AND INCONTESTABILITY UNDER SECTION 8 AND 15 FORM

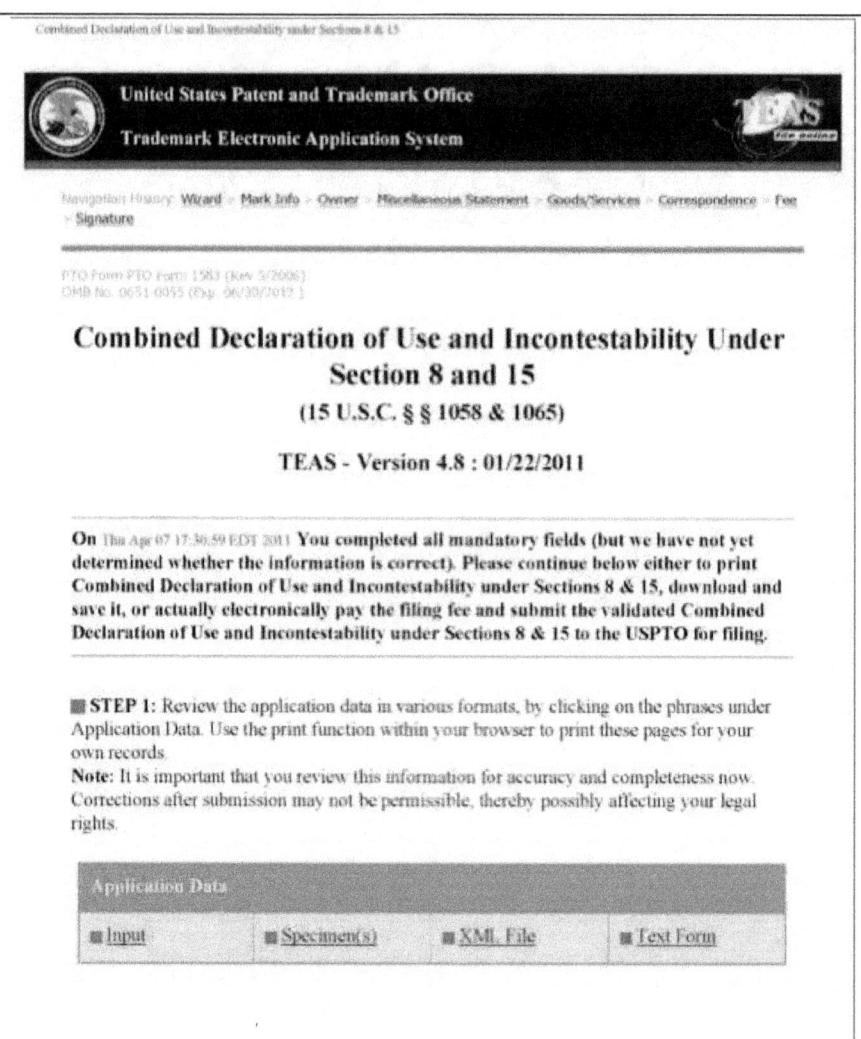

TRADEMARK MAINTENANCE

Combined Declaration of Use and Incontestability under Sections 8 & 15

■ **STEP 2:** If any of the information is incorrect, click on the Go Back to Modify button below to make changes; then re-validate using the Validate Form button at the bottom of the Combined Declaration of Use and Incontestability under Sections 8 & 15. If there are no errors and you are ready to file electronically, first use your print function within your browser to print each of these pages for your own records. Then, click on the Pay/Submit button below. This will bring up a screen for you to enter the appropriate payment information. After successful entry of the payment information, you will be able to complete the submission to the USPTO.

■ **STEP 3:** If there are no errors and you are ready to file this response electronically, confirm the email address for acknowledgment. Once you submit a response electronically, we will send an electronic acknowledgment of receipt to the email address entered below. If no email address appears, you must enter one. If we should send the acknowledgment to a different email address, or to an additional address(es), please enter the proper address or additional address(es). **For multiple addresses/receipts, please separate email addresses by either a semicolon or a comma.**

NOTE: This e-mail address is only for the purpose of receiving the acknowledgment that the transmission reached the USPTO, and is not related to the e-mail that will be used for correspondence purposes (although it could be the same address). The official e-mail address that the USPTO will use for any communication is whatever appears in the record for that purpose. If necessary, use the Change of Correspondence address form to update an e-mail address, as it will NOT be changed based on the specific entry below.

* E-mail for acknowledgment	

To ensure we can deliver your e-mail confirmation successfully, please re-enter your e-mail address(es) here:

* E-mail for acknowledgment	

■ **STEP 4:** Read and check the following:

Important Notice

Once you submit a Combined Declaration of Use and Incontestability under Sections 8 & 15, either electronically or through the mail, we will not refund your fee, because it is a processing fee for our substantive review.

☐ If you have read and understand the above notice, please check the box before you click on the **Pay/Submit** button.

TRADEMARK PROTECTION AND PROSECUTION

Combined Declaration of Use and Incontestability under Sections 8 & 15

■ **STEP 5**: To download and save the form data, click on the **Download Portable Data** button at the bottom of this page. The information will be saved to your local drive. To begin the submission process with saved data, you must open a new form, and click on the "Browse/Choose File" button displayed on the initial form wizard page, at "**[OPTIONAL] To access previously-saved data, use the "Browse/Choose File" button below to access the file from your local drive.**" **REMINDER**: Do **NOT** try to open the saved .obj form directly. You must return to the very first page of the form, *as if starting a brand new form*, and then use the specific "Browse/Choose File" button on that page to import the saved file. Clicking on the "Continue" button at the bottom of that first page will then properly open the saved version of your form.

■ **STEP 6**: If you are ready to file electronically:
Click on the Pay/Submit button, below, to access the site where you will select one of three possible payment methods. After successful entry of payment information, you can complete the submission to the USPTO. A valid transaction will result in a screen that says **SUCCESS!** Also, we will send an e-mail acknowledgment within 24 hours.

WARNING: Click on the Pay/Submit button below **ONLY** if you are now entirely prepared to complete the Pay/Submit process. After clicking the button, you can **NOT** return to the form, since you will have left the TEAS site entirely. Once in the separate payment site, you must complete the Pay/Submit process within 30 minutes. If you are not prepared to complete the process now, you should select the "Download Portable Data" option to save your form, and then complete the Pay/Submit process later. Or, if you have discovered any error, use the "Go Back to Modify" button to make a correction.

WARNING: You can **NOT** make any fee payments by *credit card* from 2 a.m. to 6 a.m. Sunday EST. To file during this specific period, you **must** use either the deposit account or electronic funds transfer payment method; or, you may use the "Download Portable Data" option to save your form, and then complete the Pay/Submit process at a later time with the credit card payment option.

[Go Back to Modify]   [Download Portable Data]   [Pay/Submit]

Help Desk | Bug Report | Feedback | TEAS Home | Trademark Home | USPTO

TRADEMARK MAINTENANCE

United States Patent and Trademark Office

System Outage- Sunday, April 10, 2011- Midnight-8am EDT.
Due to network maintenance being performed, the services provided on the Office of Finance Online Shopping Page will be unavailable on Sunday, April 10, 2011 between midnight and 8:00am EDT. We apologize for any inconvenience this may cause.

Security enhancement to EFT account maintenance and payment processing
Beginning December 19, 2010, the USPTO is implementing multi-factor authentication for EFT payments and EFT account maintenance. Whenever a customer makes a payment using their EFT account or attempts to view or modify their EFT account information, an e-mail will be sent to the address associated with the account. In order to authenticate your identity, click on the link found in this e-mail within the specified time frame and follow the instructions to complete the transaction. Please ensure your e-mail service is set up to accept e-mails from 'RAMSupport@uspto.gov' and 'donotreply@uspto.gov' to receive EFT authentication e-mails from the USPTO. (Note: Deposit account and credit card payment methods are not affected.)

The U.S. Patent and Trademark Office supports Secure Sockets Layer (SSL) for the security of all transactions. If you would like to read more about the security of your transaction click here.

Credit Card Payment

The USPTO accepts the following credit cards for payment:
Visa®, MasterCard®, Discover® and American Express®.

[Pay by Credit Card]

Deposit Account Payment

A USPTO Deposit Account is required to pay using this method.
For information about USPTO Deposit Accounts, click here.

[Pay by Deposit Account]

EFT Payment

An active EFT User Account is required to pay using this method.
For information about the EFT payment method, click here.
To sign up for an EFT User Account, click here.

TRADEMARK PROTECTION AND PROSECUTION

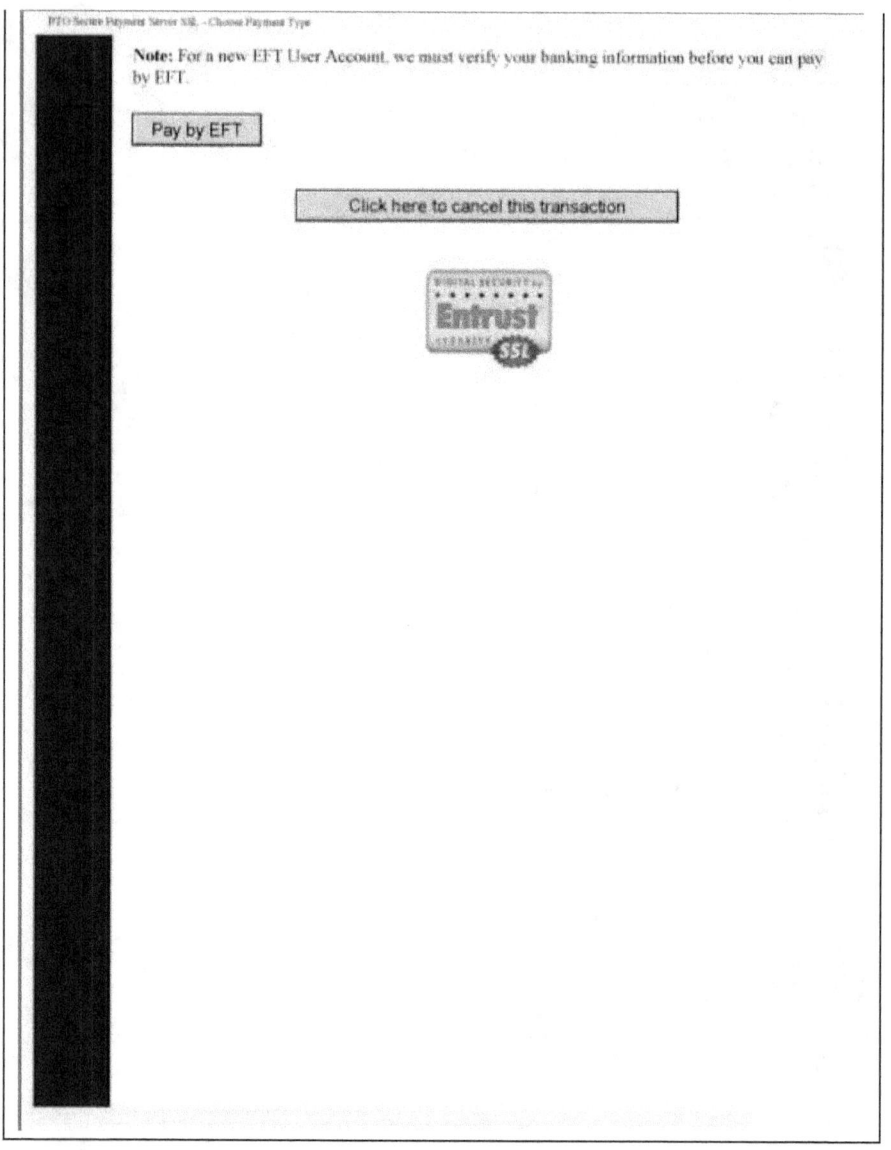

Combined Declaration of Use and/or Excusable Nonuse and Application for Renewal

Subject to the filing of Section 8 declarations and Section 9 applications for renewal, federal trademark registrations issued on or after November 16, 1989, remain in force for ten years, and may be renewed for ten-year periods. Trademark registrations issued or renewed prior to November 16, 1989 remain in force for twenty years, and may be renewed for ten-year periods.

To renew a federal trademark registration, you must file an Application for Renewal under Section 9 of the Trademark Act in conjunction with a Section 8 declaration.

The owner must file a Declaration of Use (or excusable nonuse) and an Application for Renewal between the ninth and tenth years after the registration date. The above documents will be accepted as timely if filed within six-months after the deadlines listed above with the payment of an additional fee. The USPTO has no authority to waive or extend the deadline for filing a proper Section 9 renewal application. Registrations cancelled due to the failure to file a Section 9 renewal application cannot be reinstated or "revived." A new application to pursue registration of the mark again must be filed.

Because the time period for filing the ten-year Section 8 declaration coincides with the filing of a Section 9 renewal application, the USPTO created a form entitled "Combined Declaration of Use in Commerce and Application for Renewal of Registration of a Mark Under Section 8 and 9" (combined form). As noted above, the filing of timely Section 8 declarations are required to avoid the cancellation of a registration.

The current fee for filing a Section 9 renewal is $400 per class of goods or services, and the filing fee for a combined Section 8 declaration and Section 9 renewal application is $500 per class. There is an additional surcharge of $100 per class for filing a Section 9 renewal application within the six-month grace period, or $200 per class for filing a combined Section 8 declaration and Section 9 renewal application during the grace period.

A Section 9 Renewal Application must include:

- ❖ A request to renew the registration signed by the registrant or the registrant's representative;

- ❖ The registration number, mark and date of registration;
- ❖ A name and address for correspondence; and
- ❖ The filing fee.

Section 9 Renewal Applications are reviewed by trademark specialists in the post-registration division. If the Section 9 Renewal Application is accepted, the USPTO will issue a notice granting the renewal. If the Section 9 Renewal Application is refused, the USPTO will send an Office Action stating the reasons for the refusal and any remedies available.

Declaration of Continued Use or Excusable Nonuse under Section 71 for Madrid Protocol Registrants

Holders (owners) of registered extensions of protection to the United States (also called Section 66(a) registrations, registrations resulting from 79' series applications, international registrations extended to the United States) who wish to maintain the protection granted their mark in the United States pursuant to the Madrid Protocol must file an affidavit or Declaration of Use in Commerce or Excusable Nonuse to avoid cancellation of protection in the United States. Such affidavits are required pursuant to Section 71 of the Trademark Act. The USPTO has no authority to waive or extend the deadline for filing a property Section 71 declaration. Registrations cancelled due to the failure to file a Section 71 declaration cannot be reinstated or "revived." A new application to pursue registration of the mark again must be filed.

USPTO electronic forms for filing a Section 71 declaration are available online at the USPTO website through Form #9 in the Registration Maintenance/Renewal Forms.

The owner of the registration must file a Section 71 declaration during the following time periods:

- ❖ **First Filing Deadline.** File a Declaration of Use (or excusable nonuse) on or after the fifth anniversary and no later than the sixth anniversary after the date of registration in the United States, or in the six-month grace period immediately following, with payment of the grace period surcharge.
- ❖ **Subsequent Filing Deadline.** File a Declaration of Use (or excusable nonuse) within the year preceding the end of each ten-year periods after the date of registration in the United States, or

in the six-month grace period immediately following, with payment of the grace period surcharge.

The holder of a registered extension of protection of an international registration to the United States must file an application for renewal of the international registration with the International Bureau (IB). Renewal of international registrations is governed by Article 7 of the Madrid Protocol and Rules 29 – 31 of the Common Regulations under the Madrid Agreement and Protocol.

Requests for renewal of an international registration must be filed directly with the IB. A renewal can be filed during the six-months before expiry of the period of protection or in the six-months following the expiry of the current period of protection with the payment of a surcharge.

The term of an international registration is ten years, and it may be renewed for ten years upon payment of the renewal fee. There is a renewal form available on the IB website. Online renewals may be filed through the World Intellectual Property Organization (WIPO) Marks E-Renewal System.

CHAPTER 12

TRADEMARK PORTFOLIO

As we have said, for the company, a trademark protects a product or service; for the consumer, a trademark is a promise of identity, source, and quality. Consequently, not every trademark has positive connotations. For example, some people do not like McDonald's hamburgers. You may also be wondering how trademarks and brands relate. Are they the same thing? Can you use the terms interchangeably? Think of trademarks as the legal representation and the brand as the associations that the name elicits.

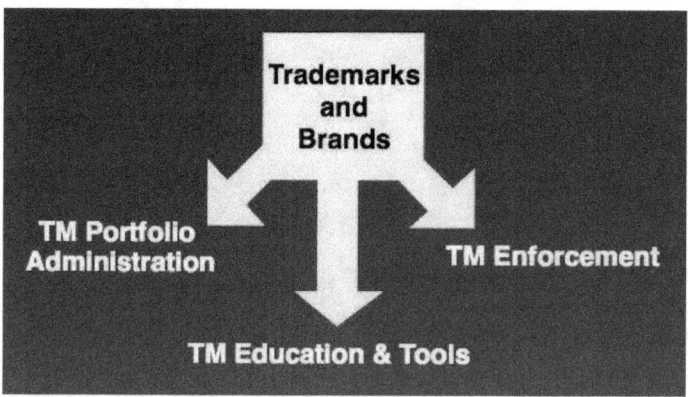

What is the value of trademarks? Trademarks add to the company' bottom line, profitability. For example, the Coca-Cola Company is over 100 years old. Financial World magazine ran an article "valuing" the company purchase price of approximately $33.5 billion. In another example, Intel ranked third most valuable brand, according to Financial World magazine, with an estimated value of $17.81 billion. It's estimated value grew 107% from its previous year, more than any other brand.

The trademark portfolio is comprised of the following parts:

- ❖ An introduction;
- ❖ Trademarks and nouns list;
- ❖ Trademark list;
- ❖ Proper usage guidelines for your trademarks and brands;
- ❖ Proper usage guidelines for your company logo;
- ❖ Proper usage guidelines for your company logo with the tagline; and
- ❖ Other guidelines.

Trademark Portfolio Introduction

Trademarks and service marks are words, acronyms, logos, symbols, taglines, or slogans that identify and distinguish a company as the source of its products and services. The owner of a valid trademark may prevent others from using its mark for particular goods or services, and may recover monetary damages caused by another's infringement.

Trademarks and service marks can be classified in two categories:

- ❖ Registered marks (indicated by the ® symbol) have undergone the appropriate legal process and are registered with the United States Patent and Trademark Office (USPTO). Marks also may be registered in individual states and foreign countries.

- ❖ Common law (unregistered) marks (indicated by the ™ or ℠ symbol) have not been formally registered, but may still be valid and enforceable (although registration provides additional legal rights).

Keep in mind that every potential company trademark must be cleared through legal searches prior to adoption to reduce potential infringement, whether or not such claimed trademarks will go through the formal registration process.

Trademark Search Process

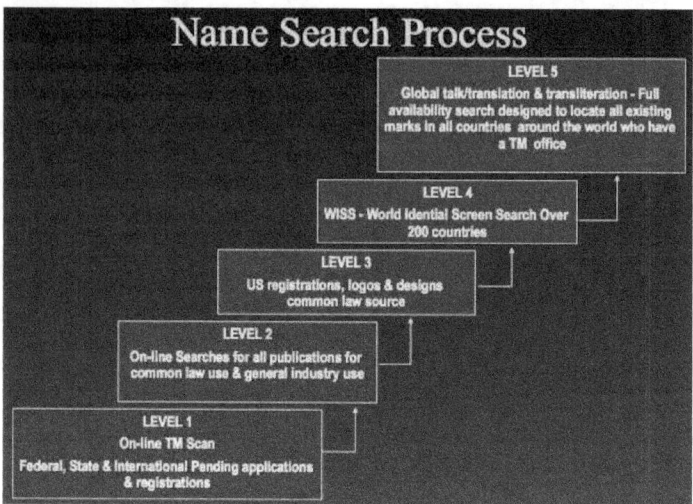

A thorough trade name or trademark search includes five processes:

1. **Level 1**. An online trademark scan for federal, state and international pending applications and registrations. If hiring a search company, expect turn-around time to be one to two days and cost to be approximately $100 per ten names searched.

2. **Level 2**. An online trademark search for all publications for common law use and general industry use via a Lexis/Nexis database. Turnaround time, one to three days and cost approximately $100 per ten names.

3. **Level 3**. A United States registration, logos and designs common law source search. Turnaround time, two weeks or sooner with premium and cost approximately $340, for example, if using such search services as Thomson & Thomson.

4. **Level 4**. A World Identical Screen Search (WISS) over two hundred countries. Turnaround time, two days and cost approximately $645 per name.

5. **Level 5**. A global talk/translation and transliteration – full availability search designed to locate all existing marks in all countries around the

TRADEMARK PORTFOLIO

world that have a trademark office via a Lexicon database. Turnaround time, two weeks and cost approximately $200 per name.

Trademark Registration Process

❖ **Actual Use**. The applicant must use the mark first (in trade) thereby gaining some common law rights of ownership in the mark before federal protection is available.

❖ **Intent-to-Use**. This allows for a form of contingent registration prior to any use at all. The applicant can file provided a "bona fide intention to use the mark in commerce."

Nonetheless, your company trademark strategy may be to not register all your trademarks with the USPTO, but instead simply designate the ™ or ℠ symbols, based on expense and time-consuming process. These kinds of decisions usually depend on whether the product or service is "key" or "non-key," life of the product, etc. and whether there is a promotional budget behind your decision process.

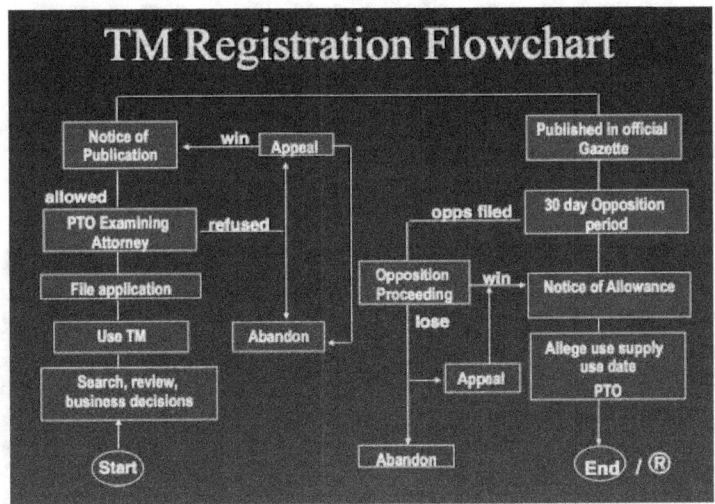

Trademark Classification Process

Classification of marks:

❖ Common Law Trademark = ™

❖ Registered Trademark = ®

TRADEMARK PROTECTION AND PROSECUTION

- Common Law Service Mark = ᔆᴹ
- Registered Service Mark = ®

The three general rules:

1. Always use a trademark as an adjective accompanied by the appropriate noun.
2. Always use the proper spelling and the proper trademark symbol when needed in superscript or subscript.
3. Always use trademarks and brand names and logos in the ways they were intended to be used.

Trademark Use Process

So with all the emphasis on brands and protecting them, why don't companies just trademark everything "to be safe"?

Again, there are a lot of factors to consider before adopting a trademark, including whether a company has the necessary marketing resources in place to establish and maintain a trademark. There are no set rules as to how to implement a trademark portfolio program and other companies may do it differently.

What is important, is that you are consistent and that the perception of the relevant market community for your products associates your brands with your company and only your company.

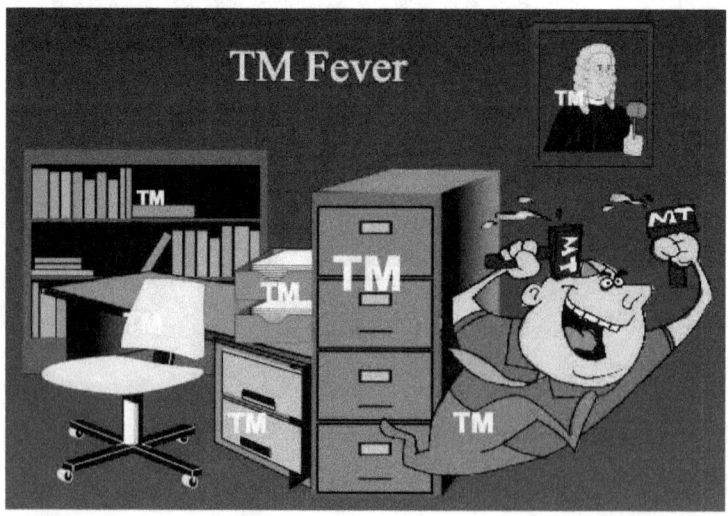

When to use it:

- ❖ Use trademark symbol in first appearance in a headline and/or first prominent use and first appearance in body of text.
- ❖ Always using it is not acceptable.
- ❖ Never use ® in place of ™ or ℠ or vice versa.

The rules apply regardless of whether it's internal or external communication.

Trademarks and Nouns Use

Your company and employees should get in the habit of using the proper noun attached to your trademarks when speaking.

Many people will argue that speech is more important than the written word and that always using the proper noun when speaking is cumbersome. Nonetheless, it's a matter of good habit. If you fail to use the proper noun in your speech, chances are you will fail to use it correctly in written communications. This can lead to losing your trademarks because the name has become generic through general use.

Third Party Trademark Use

When third parties use your trademarks, they also need to include an acknowledgment line. For example:

- ❖ "EtherLink is a registered trademark of 3Com Corporation."
- ❖ "3ComImpact is a trademark of 3Com Corporation."
- ❖ "Other brands and names are the property of their respective owners."

Note: Do not use trademark symbol and noun in the acknowledgement line.

Use of Third Party Trademarks

And when you use third parties' trademarks, apply the general rules, but do not use a ™ or a ® unless you know the status of the third-party trademark. Use a "general" acknowledgment line such as:

- ❖ "Other brands and names are the property of their respective owners."
- ❖ "Designated trademarks are the property of their respective owners."
- ❖ "Indicated names are trademarks of other companies."

TRADEMARK PROTECTION AND PROSECUTION

Trademark and Noun Use

When using a noun in a string, correct examples:

- ❖ "The ATMLink™ adapter card, EtherLink® adapter card and TokenLink® adapter card are all offered at competitive prices."

- ❖ "The ATMLink™, EtherLink® and TokenLink® adapter cards are all offered at competitive prices."

Sample Trademark and Noun List

See sample trademark and noun list in chapter 4, Trademark Protections.

TRADEMARK PORTFOLIO

Sample Trademark List

3Com Trademark List

Registered Trademarks

3Com
3ComImpact
3Com netWorking Partners
3Com Park
3Star
3Wizard
AccessBuilder
AllPoints
Bigpicture
BootWare
Boundary Routing
CELLplex
CoreBuilder
Dynamic*Access*
EtherDisk
EtherLink
Graffiti
HotSync
LANsentry
LinkBuilder
Megahertz
MultiProbe
Net Age
NETBuilder
NETBuilder II
OfficeConnect
ONsemble
PACE
Palm Computing
Parallel Tasking
SmartAgent
Sportster
SuperStack
TokenDisk
TokenLink Velocity
Total Control
Transcend
TurboPPP
U.S. Robotics
V. Everything
Winmodem
XJACK

Trademarks

3Com Connected
AirConnect
ATMDisk
ATMLink
AutoIQ
BRASICA
Connections
Courier
EdgeServer
EtherCD
FDDILink
HiPer
HomeConnect
iMessenger
Impresario
LANServant
LinkConverter
More connected.
Networks That Go the Distance
NetPrep
ONline
Palm
Palm III
Palm IIIx
Palm V
Palm VII
Palm OS
PalmPilot
PathBuilder
PowerRing
RapidComm
Simply Palm.
StorageConnect
Traffix
TriChannel
Universal Connect
V. Everywhere
Volante
WANServant
WorldPort
x2
ZipChip

Service Marks

3Com Care
3Com Facts
3Fund
3Source
Associates Program
EdgeWare
Express
Guardian
Infoline
InfoPAK
Palm.Net
Service Manager
Service Partner
Service Scout
Service Select Program
SupportPAK
Towne Square

Proper Usage Guidelines for Your Trademarks and Brands

The following general trademark rules should be applied to all company trademarks:

- ❖ **Never use the trademark in a fashion that risks making the term "generic."** In order to protect a trademark by law, you must use it appropriately.

- ❖ **Trademarks must always appear as proper adjectives, followed by an appropriate descriptive noun.** If a trademark is used as a noun, the name risks becoming generic, sacrificing the trademark status.

- ❖ **Trademark symbols must occur at least once in each piece.** The appropriate trademark symbol must appear on the first prominent reference, typically in a headline, and again on first reference in body copy. It is not necessary to repeat the designation throughout the rest of the document. However, trademark symbols should be properly designated in all sidebars, charts, tables, graphs, and slides, since they have greater potential to be used independently.

- ❖ **Use appropriate trademark symbols:** ®, ™ or ℠

- ❖ **Be consistent. Always use trademarks and brand names in the ways they were intended to be used.** Use a trademark only in the form in which it has been registered or is being claimed. It's important that all parties involved in developing communications tools be as consistent as possible in their use of trademarks. The integrity of a trademark requires that it's never used in a possessive, plural, hyphenated, or abbreviated form, or that it's never altered by adding letters or numbers. Always use the proper spelling, punctuation, or capitalization.

- ❖ **Never use trademarks as possessives.**

- ❖ **Never use trademarks in a plural form.**

- ❖ **Never hyphenate a trademark.**

- ❖ **Never abbreviate a product name in such a way that the full trademark name is left out since this can alter the meaning.**

- ❖ **Never alter a trademark.**

- ❖ **Always use the proper capitalization of a trademark.**

- ❖ Never abbreviate a product name in such a way that the noun is left out.

- ❖ Always use lower case letters for the generic noun following the trademark.

- ❖ Avoid putting descriptors between a trademark and its noun.

- ❖ Always attribute the ™ or ® correctly.

- ❖ **Differentiate trademarks and brands from trade names.** A trade name is the name of a company that is used to identify that company rather than its products. For example, 3Com uses the number/letter combination "3Com" as either a trademark or a trade name, depending on the context (for instances, "3Com® EtherLink® network interface cards" [trademark] "made by 3Com" [trade name]). Note: when using your company's name as a trade name, do not use the ® designation.

- ❖ **Trademark acknowledgment.** Always use a trademark attribution line.

- ❖ **Third-party trademarks.** Respect third-party trademarks. If you use another company's trademark, it's not necessary to use the appropriate trademark symbol within the text unless a specific contract dictates otherwise. However, always attribute the specific owner in the attribution section at the end of the document.

- ❖ **Standard attribution blocks.** Use a standard format for attribution blocks on documents. For example, "Copyright © 1999 3Com Corporation. All rights reserved. 3Com, the 3Com logo, product 1, and product 2 are registered trademarks of 3Com Corporation. More connected. and product 3 are trademarks of 3Com Corporation. Service A and service B are service marks of 3Com Corporation. Product 4 is a trademark of Y Corporation. Product 5 is a trademark of Z Corporation. (Note: list company names alphabetically.) All other company and product names may be trademarks of their respective companies which they are associated."

Proper Usage Guidelines for Your Company Logo

A logo is a graphical representation of a company or product name comprised as a symbol and artwork. Logos are not a word or something that can be reproduced in type. Logos are not to be used in body copy, headlines, possessive, plural or part of another word. Existing company logos should always be reproduced from an electronic template or logo stat sheets, which dictate the placement of the trademark symbol.

Proper display of the company logo is critical since this symbol is the brand signature of the company. The logo stat sheet should explain the most effective application of the symbol, as well as how to display it correctly using colors, clear space, and on-screen specifications. The following also offers suggestions on preferred and alternate logo usage as well as scenarios to avoid, when using the 3Com logo.

<u>Colors</u> / <u>Clear Space</u> / <u>On-Screen Specifications</u>
<u>Preferred Usage</u> / <u>Alternate Usage</u> / <u>Violations</u>

Colors

The 3Com symbol should be reproduced in 3Com Blue on a white background whenever possible. The blue logo on a white background is the best known and most effective application of the symbol. To reproduce 3Com Blue, use PANTONE® 286.

Preferred 3Com Blue logo.
(Pantone® 286)

C = 100%   R = 0
M = 60%   G = 0
Y = 0%   B = 153
K = 6%

Alternate black 3Com logo.

Clear Space

It's important to provide an adequate amount of clear space around the logo, especially when it appears with other brands. The clear space helps establish the importance of the logo in environments where it competes with other graphic elements for attention.

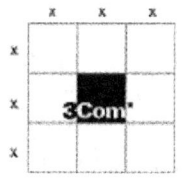
Standard Clear Space

Minimum Clear Space

When space is very limited (as sometimes happens in advertisements), it is acceptable to reduce the clear space around the logo.

TRADEMARK PORTFOLIO

On-Screen Specifications

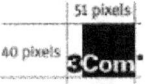 The ® should be no less than 7 pixels wide by 7 pixels tall.

 Enhanced version with drop shadow.

Preferred Usage

The 3Com Blue logo on a white background.

The logo reversed out of 3Com Blue.

The preferred 3Com Blue logo on a light colored background.

Alternate Usage

The logo reversed out of black.

The black logo on a light colored background.

The logo reversed out of a sufficiently dark background.

Violations

Do not reverse the logo on too light a background.

Do not reverse a portion of the logo on a background.

Do not use the 3Com Blue logo on too dark a background.

TRADEMARK PROTECTION AND PROSECUTION

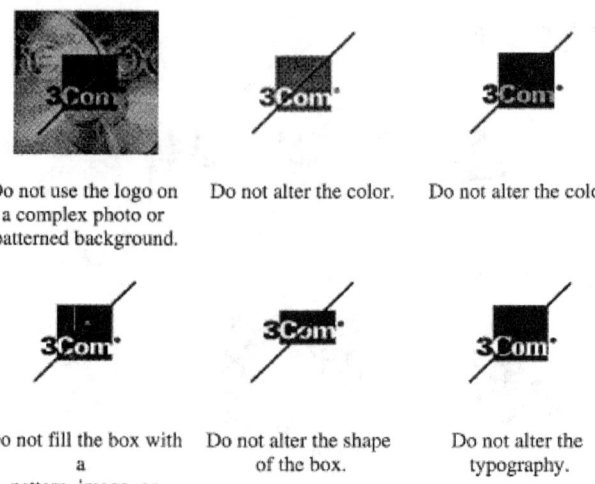

Do not use the logo on a complex photo or patterned background.

Do not alter the color.

Do not alter the color.

Do not fill the box with a pattern, image, or words.

Do not alter the shape of the box.

Do not alter the typography.

Proper Usage Guidelines for Your Company Logo with the Tagline

The 3Com logo and the tagline More connected.™ are designed to build a strong brand image for 3Com. The logo/tagline combination will be used to deliver 3Com's benefit message of industry-leading connectivity solutions for people and businesses. While this new signature does not replace the 3Com logo, it is appropriate to use the logo/tagline combination artwork to sign off 3Com branded communications, including advertising, collateral, and packaging.

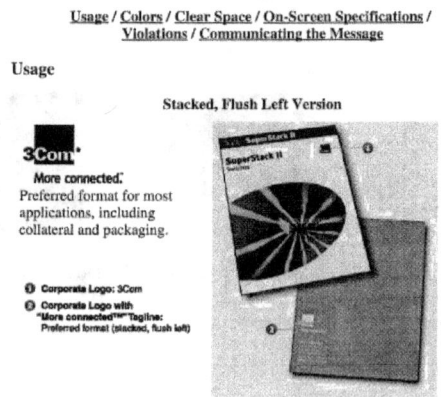

Usage / Colors / Clear Space / On-Screen Specifications / Violations / Communicating the Message

Usage

Stacked, Flush Left Version

Preferred format for most applications, including collateral and packaging.

① Corporate Logo: 3Com
② Corporate Logo with "More connected™ Tagline: Preferred format (stacked, flush left)

Single Line Version

TRADEMARK PORTFOLIO

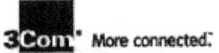

Second preferred format. Effective in wide horizontal applications, such as double page display ads.

Advertisement example using the single line version.

Stacked, Flush Right Version

Format for right alignment situations only.

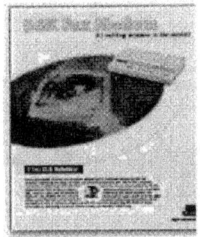

Product flyer example using the stacked, flush right version.

Colors

The 3Com symbol should be reproduced in 3Com Blue on a white background whenever possible. The blue log with the tagline on a white background is the best-known and most effective application of the symbol. To produce 3Com Blue, use PANTONE® 286.

Preferred Color Usage

Preferred 3Com Blue logo.
(Pantone 286)

Alternate black 3Com logo.

3Com Blue is represented by Pantone 286
$C = 100\%$ $R = 0$
$M = 60\%$ $G = 0$
$Y = 0\%$ $B = 153$
$K = 6\%$

Reversed out of 3Com Blue.

TRADEMARK PROTECTION AND PROSECUTION

Alternate Color Usage

Alternate black 3Com logo.   The logo reversed out of black.   The logo reversed out of a sufficiently dark background.

Clear Space

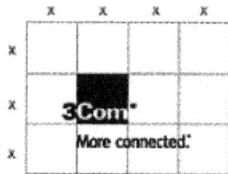

It's important to provide an adequate amount of clear space around the logo with the tagline, especially when it appears with other brands. The clear space helps establish the importance of the logo in environments where it competes with other graphic elements for attention.

On-Screen Specifications

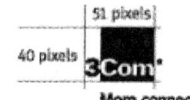 

The ® should be no less than 7 pixels wide by 7 pixels tall.   Enhanced version with drop shadow.

Violations

  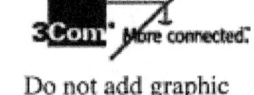

Do not move the More connected. type.   Do not alter the More connected. typography.   Do not add graphic elements to the logo.

Do not alter the colors of the logo.   Do not use a shape to obstruct the logo and the More connected. type.   Do not use the logo on a complex photo or patterned background.

TRADEMARK PORTFOLIO

Communicating the Message in Copy

Always typeset in sentence style, using an uppercase "M," a lowercase "c," a period, and, on first occurrence, a "TM" symbol: 3Com. More connected.™

Treat the message as a complete thought. Use the tagline to emphasize a point, but avoid incorporating the phrase into common, everyday usage. When emphasis is appropriate, use bold typography to distinguish the tagline's "separateness" from other material in text. Keep the trademarked words together on a line. For example, avoid breaking the trademark by leaving "More" on one line and "connected." on the next line.

Within sentences, note that it is acceptable to use the words individually or to use forms of the words: More connected. – such as "connect," "connection," "connecting," and so on – without using the tagline generically within a sentence. Of course any words that convey this message – such as "link," "tie," "increase," and so on – are appropriate.

Correct examples:

- ❖ 3Com connects more businesses and people to information and resources in more ways than any other networking company.

- ❖ For large enterprises, small to mid-size companies, providers, and individual users around the globe, 3Com means connectivity. **3Com. More connected.™**

- ❖ The value of a network increases exponentially as connectivity expands. The more connections, the better.

- ❖ 3Com understands the need for today's networks to offer greater levels of service to their users. **3Com. More connected.™**

Incorrect examples:

- ❖ 3Com builds more connected solutions for its customers.

- ❖ We recognize the needs of businesses as they move to the more connected networks of the future.

TRADEMARK PROTECTION AND PROSECUTION

Trademark Attribution Copy

Set the tagline in sentence style, using an uppercase "M," a lowercase "c," and a period. Do not use trademark symbols in attribution lines.

Correct example:

- ❖ More connected. is a trademark of 3Com Corporation.

When attributing more than one trademark, you still must use the period after the tagline.

Correct example:

- ❖ More connected., PathBuilder, and Total Control are trademarks of 3Com Corporation.

Other Guidelines

Although not mandatory under current Canadian law, it is advisable to publicly identify a trademark used in Canada by marking it. The letters TM or MC (French) should follow the mark. If the mark is registered in Canada, the symbol ® or the letters MD (French) can also be used. For example:

ABC ™ or ABC ^{MC}
ABC ® or ABC ^{MD}

Alternatively, an asterisk can be used to refer to a footnote, which identifies a trademark as follows:

ABC*
* ABC is a trademark of XYZ Ltd.

If a licensee uses a trademark, the licensee's labeling and marketing materials should, at a minimum, indicate to the public that the registrant owns the trademark and that the use is under license. For example, the use of one of the following statements is recommended:

- ❖ ABC is a trademark of XYZ Ltd., use controlled under license; or
- ❖ Used under license from XYZ Ltd.; or
- ❖ Use controlled under license from XYZ Ltd.

In advertising or literature, it is strongly recommended that a trademark be used as an adjective followed by the generic name of the goods or services, particularly in its first occurrence. Avoid using a trademark as a substitute name for the goods or services.

Correct example:

- Please buy ABC motor oil for your car.

Incorrect example:

- Please buy ABC for your car, or please ABC your car.

To enhance the value and reputation in a registered mark, it should only be used in its registered form. For a word mark, avoid pluralizing it, using it as a verb with "ed" or "ing" added, or using it in a possessive form.

Incorrect examples:

- Buy two ABCs and get the third one free.
- Has your car been ABCed for the winter yet?
- ABCing your car will make it run smoother.
- ABC's formula is the best in the industry.

For a mark registered in script form or design form, use the script or design as registered.

CHAPTER 13

TRADEMARKS AND LICENSING

Only in exceptional circumstances should other companies be permitted to use your trademarks. Since trademarks are (by law) indicators of the origin of the goods they designate, it is essential that your company maintain control over the use of its trademarks. For example, there are only two circumstances in which "Aauvi Group, Inc." will grant other companies' permission to use its "Aauvi" trademarks. The first circumstance covers licensed Aauvi partners, distributors, OEMs, etc. The second circumstance covers a limited group of authorized manufacturers of Aauvi promotional products (such as apparel, books, linens, etc.) The right of these business partners and manufacturers to use "Aauvi" trademarks will be granted only under a written license.

Use by You of the Trademarks of Others

Occasionally, your company may have reason to refer to the trademarks of its business partners, customers or even competitors. In all such instances, it should be the policy of your company to properly annotate and attribute such marks. Thus, when a trademark of another entity first appears in the text, it should be accompanied by the appropriate "™" or "®" superscript (depending on the mark's registration status) and properly attributed in a footnote. For example, if the "IBM" trademark were being used by Aauvi in an advertising brochure, the first time it appeared it would appear as "IBM®" and a conveniently located footnote would state, "IBM is a registered trademark of IBM International Business Machines, Inc."

Use of Your Trademarks by Others

When there are sound business reasons, your company may license its business partners to use its trademarks provided certain legal requirements are observed.

For instance, in all "Aauvi" trademark licenses with its business partners, each partner has: (i) acknowledged the validity of the "Aauvi" trademarks, (ii) agreed not to use deceptively similar marks of its own and (iii) agreed to use the "Aauvi" marks only in accordance with its guidelines. Moreover, in each of these licenses, "Aauvi" has retained a solid element of control over the quality of the products with which the marks will be used. With regard to the vendors of promotional goods, the concern is that Aauvi customers will regard such goods as though they were Aauvi goods. If the quality of these "external" products is not high, there is a risk that a customer's experience with them might reflect adversely on the company. Because Aauvi trademarks are a "stamp of quality", the Aauvi Trademark Committee must approve the use of Aauvi trademarks on promotional materials in advance.

It should be mentioned that not all uses of the Aauvi trademark by others would require prior authorization. For example, the "one-off" use of one or more Aauvi trademarks in third party advertising, literature, professional articles, news releases, etc. will not normally be opposed by Aauvi. However, when an Aauvi trademark is used by others, the use of the mark must nonetheless follow the rules of trademark usage, for instance, it is especially important that the use of Aauvi trademarks by others be noted with both the appropriate trademark symbol and the corresponding footnote attributing the trademark ownership to Aauvi.

All your employees should remain vigilant to the misuse of your trademarks by others. Additionally, your employees should also remain alert to the use by others of trademarks that are, or appear to be, confusingly similar to any of your company trademarks. Any employee who becomes aware of an unauthorized or incorrect use of your company's trademark should immediately notify your legal department so that appropriate corrective action may be taken.

Trade Name License Agreement

The following agreement is not intended to be comprehensive or an absolute statement of the governing law. This agreement is not legal advice. It does not analyze any specific fact patterns from any parties but rather discusses broadly points of law, which may or may not be the most accurate, according to current case law interpretation or even case law interpretation that is very in-depth on very narrowly presented issues. Sound legal advice arises from interaction between client and attorney in a question-and-answer dialogue where facts are provided by a client as the attorney probes for issues and then conducts appropriate research if need be, to ascertain the applicable law. Anyone seeking

TRADEMARK PROTECTION AND PROSECUTION

specific advice to specific legal questions should present their facts to an attorney.

SAMPLE
TRADE NAME LICENSE AGREEMENT

This Trade Name License Agreement ("Agreement") is made and effective the [Date]

BETWEEN: [LICENSOR NAME] (the "Licensor"), a corporation organized and existing under the laws of the [STATE/PROVINCE], with its headquarters located at _____.

AND: [LICENSEE NAME] (the "Licensee"), a corporation organized and existing under the laws of the [STATE/PROVINCE], with its headquarters located at _____.

WHEREAS, Licensee acknowledges that Licensor is the owner of the name "[BRAND NAME]" and any variation thereof (the "Name"); and

WHEREAS, Licensee is desirous of using the Name in connection with [DESCRIBE].

NOW, THEREFORE, in consideration of the mutual promises herein contained, the parties hereto agree as follows:

1. Grant of License. Licensor hereby grants to Licensee and Licensee hereby accepts the right, privilege and nonexclusive license to use the Name solely in connection with [DESCRIBE] (the "Business"). Licensee shall use the Name at all times for the Business and no other purposes. Licensor represents and warrants that, to the best of its knowledge, it owns the rights to the Name.

2. Term. The term of the license hereby granted shall be effective upon the date of execution of this Agreement and shall continue for [number] years, unless sooner terminated in accordance with the provisions hereof.

3. License Fee. Licensee shall pay to Licensor, as a license fee for the use of the Name, [amount], payable [on the date hereof] [set forth payment date or dates].

4. Non-exclusivity. Nothing in this Agreement shall be construed to prevent Licensor from granting any other licenses for the use of the Name or from utilizing the Name in any manner whatsoever.

5. Good Will. Licensee recognizes that there exists great value and good will associated with the Name, and acknowledges that the Name and all rights therein and good will pertaining thereto belong exclusively to Licensor, and that the Name has a secondary meaning in the mind of the public.

TRADEMARKS AND LICENSING

6. **Licensor's Title and Protection of Licensor's Rights**

   a. Licensee agrees that it will not during the term of this Agreement, or thereafter, attack the title or any rights of Licensor in and to the Name or attack the validity of the license granted herein.

   b. Licensee agrees to assist Licensor to the extent necessary in the procurement of any protection or to protect any of Licensor's right to the Name, and Licensor, if it so desires, may commence or prosecute any claims or suits in its own name or in the name of Licensee or join Licensee as a party thereto. Licensee shall notify Licensor in writing of any infringements or imitations by others of the Name which may come to Licensee's attention, and Licensor shall have the sole right to determine whether or not any action shall be taken on account of any such infringements or imitations. Licensee shall not institute any suit or take any action on account of any such infringements or imitation without first obtaining the written consent of the Licensor so to do.

   c. Licensee agrees to cooperate fully and in good faith with Licensor for the purpose of securing and preserving Licensor's rights in and to the Name, and Licensor shall reimburse Licensee its reasonable costs for such cooperation (unless Licensee is in breach of this Agreement). It is agreed that nothing contained in this Agreement shall be construed as an assignment or grant to the Licensee of any right, title or interest in or to the Name, it being understood that all rights relating thereto are reserved by Licensor, expect for the license hereunder to Licensee of the right to use and utilize the Name only as specifically and expressly provided in this Agreement. Licensee hereby agrees that at the termination or expiration of this Agreement, Licensee will be deemed to have assigned, transferred and conveyed to Licensor any trade rights, equities, good will, titles or other rights in and to the Name which may have been obtained by Licensee or which may have vested in Licensee in pursuance of any endeavors covered hereby, and that Licensee will execute any instruments requested by Licensor to accomplish or conform the foregoing. Any such assignment, transfer or conveyance shall be without other consideration than the mutual covenants and considerations of this Agreement.

7. **Inspection.** Licensor, or its nominee, shall have access to the Business during normal business hours and to books and records of Licensee for the purpose of ensuring compliance with this Agreement.

8. **Use of Name.** Licensee shall have no right to affix the Name to any building, sign, merchandise or other item without first obtaining Licensor's express written consent, which consent shall be within the reasonable discretion of Licensor.

9. **Termination**

   a. Licensee may not terminate this Agreement.

   b. The license rights granted hereunder may be terminated by Licensor upon immediate notice without the opportunity to cure should any of the following events occur:

   i. If Licensee shall: (A) admit in writing its inability to pay its debts generally as they become due; (B) file a petition in bankruptcy or a petition to take advantage of any insolvency act; (C) make an assignment for the benefit of its creditors; (D) consent to the appointment of a receiver of itself or of the whole or any substantial part of its property;

TRADEMARK PROTECTION AND PROSECUTION

(E) on a petition in bankruptcy filed against it, be adjudicated as bankrupt; (F) file a petition or answer seeking reorganization or arrangement under the bankruptcy laws or any other applicable law or statute; (G) become subject to a final order, judgment or decree entered by a court of competent jurisdiction appointing, without the consent of Licensee, a receiver of Licensee or of the whole or any substantial part of its property or approving a petition filed against Licensee seeking reorganization or arrangement of Licensee under the bankruptcy laws or any other applicable law or statute; or

   ii. Licensee shall fail or refuse to perform any other obligation created by this Agreement of Licensee breaches any term or condition of this Agreement or any other agreement between Licensee and Licensor or its affiliates; or

   iii. Licensee has made any misrepresentations relating to the acquisition of the license granted herein, or Licensee or any of Licensee's shareholders, officers, directors, or managing personnel engages in conduct which reflects unfavorable on the Name or upon the operation and reputation of the Licensor's business; or

   iv. Licensee or any of Licensee's shareholders, officers, directors, or managing personnel is convicted of a felony or any other criminal misconduct which is relevant to the operation of the business of Licensee.

In the event of termination of this License for any reason, Licensee shall immediately cease all use of the Name and shall not thereafter use any name, mark or trade name similar thereto. Termination of the license under the provisions of this Section 9 shall be without prejudice to any rights, which Licensor may otherwise have against Licensee.

10. Compliance with Laws and Regulations. Licensee shall, and shall cause its shareholders, officers, directors, and managing personnel to, comply with all laws, rules and government regulations pertaining to its business and shall not violate any laws, which would create an adverse effect on the Name.

11. Relationship of Parties. Licensee shall not in any manner or respect be the legal representative or agent of Licensor and shall not enter into or create any contracts, agreements, or obligations on the part of Licensor, either expressed or implied, nor bind Licensor in any manner or respect whatsoever; it being understood that this Agreement is only a contract for the license of the Name.

12. Name Ownership. Licensee agrees that the Name is the sole property of Licensor and that Licensee has no interest whatsoever in such Name, and Licensee shall use the Name only for so long as the license granted hereby remains in full force and effect. Licensee shall not take any actions, or aid or assist any other party to take any actions that would infringe upon, harm or contest the proprietary rights of Licensor in and to the Name.

13. Other Licensees. Licensee agrees not to interfere in any manner with, or attempt to prohibit the use of the Name by, any other Licensee duly licensed by Licensor. Licensee further agrees to execute any and all documents and assurances reasonably requested by Licensor to effectuate the licensing of the Name to any other party and agrees to cooperate fully with Licensor or any other Licensees of Licensor to protect Licensor's lawful authority to use the Name.

14. Indemnification and Insurance

TRADEMARKS AND LICENSING

a. Licensee agrees to defend, indemnify and hold harmless Licensor, its officers, affiliates, directors, agents, and employees from and against any and all property damage, personal injuries or death and other liability, loss, cost, expense, or damage, including, without limitation, court costs and reasonable attorney's fees arising out of operations of the Business and from Licensee's breach of any of the terms contained herein.

b. Licensee agrees that it will obtain, at its own expense, liability insurance from a recognized insurance company which is qualified to do business in the State of [state/province], providing protection which is standard in the industry for businesses similar to the Business for the benefit of Licensor and its affiliates and their officers, directors, agents, and employees (as well for Licensee) against any claims, suits, loss or damage arising out of or in connection with the Business. As proof of such insurance, a fully paid certificate of insurance naming Licensor as an insured party will be submitted to Licensor by Licensee for Licensor's approval within thirty (30) days after the date of execution of this Agreement. Any proposed change in certificates of insurance shall be submitted to Licensor for its prior approval.

15. **Notices.** All notices and statements and all payments to be made hereunder, shall be given or made at the respective addresses of the parties as set forth below such party's name unless notification of a change of address is given in writing, and the date of mailing shall be deemed the date the notice or statement is given.

16. **No Joint Venture.** Nothing herein contained shall be construed to place the parties in the relationship of partners or joint venturers or of franchisor/franchisee.

17. **No Assignment or Sublicense by Licensee.** This Agreement and all rights an duties hereunder are personal to Licensee and Licensee shall not, without the written consent of Licensor, which consent shall be granted or denied in the sole and absolute discretion of Licensor, be assigned, mortgaged, sublicensed or otherwise encumbered by Licensee or by operation of law.

18. **No Waiver, Etc.** This Agreement may not be waived or modified except by an express agreement in writing signed by both parties. There are no representations, promises, warranties, covenants or undertakings other than those contained in this Agreement with respect to its subject matter, which represents the entire understanding of the parties. The failure of either party hereto to enforce, or the delay by either party in enforcing, any of its rights under this Agreement shall not be deemed a continuing waiver or a modification thereof and either party may, within the time provided by applicable law, commence appropriate legal proceedings to enforce any or all of such rights.

19. **Governing Law.** This Agreement shall be construed under the laws of the State of [state/province].

20. **Severability.** Whenever possible each provision of this Agreement shall be interpreted in such a manner as to be effective and valid under applicable law, but if any provision of this Agreement shall be prohibited, void, invalid, or unenforceable under applicable law, such provision shall be ineffective to the extent of such prohibition, invalidity, voidability, or enforceability without invalidating the remainder of such provision or the remaining provisions of this Agreement.

21. **Survival.** All obligations of the Licensee shall survive the termination of this

TRADEMARK PROTECTION AND PROSECUTION

Agreement.

22. Attorneys' Fees. Should any litigation be commenced between the parties to this Agreement concerning this Agreement, or the rights and duties of either in relation thereto, the party prevailing in such litigation shall be entitled, in addition to such relief as may be granted, to its attorneys' fees and costs in the litigation.

IN WITNESS WHEREOF, the parties have executed this Agreement as of the date first above written.

LICENSOR   LICENSEE

_____   _____
Authorized Signature   Authorized Signature

_____   _____
Print Name and Title   Print Name and Title

Trademark Ownership and License Agreement

The following agreement is not intended to be comprehensive or an absolute statement of the governing law. This agreement is not legal advice. It does not analyze any specific fact patterns from any parties but rather discusses broadly points of law, which may or may not be the most accurate, according to current case law interpretation or even case law interpretation that is very in-depth on very narrowly presented issues. Sound legal advice arises from interaction between client and attorney in a question-and-answer dialogue where facts are provided by a client as the attorney probes for issues and then conducts appropriate research if need be to ascertain the applicable law. Anyone seeking specific advice to specific legal questions should present their facts to an attorney.

SAMPLE
TRADEMARK OWNERSHIP AND LICENSE AGREEMENT

This Trademark Ownership and License Agreement (the "Agreement") is effective as of _____ (the "Effective Date"), between XYZ Corporation, a _____ corporation ("XYZ"), having an office at _____, and ABC, Inc., a _____ corporation ("ABC"), having an office at _____.

WHEREAS, the Board of Directors of XYZ has determined that it is in the best interest of XYZ and its stockholders to separate XYZ's existing businesses into two independent businesses;

WHEREAS, as part of the foregoing, XYZ and ABC have entered into a Separation Agreement (as defined below) which provides, among other things, for the separation of certain ABC assets and ABC liabilities, the initial public offering of ABC stock,

TRADEMARKS AND LICENSING

the distribution of such stock and the execution and delivery of certain other agreements in order to facilitate and provide for the foregoing;

WHEREAS, the parties desire that XYZ assign and transfer to ABC the ABC Business Marks (as defined below); and

WHEREAS, the parties further desire that XYZ license the Licensed Marks (as defined below) to ABC after the separation of the ABC businesses.

NOW, THEREFORE, in consideration of the mutual promises of the parties, and of good and valuable consideration, it is agreed by and between the parties as follows:

ARTICLE I
DEFINITIONS

For the purpose of this Agreement, the following capitalized terms are defined in this Article I and shall have the meaning specified herein:

1.1 ABC BUSINESS. "ABC Business" means (a) the business and operations of the following business entities of XYZ, as described in the IPO Registration Statement (as defined in the Separation Agreement):

1.2 ABC BUSINESS MARKS. **[Need to determine if there are ABC trademarks owned by XYZ that need to be assigned to ABC.]** "ABC Business Marks" means the Marks listed in the ABC Business Marks Database.

1.3 ABC BUSINESS MARKS DATABASE. "ABC Business Marks Database" means the ABC Business Marks Database, as it may be updated by the parties upon mutual agreement to add additional Marks as of the Separation Date.

1.4 ABC BUSINESS PRODUCTS means **[Need to determine what products and new versions may keep the XYZ mark after termination]**

1.5 AFFILIATED COMPANY. "Affiliated Company" means, with respect to XYZ, any entity in which XYZ holds a 50% or less ownership interest and that is listed on Exhibit A hereto and, with respect to ABC, any entity in which ABC holds a 50% or less ownership interest and that is listed on Exhibit A hereto; provided, however, that any such entity listed in Exhibit A shall be considered to be an Affiliated Company under this Agreement only if it agrees in writing to be bound by the terms and conditions of this Agreement. Exhibit A may be amended from time to time after the date hereof upon mutual consent of the parties. **[Need to determine if there are any non-controlled subsidiaries (i.e. joint ventures) that should be under this Agreement.]**

1.6 AUTHORIZED DEALERS. "Authorized Dealers" means any distributor, dealer, OEM customer, VAR customer, VAD customer, systems integrator or other agent that on or after the Separation Date is authorized to market, advertise, sell, lease, rent, service or otherwise offer ABC Business Products. ABC will provide XYZ a list of the then current Authorized Dealers within a reasonable period after XYZ's request.

TRADEMARK PROTECTION AND PROSECUTION

1.7 COLLATERAL MATERIALS. "Collateral Materials" means all packaging, tags, labels, advertising, promotions, display fixtures, instructions, warranties and other materials of any and all types associated with the ABC Business Products that are marked with at least one of the Licensed Marks.

1.8 CORPORATE IDENTITY MATERIALS. "Corporate Identity Materials" means materials that are not products or product-related and that ABC may now or hereafter use to communicate its identity, including, by way of example and without limitation, business cards, letterhead, stationery, paper stock and other supplies, signage on real property, buildings, fleet and uniforms.

1.9 DISTRIBUTION DATE. "Distribution Date" has the meaning set forth in the Separation Agreement.

1.10 LICENSED MARKS. **[Does ABC need a transitional license to XYZ trademarks?]** "Licensed Marks" means the Marks set forth on Exhibit A hereto.

1.11 MAINTENANCE CONTRACTS. "Maintenance Contracts" means agreements pursuant to which ABC, its Subsidiaries or Affiliated Companies or its or their Authorized Dealers or their designees provide repair and maintenance services (whether preventive, diagnostic, remedial, warranty or non-warranty) in connection with ABC Business Products, including without limitation agreements entered into by XYZ prior to the Separation Date and assigned to ABC pursuant to the Separation Agreement or the Ancillary Agreements (as such term is defined in the Separation Agreement).

1.12 MARK. "Mark" means any trademark, service mark, trade name, domain name, and the like, or other word, name, symbol or device, or any combination thereof, used or intended to be used by a Person to identify and distinguish the products or services of that Person from the products or services of others and to indicate the source of such goods or services, including without limitation all registrations and applications therefor throughout the world and all common law and other rights therein throughout the world.

1.13 PERSON. "Person" means an individual, a partnership, a corporation, a limited liability company, an association, a joint stock company, a trust, a joint venture, an unincorporated organization, and a governmental entity or any department, agency or political subdivision thereof.

1.14 QUALITY STANDARDS. "Quality Standards" means standards of quality applicable to the ABC Business Products, as in use immediately prior to the Separation Date, unless otherwise communicated in writing by XYZ from time to time.

TRADEMARKS AND LICENSING

1.15   SELL. To "Sell" a product means to sell, transfer, lease or otherwise dispose of a product. "Sale" and "Sold" have the corollary meanings ascribed thereto.

1.16   SEPARATION AGREEMENT. "Separation Agreement" means the Separation and Distribution Agreement between the parties.

1.17   SEPARATION DATE. "Separation Date" means _____ or such other date as may be fixed by the Board of Directors of XYZ.

1.18   SUBSIDIARY. "Subsidiary" means with respect to any specified Person, any corporation, any limited liability company, any partnership or other legal entity of which such Person owns, directly or indirectly, more than 50% of the stock or other equity interest entitled to vote on the election of the members of the board of directors or similar governing body. Unless the context otherwise requires, reference to XYZ and its Subsidiaries shall not include the subsidiaries of XYZ that will be transferred to ABC after giving effect to the Separation (as defined in the Separation Agreement), including the actions taken pursuant to the Non-US Plan (as defined in the Separation Agreement). For example, if XYZ owns 70% of the stock of another corporation, and that corporation owns 60% of the equity interest of a limited liability company, then that corporation is a Subsidiary of XYZ but that limited liability company is not. However, if such corporation owns 90% of the equity interest of a limited liability company, then that limited liability company is a Subsidiary of XYZ. For the avoidance of doubt, this definition of Subsidiary is different from the definition of Subsidiary in the Separation Agreement.

1.19   THIRD PARTY. "Third Party" means a Person other than XYZ and its Subsidiaries and Affiliated Companies and ABC and its Subsidiaries and Affiliated Companies.

1.20   TRADEMARK USAGE GUIDELINES. "Trademark Usage Guidelines" means the guidelines for proper usage of the Licensed Marks, as in use immediately prior to the Separation Date, as such guidelines may be revised and updated in writing by XYZ from time to time.

ARTICLE II
ASSIGNMENT

2.1   ASSIGNMENT OF ABC BUSINESS MARKS. **[Need to determine if there are ABC trademarks owned by XYZ that need to be assigned to ABC.]** Subject to Sections 2.2 and 2.3 below, XYZ hereby grants, conveys and assigns (and agrees to cause its appropriate Subsidiaries to grant, convey and assign) to ABC, by execution hereof (or, where appropriate or required, by execution of separate instruments of assignment), all its (and their) right, title and interest in and to the ABC Business Marks, including all goodwill of the ABC Business appurtenant thereto, to be held and enjoyed by ABC, its successors and assigns. XYZ further grants, conveys and assigns (and agrees to cause its appropriate Subsidiaries to grant, convey and assign) to ABC all its (and their) right, title and interest in and to any and all causes of action and rights of recovery for past infringement of the ABC

TRADEMARK PROTECTION AND PROSECUTION

Business Marks. XYZ will, without demanding any further consideration therefor, at the request and expense of ABC (except for the value of the time of XYZ employees), do (and to cause its Subsidiaries to do) all lawful and just acts that may be or become necessary for evidencing, maintaining, recording and perfecting ABC's rights to such ABC Business Marks consistent with XYZ's general business practice as of the Separation Date, including but not limited to execution and acknowledgement of (and causing its Subsidiaries to execute and acknowledge) assignments and other instruments in a form reasonably required by ABC or the relevant governmental or other authorities for each Mark in all jurisdictions in which XYZ owns rights thereto.

2.2 PRIOR GRANTS. ABC acknowledges and agrees that the foregoing assignment is subject to any and all licenses or other rights that may have been granted by XYZ or its Subsidiaries with respect to the ABC Business Marks prior to the Separation Date. XYZ shall respond to reasonable inquiries from ABC regarding any such prior grants.

2.3 ASSIGNMENT DISCLAIMER. ABC ACKNOWLEDGES AND AGREES THAT THE FOREGOING ASSIGNMENTS ARE MADE ON AN "AS-IS," QUITCLAIM BASIS AND THAT NEITHER XYZ NOR ANY SUBSIDIARY OR AFFILIATED COMPANY OF XYZ HAS MADE OR WILL MAKE ANY WARRANTY WHATSOEVER, EXPRESS, IMPLIED OR STATUTORY, INCLUDING, WITHOUT LIMITATION, ANY IMPLIED WARRANTIES OF TITLE, ENFORCEABILITY OR NON-INFRINGEMENT.

ARTICLE III
LICENSE

3.1 LICENSE GRANT. **[Does ABC need a transitional license to XYZ trademarks? Need to determine if license should be perpetual or limited and tax implications of such choice.]** XYZ grants (and agrees to cause its appropriate Subsidiaries to grant) to ABC a personal, irrevocable, nonexclusive, perpetual, worldwide, fully-paid and non-transferable (except as set forth in Section 14.9) license to use the Licensed Marks on the ABC Business Products and in connection with the Sale and offer for Sale of ABC Business Products (or, in the case of ABC Business Products in the form of software, in connection with licensing of ABC Business Products) and to use the Licensed Marks in the advertisement and promotion of such ABC Business Products.

3.2 LICENSE RESTRICTIONS.

3.2.1 Once ABC abandons the use of all of the Licensed Marks on a particular ABC Business Product, then ABC agrees that its license granted hereunder with respect to that ABC Business Product shall thereupon terminate.

3.2.2 ABC may not make any use whatsoever, in whole or in part, of the Licensed Marks, or any other Mark owned by XYZ, in connection with ABC's corporate, doing business as, or fictitious name, or on Corporate Identity Materials without the prior written consent of XYZ, except as expressly set forth in this Section 3.2(b) or in Section 3.4 below. Notwithstanding the foregoing, ABC may use any business cards, letterhead, stationery, paper stock and other supplies, uniforms and the like throughout their useful life in connection with the conduct of the ABC Business, to the extent that, as of the Separation Date, they are in use, in inventory or on order.

TRADEMARKS AND LICENSING

3.2.3 ABC may not use any Licensed Mark in direct association with another Mark such that the two Marks appear to be a single Mark or in any other composite manner with any Marks of ABC or any Third Party (other than the ABC Business Marks as permitted herein).

3.2.4 In all respects, ABC's usage of the Licensed Marks pursuant to the license granted hereunder shall be in a manner consistent with the high standards, reputation and prestige represented by the Licensed Marks, and any usage by ABC that is inconsistent with the foregoing shall be deemed to be outside the scope of the license granted hereunder. As a condition to the license granted hereunder, ABC shall at all times present, position and promote the ABC Business Products marked with one or more of the Licensed Marks in a manner consistent with the high standards and prestige represented by the Licensed Marks.

3.3 LICENSEE UNDERTAKINGS. As a condition to the licenses granted hereunder, ABC undertakes to XYZ that:

3.3.1 ABC shall not use the Licensed Marks (or any other Mark of XYZ) in any manner contrary to public morals, in any manner which is deceptive or misleading, which ridicules or is derogatory to the Licensed Marks, or which compromises or reflects unfavorably upon the goodwill, good name, reputation or image of XYZ or the Licensed Marks, or which might jeopardize or limit XYZ's proprietary interest therein.

3.3.2 ABC shall not use the Licensed Marks in connection with any products or services other than the ABC Business Products, including, without limitation, any other products of the ABC Business.

3.3.3 ABC shall not (i) misrepresent to any Person the scope of its authority under this Agreement, (ii) incur or authorize any expenses or liabilities chargeable to XYZ, or (iii) take any actions that would impose upon XYZ any obligation or liability to a Third Party other than obligations under this Agreement, or other obligations which XYZ expressly approves in writing for ABC to incur on its behalf.

3.3.4 All press releases and corporate advertising and promotions that embody the Licensed Marks and messages conveyed thereby shall be consistent with the high standards and prestige represented by the Licensed Marks.

3.4 NON-TRADEMARK USE. Each party may make appropriate and truthful references to the other party and the other party's products and technology.

3.5 RESERVATION OF RIGHTS. Except as otherwise expressly provided in this Agreement, XYZ shall retain all rights in and to the Licensed Marks, including without limitation:

3.5.1 All rights of ownership in and to the Licensed Marks;

3.5.2 The right to use (including the right of XYZ's Subsidiaries and Affiliated Companies to use) the Licensed Marks, either alone or in combination with other Marks, in connection with the marketing, offer or provision of any product or service, including any product or service which competes with ABC Business products; and

3.5.3 The right to license Third Parties to use the Licensed Marks.

3.6 THIRD PARTY LICENSES. **[Need to determine if this restriction is appropriate.]** XYZ agrees that it and its Subsidiaries and Affiliated Companies will not

TRADEMARK PROTECTION AND PROSECUTION

license or transfer the Licensed Marks to Third Parties (other than to and among Subsidiaries of XYZ) for use in connection with products or services which compete with ABC Business Products that are listed on an ABC corporate price list as of the Distribution Date until three (3) years after the Separation Date. Such restriction shall be binding on any successors and assigns of the Licensed Marks.

ARTICLE IV
PERMITTED SUBLICENSES

 a. SUBLICENSES

  i. SUBLICENSES TO SUBSIDIARIES AND AFFILIATED COMPANIES. Subject to the terms and conditions of this Agreement, including all applicable Quality Standards and Trademark Usage Guidelines and other restrictions in this Agreement, ABC may grant sublicenses to its Subsidiaries and Affiliated Companies to use the Licensed Marks in accordance with the license grant in Section 3.1 above; provided, that (i) ABC enters into a written sublicense agreement with each such Subsidiary and Affiliated Company sublicensee, and (ii) such agreement does not include the right to grant further sublicenses other than, in the case of a sublicensed Subsidiary of ABC, to another Subsidiary of ABC. ABC shall provide copies of such written sublicense agreements to XYZ upon request. If ABC grants any sublicense rights pursuant to this Section 4.1(a) and any such sublicensed Subsidiary ceases to be a Subsidiary or ABC ceases to hold at least a thirty percent (30%) ownership interest in such sublicensed Affiliated Company, then the sublicense granted to such Subsidiary or Affiliated Company pursuant to this Section 4.1(a) shall terminate ____ (__) days from the date of such cessation.

  ii. SUBLICENSES TO TRANSFEREES. In addition, if ABC, within ____ (__) years after the Separation Date, transfers a going business (but not all or substantially all of its business or assets), and such transfer includes at least one marketable product and tangible assets having a net value of at least ____ U.S. dollars ($____) then, subject to the terms and conditions of this Agreement, including all applicable Quality Standards and Trademark Usage Guidelines and other restrictions in this Agreement, ABC may grant sublicenses to the transferee of such business to use the Licensed Marks on the ABC Business Products that are in the transferred business as of the effective date of the transfer in accordance with the license grant in Section 3.1 above; provided, that (i) ABC enters into a written sublicense agreement with the sublicensee, (ii) such agreement does not include the right to grant further sublicenses and (iii) in any event, such sublicense shall terminate one hundred eighty (180) days after the effective date of the transfer. ABC shall provide copies of such written sublicense agreements to XYZ upon request.

 b. AUTHORIZED DEALERS' USE OF MARKS. Subject to the terms and conditions of this Agreement, including all applicable Quality Standards and Trademark Usage Guidelines and other restrictions in this Agreement, ABC (and those Subsidiaries and Affiliated Companies sublicensed to use the Licensed Marks pursuant to Section 4.1) may allow Authorized Dealers to, and may allow such Authorized Dealers to allow other Authorized Dealers to, use the Licensed Marks in the advertisement and promotion of ABC Business Products Sold by such Authorized Dealers.

 c. ENFORCEMENT OF AGREEMENTS. ABC shall take all appropriate measures at ABC's expense promptly and diligently to enforce the terms of any sublicense

TRADEMARKS AND LICENSING

agreement or other agreement with any Subsidiary, Affiliated Company or Authorized Dealer, or of any existing agreement with any Authorized Dealer, and shall restrain any such Subsidiary, Affiliated Company or Authorized Dealer from violating such terms, including without limitation (i) monitoring the Subsidiaries', Affiliated Companies' and Authorized Dealers' compliance with the relevant Trademark Usage Guidelines and Quality Standards and causing any noncomplying Subsidiary, Affiliated Company or Authorized Dealer promptly to remedy any failure, (ii) terminating such agreement and/or (iii) commencing legal action, in each case, using a standard of care consistent with XYZ's practices as of the Separation Date. In the event that XYZ determines that ABC has failed promptly and diligently to enforce the terms of any such agreement using such standard of care, XYZ reserves the right to enforce such terms, and ABC shall reimburse XYZ for its fully allocated direct costs and expenses incurred in enforcing such agreement, plus all out-of-pocket costs and expenses, plus five percent (5%) (or, if such costs and expenses are incurred more than two (2) years after the Separation Date, ten percent (10%)). **[Need to determine what appropriate remedy should be for failing to enforce a trademark agreement.]**

ARTICLE V
ROYALTIES

5.1   ROYALTIES **[Will there be any royalties? Tax concerns may drive this section.]**.

5.1.1   Upon (i) any Sale occurring more than five (5) years after the Separation Date by ABC, its Subsidiaries or Affiliated Companies of tangible ABC Business Products that are marked with one or more of the Licensed Marks (other than repaired, refurbished or reconstructed ABC Business Products or repair parts and other than Sales to XYZ, its Subsidiaries and its Affiliated Companies), and (ii) the use by ABC, its Subsidiaries or Affiliated Companies of one or more of the Licensed Marks as a service mark in connection with the sale of services associated with ABC Business Products (other than repair, maintenance and calibration services and other than sales to XYZ, its Subsidiaries and its Affiliated Companies), ABC shall pay to XYZ a royalty on the Net Sales earned by ABC in each ABC fiscal quarter as a result of such sale. The royalty rate shall be the standard royalty rate that is charged by XYZ to the ABC Business as of the Separation Date for use of the Licensed Marks.

5.1.2   As used in this Article V, "Net Sales" means the gross invoice price from (i) royalty-bearing Sales under Section 5.1(a)(i) above and (ii) royalty-bearing sales of services under Section 5.1(a)(ii) above, in any case less (A) charges for handling, freight, sales taxes, insurance costs and import duties where such items are included in the invoiced price, (B) point-of-sale credits (or other similar adjustments to price) granted to independent distributors and (C) credits actually granted or refunds actually given for returns during such ABC fiscal quarter. In the event that the foregoing ABC Business Products are Sold for no or nominal consideration or to a Subsidiary or Affiliated Company or in any other circumstances in which the selling price is established on other than an arms-length basis, the Net Sales on such Sales shall be determined on the average selling price earned by ABC during the preceding ABC fiscal quarter on Sales of like volumes of the applicable ABC Business Products to unaffiliated customers in arms-length sales. However, in the event that the foregoing ABC Business Products are Sold to ABC's Subsidiaries or Affiliated Companies for resale to Third Parties, then the royalties will be based on Net Sales from the Subsidiaries or Affiliated Companies to the Third Parties and no royalties will be due on the Sales to the Subsidiaries and Affiliated Companies.

TRADEMARK PROTECTION AND PROSECUTION

5.1.3   For the purposes of clarification, no royalty is due under this Article V for uses of the Licensed Marks that are covered by Section 3.4.

5.2   PAYMENTS AND ACCOUNTING.

5.2.1   With respect to the royalties set forth herein, ABC shall keep full, clear and accurate records until otherwise provided in Section 5.2(b). These records shall be retained for a period of three (3) years from the date of payment notwithstanding the expiration or other termination of this Agreement. XYZ shall have the right, through a mutually agreed upon independent certified public accountant (consent to which shall not be unreasonably withheld or delayed by ABC), and at XYZ's expense, to examine and audit, not more than once a year, and during normal business hours, all such records and such other records and accounts as may under recognized accounting practices contain information bearing upon the amount of royalty payable to XYZ under this Agreement. Prompt adjustment shall be made by either party to compensate for any errors and/or omissions disclosed by such examination or audit. Should any such error and/or omission result in an underpayment of more than five percent (5%) of the total royalties due for the period under audit, ABC shall upon XYZ's request pay for the cost of the audit and pay XYZ an additional fee equal to a compound annual interest rate of ten percent (10%) of such error and/or omission.

5.2.2   Within forty-five (45) days after the end of each ABC fiscal quarter, ABC shall furnish to XYZ a statement in suitable form showing all ABC Business Products and related services subject to royalties that were sold, during such quarter, and the amount of royalty payable thereon. If no products or services subject to royalty have been sold, that fact shall be shown on such statement. Also, within such forty-five (45) days, ABC shall pay to XYZ the royalties payable hereunder for such quarter. XYZ and ABC will determine the form of the statement prior to submission of the first such statement. All royalty and other payments to XYZ hereunder shall be in United States dollars. Royalties based on sales in other currencies shall be converted to United States dollars according to the official rate of exchange for that currency, as published in the Wall Street Journal on the last day of the calendar month in which the royalty accrued (or, if not published on that day, the last publication day for the Wall Street Journal during that month). If two consecutive ABC fiscal quarters pass in which no royalties are due under this Agreement and ABC reasonably believes no royalties will be due, the obligations pursuant to this Article V shall terminate. If ABC resumes sale of ABC Business Products or related services that are subject to royalties, the obligations of this Article V shall automatically resume.

ARTICLE VI
TRADEMARK USAGE GUIDELINES

6.1   TRADEMARK USAGE GUIDELINES. ABC and its Subsidiaries, Affiliated Companies and Authorized Dealers shall use the Licensed Marks only in a manner that is consistent with the Trademark Usage Guidelines.

6.2   TRADEMARK REVIEWS. At XYZ's request, ABC agrees to furnish or make available for inspection to XYZ samples of all ABC Business Products and Collateral Materials of ABC, its Subsidiaries, Affiliated Companies and Authorized Dealers that are marked with one or more of the Licensed Marks (to the extent that ABC has the right to obtain such samples). If ABC is notified or determines that it or any of its Subsidiaries, Affiliated Companies or Authorized Dealers is not complying with any

TRADEMARKS AND LICENSING

Trademark Usage Guidelines, it shall notify XYZ and the provisions of Article VII and Section 4.3 shall apply to such noncompliance.

ARTICLE VII
TRADEMARK USAGE GUIDELINE ENFORCEMENT

7.1 INITIAL CURE PERIOD. If XYZ becomes aware that ABC or any Subsidiary, Affiliated Company or Authorized Dealer is not complying with any Trademark Usage Guidelines, XYZ shall notify ABC in writing, setting forth in reasonable detail a written description of the noncompliance and any requested action for curing such noncompliance. ABC shall then have sixty (60) days with regard to noncompliance by Authorized Dealers and thirty (30) days with regard to noncompliance by ABC or any Subsidiary or Affiliated Company after receipt of such notice ("Guideline Initial Cure Period") to correct such noncompliance or submit to XYZ a written plan to correct such noncompliance which written plan is reasonably acceptable to XYZ.

7.2 SECOND CURE PERIOD. If noncompliance with the Trademark Usage Guidelines continues beyond the Guideline Initial Cure Period, ABC and XYZ shall each promptly appoint a representative to negotiate in good faith actions that may be necessary to correct such noncompliance. The parties shall have thirty (30) days following the expiration of the Guideline Initial Cure Period to agree on corrective actions, and ABC shall have thirty (30) days from the date of an agreement of corrective actions to implement such corrective actions and cure or cause the cure of such noncompliance ("Second Guideline Cure Period").

7.3 FINAL CURE PERIOD. If the noncompliance with the Trademark Usage Guidelines remains uncured after the expiration of the Second Guideline Cure Period, then at XYZ's election, ABC, or the noncomplying Subsidiary, Affiliated Company or Authorized Dealer, whichever is applicable, promptly shall cease using the noncomplying Collateral Materials until XYZ determines that ABC, or the noncomplying Subsidiary, Affiliated Company or Authorized Dealer, whichever is applicable, has demonstrated its ability and commitment to comply with the Trademark Usage Guidelines. Nothing in this Article VII shall be deemed to limit ABC's obligations under Section 4.3 above or to preclude XYZ from exercising any rights or remedies under Section 4.3 above.

ARTICLE VIII
QUALITY STANDARDS

8.1 GENERAL. ABC acknowledges that the ABC Business Products permitted by this Agreement to be marked with one or more of the Licensed Marks must continue to be of sufficiently high quality as to provide protection of the Licensed Marks and the goodwill they symbolize, and ABC further acknowledges that the maintenance of the high-quality standards associated with such products is of the essence of this Agreement.

8.2 QUALITY STANDARDS. ABC and its Authorized Dealers, Affiliated Companies and Subsidiaries shall use the Licensed Marks only on and in connection with ABC Business Products that meet or exceed in all respects the Quality Standards.

8.3 QUALITY CONTROL REVIEWS. At XYZ's request, ABC agrees to furnish or make available to XYZ for inspection sample ABC Business Products marked

TRADEMARK PROTECTION AND PROSECUTION

with one or more of the Licensed Marks. XYZ may also independently conduct customer satisfaction surveys to determine if ABC and its Subsidiaries, Affiliated Companies and Authorized Dealers are meeting the Quality Standards. ABC shall cooperate with XYZ fully in the distribution of such surveys. In the event of a challenge by XYZ, XYZ shall, at the request of ABC, provide ABC with copies of customer surveys used by XYZ to determine if ABC is meeting the Quality Standards. If ABC is notified or determines that it or any of its Subsidiaries, Affiliated Companies or Authorized Dealers is not complying with any Quality Standards, it shall notify XYZ and the provisions of Article IX and Section 4.3 shall apply to such noncompliance.

        8.4   PRODUCT DISCONTINUATION. If, at any time during or after the term of this Agreement, ABC discontinues the sale of a ABC Business Product that has been marked with one or more of the Licensed Marks, ABC shall substantially comply with the discontinuation procedure used by XYZ for such or similar products immediately prior to Separation Date.

ARTICLE IX
QUALITY STANDARD ENFORCEMENT

        9.1   INITIAL CURE PERIOD. If XYZ becomes aware that ABC or any Subsidiary, Affiliated Company or Authorized Dealer sublicensee is not complying with any Quality Standards, XYZ shall notify ABC in writing, setting forth in reasonable detail a written description of the noncompliance and any requested action for curing such noncompliance. ABC shall then have thirty (30) days after receipt of such notice ("Initial Cure Period") to correct such noncompliance or submit to XYZ a written plan to correct such noncompliance which written plan is reasonably acceptable to XYZ.

        9.2   SECOND CURE PERIOD. If noncompliance with the Quality Standards continues beyond the Initial Cure Period, ABC and XYZ shall each promptly appoint a representative to negotiate in good faith actions that may be necessary to correct such noncompliance. The parties shall have thirty (30) days following the expiration of the Initial Cure Period to agree on corrective actions, and ABC shall have thirty (30) days from the date of an agreement of corrective actions to implement such corrective actions and cure or cause the cure of such noncompliance ("Second Cure Period").

        9.3   FINAL CURE PERIOD. If the noncompliance with the Quality Standards remains uncured after the expiration of the Second Cure Period, then at XYZ's election, ABC, or the noncomplying Subsidiary, Affiliated Company or Authorized Dealer, whichever is applicable, promptly shall cease offering the noncomplying ABC Business Products under the Licensed Marks until XYZ determines that ABC, or the noncomplying Subsidiary, Affiliated Company or Authorized Dealer, whichever is applicable, has demonstrated its ability and commitment to comply with the Quality Standards. Nothing in this Article IX shall be deemed to limit ABC's obligations under Section 4.3 above or to preclude XYZ from exercising any rights or remedies under Section 4.3 above.

ARTICLE X
PROTECTION OF LICENSED MARKS

        10.1   OWNERSHIP AND RIGHTS. ABC agrees not to challenge the ownership or validity of the Licensed Marks. ABC shall not disparage, dilute or adversely

TRADEMARKS AND LICENSING

affect the validity of the Licensed Marks. ABC's use of the Licensed Marks shall inure exclusively to the benefit of XYZ, and ABC shall not acquire or assert any rights therein. ABC recognizes the value of the goodwill associated with the Licensed Marks, and that the Licensed Marks may have acquired secondary meaning in the minds of the public.

10.2 PROTECTION OF MARKS. ABC shall assist XYZ, at XYZ's request and expense, in the procurement and maintenance of XYZ's intellectual property rights in the Licensed Marks. ABC will not grant or attempt to grant a security interest in the Licensed Marks, or to record any such security interest in the United States Patent and Trademark Office or elsewhere, against any trademark application or registration belonging to XYZ. ABC agrees to, and to cause its Subsidiaries and Affiliated Companies to, execute all documents reasonably requested by XYZ to effect further registration of, maintenance and renewal of the Licensed Marks, recordation of the license relationship between XYZ and ABC, and recordation of ABC as a registered user. XYZ makes no warranty or representation that trademark registrations have been or will be applied for, secured or maintained in the Licensed Marks throughout, or anywhere within, the world. ABC shall cause to appear on all ABC Business Products, and all Collateral Materials, such legends, markings and notices as may be required by applicable law or reasonably requested by XYZ.

10.3 SIMILAR MARKS. ABC agrees not to use or register in any country any Mark that infringes XYZ's rights in the Licensed Marks, or any element thereof. If any application for registration is, or has been, filed in any country by ABC which relates to any Mark that infringes XYZ's rights in the Licensed Marks, ABC shall immediately abandon any such application or registration or assign it to XYZ. ABC shall not challenge XYZ's ownership of or the validity of the Licensed Marks or any application for registration thereof throughout the world. ABC shall not use or register in any country any copyright, domain name, telephone number or any other intellectual property right, whether recognized currently or in the future, or other designation which would affect the ownership or rights of XYZ in and to the Licensed Marks, or otherwise to take any action which would adversely affect any of such ownership rights, or assist anyone else in doing so. ABC shall cause its Subsidiaries, Affiliated Companies and Authorized Dealers to comply with the provisions of this Section 10.3.

10.4 INFRINGEMENT PROCEEDINGS. In the event that the ABC Director of Intellectual Property or ABC Trademark Counsel learns of any infringement or threatened infringement of the Licensed Marks, or any unfair competition, passing-off or dilution with respect to the Licensed Marks, ABC shall notify XYZ or its authorized representative giving particulars thereof, and ABC shall provide necessary information and assistance to XYZ or its authorized representatives at XYZ's expense in the event that XYZ decides that proceedings should be commenced. Notwithstanding the foregoing, ABC is not obligated to monitor, or police use of the Licensed Marks by Third Parties other than as specifically set forth in Section 4.3. XYZ shall have exclusive control of any litigation, opposition, cancellation or related legal proceedings. The decision whether to bring, maintain or settle any such proceedings shall be at the exclusive option and expense of XYZ, and all recoveries shall belong exclusively to XYZ. ABC shall not and shall have no right to initiate any such litigation, opposition, cancellation or related legal proceedings in its own name, but, at XYZ's request, agrees to be joined as a party in any action taken by XYZ to enforce its rights in the Licensed Marks. XYZ shall incur no liability to ABC or any other

TRADEMARK PROTECTION AND PROSECUTION

Person under any legal theory by reason of XYZ's failure or refusal to prosecute or by XYZ's refusal to permit ABC to prosecute, any alleged infringement by Third Parties, nor by reason of any settlement to which XYZ may agree.

ARTICLE XI
TERMINATION

11.1 VOLUNTARY TERMINATION. By written notice to XYZ, ABC may voluntarily terminate all or a specified portion of the licenses and rights granted to it hereunder by XYZ. Such notice shall specify the effective date of such termination and shall clearly specify any affected Licensed Marks, ABC Business Products or services.

11.2 SURVIVAL. Any voluntary termination of licenses and rights of ABC under Section 11.1 shall not affect ABC's licenses and rights with respect to any ABC Business Products made or furnished prior to such termination.

11.3 OTHER TERMINATION. XYZ acknowledges and agrees that its rights to terminate the licenses granted to ABC hereunder are solely as set forth in Section 4.3 and Articles VII and IX.

ARTICLE XII
DISPUTE RESOLUTION

12.1 NEGOTIATION. The parties shall make a good faith attempt to resolve any dispute or claim arising out of or related to this Agreement through negotiation. Within thirty (30) days after notice of a dispute or claim is given by either party to the other party, the parties' first tier negotiating teams (as determined by each party's Director of Intellectual Property or his or her delegate) shall meet and make a good faith attempt to resolve such dispute or claim and shall continue to negotiate in good faith in an effort to resolve the dispute or claim or renegotiate the applicable section or provision without the necessity of any formal proceedings. If the first tier negotiating teams are unable to agree within thirty (30) days of their first meeting, then the parties' second tier negotiating teams (as determined by each party's Director of Intellectual Property or his or her delegate) shall meet within thirty (30) days after the end of the first thirty (30) day negotiating period to attempt to resolve the matter. During the course of negotiations under this Section 12.1, all reasonable requests made by one party to the other for information, including requests for copies of relevant documents, will be honored. The specific format for such negotiations will be left to the discretion of the designated negotiating teams but may include the preparation of agreed upon statements of fact or written statements of position furnished to the other party.

12.2 NONBINDING MEDIATION. In the event that any dispute or claim arising out of or related to this Agreement is not settled by the parties within fifteen (15) days after the first meeting of the second tier negotiating teams under Section 12.1, the parties will attempt in good faith to resolve such dispute or claim by nonbinding mediation in accordance with the American Arbitration Association Commercial Mediation Rules. The mediation shall be held within thirty (30) days of the end of such fifteen (15) day negotiation period of the second tier negotiating teams. Except as provided below in Section 12.3, no litigation for the resolution of such dispute may be commenced until the parties try in good

TRADEMARKS AND LICENSING

faith to settle the dispute by such mediation in accordance with such rules, and either party has concluded in good faith that amicable resolution through continued mediation of the matter does not appear likely. The costs of mediation shall be shared equally by the parties to the mediation. Any settlement reached by mediation shall be recorded in writing, signed by the parties, and shall be binding on them.

12.3 PROCEEDINGS. Nothing herein, however, shall prohibit either party from initiating litigation or other judicial or administrative proceedings if such party would be substantially harmed by a failure to act during the time that such good faith efforts are being made to resolve the dispute or claim through negotiation or mediation. In the event that litigation is commenced under this Section 12.3, the parties agree to continue to attempt to resolve any dispute or claim according to the terms of Sections 12.1 and 12.2 during the course of such litigation proceedings under this Section 12.3.

ARTICLE XIII
LIMITATION OF LIABILITY

IN NO EVENT SHALL EITHER PARTY OR ITS SUBSIDIARIES OR AFFILIATED COMPANIES BE LIABLE TO THE OTHER PARTY OR ITS SUBSIDIARIES OR AFFILIATED COMPANIES FOR ANY DAMAGES, INCLUDING WITHOUT LIMITATION SPECIAL, CONSEQUENTIAL, INDIRECT, INCIDENTAL OR PUNITIVE DAMAGES OR LOST PROFITS OR ANY OTHER DAMAGES, HOWEVER CAUSED AND ON ANY THEORY OF LIABILITY (INCLUDING NEGLIGENCE) ARISING IN ANY WAY OUT OF THIS AGREEMENT, WHETHER OR NOT SUCH PARTY HAS BEEN ADVISED OF THE POSSIBILITY OF SUCH DAMAGES; PROVIDED, HOWEVER, THAT THE FOREGOING LIMITATIONS SHALL NOT LIMIT EACH PARTY'S OBLIGATIONS EXPRESSLY ASSUMED IN EXHIBIT K OF THE SEPARATION AGREEMENT; PROVIDED FURTHER THAT THE EXCLUSION OF PUNITIVE DAMAGES SHALL APPLY IN ANY EVENT.

ARTICLE XIV
MISCELLANEOUS PROVISIONS

14.1 DISCLAIMER. EACH PARTY ACKNOWLEDGES AND AGREES THAT ALL LICENSED MARKS AND ANY OTHER INFORMATION OR MATERIALS LICENSED OR PROVIDED HEREUNDER ARE LICENSED OR PROVIDED ON AN "AS IS" BASIS AND THAT NEITHER PARTY NOR ANY OF ITS SUBSIDIARIES OR AFFILIATED COMPANIES MAKES ANY REPRESENTATIONS OR EXTENDS ANY WARRANTIES WHATSOEVER, EXPRESS, IMPLIED OR STATUTORY, WITH RESPECT THERETO INCLUDING WITHOUT LIMITATION ANY IMPLIED WARRANTIES OF TITLE, ENFORCEABILITY OR NON-INFRINGEMENT. Without limiting the generality of the foregoing, neither XYZ nor any of its Subsidiaries or Affiliated Companies makes any warranty or representation as to the validity of any Mark licensed by it to ABC or any warranty or representation that any use of any Mark with respect to any product or service will be free from infringement of any rights of any Third Party.

14.2 NO IMPLIED LICENSES. Nothing contained in this Agreement shall be construed as conferring any rights by implication, estoppel or otherwise, under any

TRADEMARK PROTECTION AND PROSECUTION

intellectual property right, other than the rights expressly granted in this Agreement with respect to the Licensed Marks. Neither party is required hereunder to furnish or disclose to the other any information (including copies of registrations of the Marks), except as specifically provided herein.

14.3   INFRINGEMENT SUITS. Except as set forth in Section 4.3, (i) neither party shall have any obligation hereunder to institute any action or suit against Third Parties for infringement of any of the Licensed Marks or to defend any action or suit brought by a Third Party which challenges or concerns the validity of any of the Licensed Marks and (ii) ABC shall not have any right to institute any action or suit against Third Parties for infringement of any of the Licensed Marks.

14.4   NO OTHER OBLIGATIONS. NEITHER PARTY ASSUMES ANY RESPONSIBILITIES OR OBLIGATIONS WHATSOEVER, OTHER THAN THE RESPONSIBILITIES AND OBLIGATIONS EXPRESSLY SET FORTH IN THIS AGREEMENT OR A SEPARATE WRITTEN AGREEMENT BETWEEN THE PARTIES. Without limiting the generality of the foregoing, neither party, nor any of its Subsidiaries or Affiliated Companies, is obligated to (i) file any application for registration of any Mark, or to secure any rights in any Marks, (ii) to maintain any Mark registration, or (iii) provide any assistance, except for the obligations expressly assumed in this Agreement.

14.5   ENTIRE AGREEMENT. This Agreement, the Separation Agreement and the other Ancillary Agreements (as defined in the Separation Agreement) constitute the entire agreement between the parties with respect to the subject matter hereof and shall supersede all prior written and oral and all contemporaneous oral agreements and understandings with respect to the subject matter hereof. To the extent there is a conflict between this Agreement and the General Assignment and Assumption Agreement between the parties, the terms of this Agreement shall govern.

14.6   GOVERNING LAW. This Agreement shall be governed by and construed and enforced in accordance with the laws of the State of _____ as to all matters regardless of the laws that might otherwise govern under principles of conflicts of laws applicable thereto.

14.7   DESCRIPTIVE HEADINGS. The descriptive headings herein are inserted for convenience of reference only and are not intended to be part of or to affect the meaning or interpretation of this Agreement.

14.8   NOTICES. All notices and other communications hereunder shall be in writing and shall be deemed to have been duly given when delivered in person, by telecopy with answer back, by express or overnight mail delivered by a nationally recognized air courier (delivery charges prepaid), by registered or certified mail (postage prepaid, return receipt requested) or by e-mail with receipt confirmed by return e-mail to the respective parties as follows:

TRADEMARKS AND LICENSING

    if to XYZ:
        XYZ Corporation
        _____

        _____
        Attention: _____
        Telecopy: _____
    if to ABC, Inc.:

        _____

        _____
        Attention: _____
        Telecopy: _____

or to such other address as the party to whom notice is given may have previously furnished to the other in writing in the manner set forth above. Any notice or communication delivered in person shall be deemed effective on delivery. Any notice or communication sent by e-mail, telecopy or by air courier shall be deemed effective on the first Business Day following the day on which such notice or communication was sent. Any notice or communication sent by registered or certified mail shall be deemed effective on the third Business Day following the day on which such notice or communication was mailed. As used in this Section 14.8, "Business Day" means day other than a Saturday, a Sunday or a day on which banking institutions located in the State of _____ are authorized or obligated by law or executive order to close.

    14.9   NONASSIGNABILITY. Neither party may, directly or indirectly, in whole or in part, whether by operation of law or otherwise, assign or transfer this Agreement, without the other party's prior written consent, and any attempted assignment, transfer or delegation without such prior written consent shall be voidable at the sole option of such other party. Notwithstanding the foregoing, each party (or its permitted successive assignees or transferees hereunder) may assign or transfer this Agreement as a whole without consent to a Person that succeeds to all or substantially all of the business or assets of such party. Without limiting the foregoing, this Agreement will be binding upon and inure to the benefit of the parties and their permitted successors and assigns.

    14.10   SEVERABILITY. If any term or other provision of this Agreement is determined by a non-appealable decision of a court, administrative agency or arbitrator to be invalid, illegal or incapable of being enforced by any rule of law or public policy, all other conditions and provisions of this Agreement shall nevertheless remain in full force and effect so long as the economic or legal substance of the transactions contemplated hereby is not affected in any manner materially adverse to either party. Upon such determination that any term or other provision is invalid, illegal or incapable of being enforced, the parties hereto shall negotiate in good faith to modify this Agreement so as to affect the original intent of the parties as closely as possible in an acceptable manner to the end that the transactions contemplated hereby are fulfilled to the fullest extent possible.

    14.11   FAILURE OR INDULGENCE NOT WAIVER; REMEDIES CUMULATIVE. No failure or delay on the part of either party hereto in the exercise of any right hereunder shall impair such right or be construed to be a waiver of, or acquiescence in, any breach of any representation, warranty or agreement herein, nor shall any single or

TRADEMARK PROTECTION AND PROSECUTION

partial exercise of any such right preclude other or further exercise thereof or of any other right. All rights and remedies existing under this Agreement are cumulative to, and not exclusive of, any rights or remedies otherwise available.

    14.12   AMENDMENT. No change or amendment will be made to this Agreement except by an instrument in writing signed on behalf of each of the parties to such agreement.

    14.13   COUNTERPARTS. This Agreement may be executed in two or more counterparts, all of which, taken together, shall be considered to be one and the same instrument.

    WHEREFORE, the parties have signed this Trademark Ownership and License Agreement effective as of the date first set forth above.

XYZ Corporation	ABC, Inc.
By: _____	By: _____
Name: _____	Name: _____
Title: _____	Title: _____

CHAPTER 14

TRADEMARK ASSIGNMENTS

During the examination of a pending trademark application as well as after a trademark has registered, the owner of a trademark may change for various reasons. Some trademark owners transfer the ownership of a mark to another entity, which is called an assignment. In addition, some trademark owners change their names while retaining ownership. In both instances, the USPTO advises trademark owners to record the ownership transfer (assignment) or (name change) with the Assignment Recordation Branch of the USPTO.

Note: An applicant cannot assign an intent to use application before the application files an amendment to allege use except to a successor to the applicant's business, or portion of the business to which the mark pertains, if that business is ongoing and existing.

Recording an Assignment Online

To record an assignment or name change, the owner must file a Recordation Form Cover Sheet along with a copy of the actual assignment or proof of name change. Requests to record documents in the Assignment Recordation Branch can be filed through the USPTO website.

Recording an Assignment by Paper

Paper documents and cover sheets to be recorded in the Assignment Recordation Branch should be sent to: Mail Stop Assignment Recordation Branch, Director of the United States Patent and Trademark Office, PO Box 1450, Alexandria, VA 22313-1450.

TRADEMARK PROTECTION AND PROSECUTION

SAMPLE RECORDATION FORM COVER SHEET FORM

Form PTO-1594 (Rev. 03-11)
OMB Collection 0651-0027 (exp. 03/31/2012)

U.S. DEPARTMENT OF COMMERCE
United States Patent and Trademark Office

RECORDATION FORM COVER SHEET
TRADEMARKS ONLY

To the Director of the U. S. Patent and Trademark Office: Please record the attached documents or the new address(es) below

1. Name of conveying party(ies):

- [ ] Individual(s)
- [ ] Association
- [ ] General Partnership
- [ ] Limited Partnership
- [ ] Corporation- State: _____
- [ ] Other _____

Citizenship (see guidelines) _____

Additional names of conveying parties attached? [ ] Yes [ ] No

2. Name and address of receiving party(ies)

Additional names, addresses, or citizenship attached? [ ] Yes [ ] No

Name: _____
Internal Address: _____
Street Address: _____
City: _____
State: _____
Country: _____ Zip: _____

- [ ] Association Citizenship _____
- [ ] General Partnership Citizenship _____
- [ ] Limited Partnership Citizenship _____
- [ ] Corporation Citizenship _____
- [ ] Other _____ Citizenship _____

If assignee is not domiciled in the United States, a domestic representative designation is attached [ ] Yes [ ] No
(Designations must be a separate document from assignment)

3. Nature of conveyance)/Execution Date(s) :

Execution Date(s) _____

- [ ] Assignment
- [ ] Merger
- [ ] Security Agreement
- [ ] Change of Name
- [ ] Other _____

4. Application number(s) or registration number(s) and identification or description of the Trademark.

A. Trademark Application No.(s) _____

B. Trademark Registration No.(s) _____

Additional sheet(s) attached? [ ] Yes [ ] No

C. Identification or Description of Trademark(s) (and Filing Date if Application or Registration Number is unknown):

5. Name & address of party to whom correspondence concerning document should be mailed:

Name: _____
Internal Address: _____
Street Address: _____
City: _____
State: _____ Zip: _____
Phone Number: _____
Fax Number: _____
Email Address: _____

6. Total number of applications and registrations involved: _____

7. Total fee (37 CFR 2.6(b)(6) & 3.41) $ _____

- [ ] Authorized to be charged to deposit account
- [ ] Enclosed

8. Payment Information:

Deposit Account Number _____
Authorized User Name _____

9. Signature:

_____ _____
Signature Date

_____
Name of Person Signing

Total number of pages including cover sheet, attachments, and document: _____

Documents to be recorded (including cover sheet) should be faxed to (571) 273-0140, or mailed to:
Mail Stop Assignment Recordation Services, Director of the USPTO, P.O. Box 1450, Alexandria, VA 22313-1450

TRADEMARK ASSIGNMENTS

SAMPLE RECORDATION FORM COVER SHEET FORM

Guidelines for Completing Trademarks Cover Sheets (PTO-1594)

Cover Sheet information must be submitted with each document to be recorded. If the document to be recorded concerns both patents and trademarks, separate patent and trademark cover sheets, including any attached pages for continuing information, must accompany the document. All pages of the cover sheet should be numbered consecutively for example, if both a patent and trademark cover sheet is used, and information is continued on an additional page for both patents and trademarks, the pages of the cover sheet would be numbered from 1 to 4.

Item 1. Name of Conveying Party(ies).
Enter the full name of the party(ies) conveying the interest. If there is more than one conveying party, enter a check mark in the "Yes" box to indicate that additional information is attached. The name of the second and any subsequent conveying party(ies) should be placed on an attached page clearly identified as a continuation of the information in Item 1. Enter a check mark in the "No" box, if no information is contained on an attached page.

Item 2. Name and Address of Receiving Party(ies).
Enter the name and full address of the first party receiving the interest. If there is more than one party receiving the interest, enter a check mark in the "Yes" box to indicate that additional information is attached. If the receiving party is an individual, check the "other" box, place the word "individual" in the following line, and enter the citizenship of the receiving individual. If the receiving party is a legal entity, designate the legal entity of the receiving party by checking the appropriate box. If the receiving party has more than one citizenship, then the citizenship of each partner should be specified on an additional sheet, and "See additional sheet" should be written on the line for citizenship. A corporation must set forth the state, if applicable, or country of incorporation. An association must set forth the state, if applicable, or country under which they are organized. If the receiving party is not domiciled in the United States, a designation of domestic representative is encouraged. Place a check mark in the appropriate box to indicate whether or not a designation of domestic representative is attached. Enter a check mark in the "No" box if no information is contained on an attached page.

Item 3. Nature of Conveyance/Execution Date(s).
Enter the execution date(s) of the document. It is preferable to use the name of the month, or an abbreviation of that name, to minimize confusion over dates. In addition, place a check mark in the appropriate box describing the nature of the conveying document. If the "Other" box is checked, specify the nature of the conveyance. The "Other" box should be checked if the conveying/receiving party is correcting a previously filed document.

Item 4. Application Number(s) or Registration Number(s).
Indicate the application number(s) including series code and serial number, and/or registration number(s) against which the document is to be recorded. The identification of the trademark should be provided for all properties to avoid recordation against the wrong property. A filing date should be provided only when the application or registration number is unknown. Enter a check mark in the appropriate box. "Yes" or "No" if additional numbers appear on attached pages. Be sure to identify numbers included on attached pages as the continuation of Item 4.

Item 5. Name and Address of Party to whom correspondence concerning document should be mailed.
Enter the name and full address of the party to whom correspondence is to be mailed.

Item 6. Total Applications and Trademarks Involved.
Enter the total number of applications and trademarks identified for recordation. Be sure to include all applications and registrations identified on the cover sheet and on additional pages.

Block 7. Total Fee Enclosed.
Enter the total fee enclosed or authorized to be charged. A fee is required for each application and registration against which the document is recorded.

Item 8. Payment Information.
Enter the deposit account number and authorized user name to authorize charges.

Item 9. Signature.
Enter the name of the person submitting the document. The submitter must sign and date the cover sheet. Enter the total number of pages including the cover sheet, attachments, and document.

This collection of information is required by 35 USC 261 and 262 and 15 USC 1057 and 1060. The information is used by the public to submit (and by the USPTO to process) patent and trademark assignment requests. After the USPTO records the information, the records for patent and trademark assignments and other associated documents can be inspected by the public. To view documents recorded under secrecy orders or documents recorded due to the interest of the federal government, a written authorization must be submitted. This collection is estimated to take 30 minutes to complete, including gathering, preparing, and submitting the form to the USPTO. Any comments on the amount of time you require to complete this form and/or suggestions for reducing this burden, should be sent to the Manager of the Assignment Division, Crystal Gateway 4, Room 310, 1213 Jefferson Davis Highway, Arlington, VA 22202. DO NOT SEND FEES OR COMPLETED FORMS TO THIS ADDRESS. SEND TO: Mail Stop Assignment Recordation Services, Director of the USPTO, P.O. Box 1450, Alexandria, VA 22313-1450.

Privacy Act Statement for Patent Assignment Recordation Form Cover Sheet

The Privacy Act of 1974 (P.L. 93-579) requires that you be given certain information in connection with the above request for information. This collection of information is authorized by 35 U.S.C. 1, 2, 261 and E.O. 9424. This information will primarily be used by the USPTO for the recordation of assignments related to patents and patent applications. Submission of this information is voluntary but is required in order for the USPTO to record the requested assignment. If you do not provide the information required on the cover sheet, the assignment will not be recorded, and all documents will be returned to you.

After the information is recorded, the records and associated documents can be inspected by the public and are not confidential, except for documents that are sealed under secrecy orders or related to unpublished patent applications. Assignment records relating to unpublished patent applications are maintained in confidence in accordance with 35 U.S.C. 122. Records open to the public are searched by users for the purpose of determining ownership for other property rights with respect to patents and trademarks.

Routine uses of the information you provide may also include disclosure to appropriate Federal, state, local, or foreign agencies in support of their enforcement duties and statutory or regulatory missions, including investigating potential violations of law or contract and awarding contracts or other benefits; to a court, magistrate, or administrative tribunal in the course of presenting evidence; to members of Congress responding to requests for assistance from their constituents; to the Office of Management and Budget in connection with the review of private relief legislation; to the Department of Justice in connection with a Freedom of Information Act request; to a contractor in the performance of their duties; to the Office of Personnel Management for personnel studies; and to the General Services Administration (GSA) as part of their records management responsibilities under the authority of 44 U.S.C. 2904 and 2906. Such disclosure to GSA shall not be used to make determinations about individuals.

TRADEMARK ASSIGNMENTS

Assignment Agreement

The following agreement is not intended to be comprehensive or an absolute statement of the governing law. This agreement is not legal advice. It does not analyze any specific fact patterns from any parties but rather discusses broadly points of law, which may or may not be the most accurate, according to current case law interpretation or even case law interpretation that is very in-depth on very narrowly presented issues. Sound legal advice arises from interaction between client and attorney in a question-and-answer dialogue where facts are provided by a client as the attorney probes for issues and then conducts appropriate research if need be, to ascertain the applicable law. Anyone seeking specific advice to specific legal questions should present their facts to an attorney.

SAMPLE
ASSIGNMENT OF SERVICE MARKS AND TRADEMARKS

ASSIGNMENT OF SERVICE MARKS AND TRADEMARKS made as of _____, 20__, by and among XYZ Inc., a _____ corporation with its principal place of business at _____ ("XYZ"), and ABC Corporation, a _____ corporation with its principal place of business at _____ ("ABC") (XYZ and ABC are referred to as "Assignor"), to NYC Corporation, a _____ corporation with its principal place of business _____ ("Assignee").

RECITAL

Assignee and Assignor are parties to an Asset Purchase Agreement dated as of _____, 20__ (the "Agreement"), pursuant to which Assignor has agreed to sell to Assignee and Assignee has agreed to buy from Assignor the Assets (as defined in the Agreement), including without limitation the service marks, trademarks and trade names of Assignor. Pursuant to the Agreement, Assignor has agreed to execute such instruments as the Assignee may reasonably request in order to more effectively assign, transfer, grant, convey, assure and confirm to Assignee and its successors and assigns, or to aid and assist in the collection of or reducing to possession by the Assignee of, all of such assets.

In accordance therewith, Assignor desires to transfer and assign to Assignee, and Assignee desires to accept the transfer and assignment of, all of Assignor's worldwide right, title and interest in, to and under Assignor's registered and unregistered domestic and foreign service marks, trademarks, trademark applications and trade names, including without limitation the service marks, trademarks, service mark and trademark applications and trade names listed on Schedule A annexed hereto and incorporated herein by reference (all of the foregoing being referred to herein as the "Marks").

NOW, THEREFORE, Assignor, for and in exchange for the payment of the purchase price set forth in the Agreement, the receipt of which is hereby acknowledged, does hereby transfer and assign to Assignee, and Assignee hereby accepts the transfer and assignment of, all of Assignor's worldwide right, title and interest in, to and under the Marks, together

TRADEMARK PROTECTION AND PROSECUTION

with the goodwill of the business associated therewith and which is symbolized thereby, all rights to sue for infringement of any Mark, whether arising prior to or subsequent to the date of this Assignment of Service Marks and Trademarks, and any and all renewals and extensions thereof that may hereafter be secured under the laws now or hereafter in effect in the United States, Canada and in any other jurisdiction, the same to be held and enjoyed by the said Assignee, its successors and assigns from and after the date hereof as fully and entirely as the same would have been held and enjoyed by the said Assignor had this Assignment of Service Marks and Trademarks not been made.

Except to the extent that federal law preempts state law with respect to the matters covered hereby, this Assignment of Service Marks and Trademarks shall be governed by and construed in accordance with the laws of the State of _____ without giving effect to the principles of conflicts of laws thereof.

IN WITNESS WHEREOF, Assignor has caused its duly authorized officer to execute this Assignment of Service Marks and Trademarks as of the date first above written.

NYC CORPORATION   ABC CORPORATION
(Assignee):   (Assignor):
By: _____   By: _____
Name: _____   Name: _____
Title: _____   Title: _____

XYZ INC. (Assignor):
By: _____
Name: _____
Title: _____

[SEAL]

State of _____)
County of _____)

On this _____ day of _____, 20__, before me, _____, personally appeared _____ of _____, personally known to me (or proved to me on the basis of satisfactory evidence) to be the person whose name is subscribed to the within instrument and acknowledged to me that he executed the same in his authorized capacity and that by his signature on the instrument the person, or the entity upon behalf of which the person acted, executed the instrument.

Witness my hand and official seal.

_____
Notary Public

TRADEMARK ASSIGNMENTS

SCHEDULE A

Mark	**Description**
XYZ Inc.	Corporate name
ABC Corporation	Corporate name
Corporate logo	Corporate logo with "XYZ Inc."
MSDS	Metabolic Screening Database System (software)
CMS	Case Management System (software)
CEM	Data Reduction System (software)
DR	Data Repository (software)
VRS	Voice Response System (software)
EBP	Electronic Birth Pages (software)
WebEBP	Web Based Electronic Birth Pages (software)
WebEAR	Web Based Early Auditory Reporting (software)
RDES	Remote Data Entry System (software)
NBS	Newborn Supply System (software)

CHAPTER 15

TRADEMARK ENFORCEMENT

The International Trademark Association (INTA) is a worldwide not-for-profit association of member companies and firms that supports and advances trademarks and intellectual property as elements of fair and effective global commerce. INTA, originally known as the United States Trademark Association (USTA), was established in November 1878 in New York City by seventeen merchants and manufacturers to protect and promote the rights of trademark owners, secure useful legislation, and give aid and encouragement to all efforts for the advancement and observance of trademark rights.

- ❖ In 1908, the Association became a business corporation under the Business Corporation Law of the State of New York, and it was given broad powers to act for the protection of trademarks in the United States and around the world.

- ❖ In 1926, the USTA became a not-for-profit member organization.

- ❖ In 1946, the USTA worked in support of the Lanham Act, which remains the federal trademark law in the United States. The Act defines a trademark as "any word, name, symbol, or device or any combination thereof adopted by a manufacturer or merchant to define his or her goods or services and distinguish them from those manufactured or sold by others."

- ❖ In 1949, USTA's advocacy led to the creation of the Model State Trademark Bill (MSTB) which addressed the threat of mandatory state trademark registration and legislation. The MSTB is the foundation for trademark statutes across the United States and provides a set of standards for the establishment, maintenance and enforcement of United States trademark rights.

- In 1985, the USTA created a Trademark Review Commission to review the United States trademark system, including the Lanham Act, and to recommend updates to meet the changing intellectual property landscape. In 1990, Congress enacted the Trademark Law Revision Act.

- In 1993, the Association changed its name to the International Trademark Association to reflect the diversity of its membership and the breadth of its activities.

- In 1995, The Agreement on Trade-Related Aspects of Intellectual Property Rights (TRIPS), which stresses the importance of harmonization of enforcement standards, went into effect under the jurisdiction of the World Trade Organization (WTO).

- In 1996, the United States Congress passed the Federal Trademark Dilution Act (FTDA), a federal statute meant to prevent the dilution of the value of famous trademarks by blurring or tarnishment.

- In 2005, The Association released a Model Free Trade Agreement to provide the parties of free trade agreements with a set of baseline proposals to consider when negotiating trademark-related provisions.

- In 2006, a new United States trademark dilution statute that protects famous marks from uses that blur their distinctiveness or tarnish their reputation was signed into law on October 6.

- In February 2009, INTA embraced the social media trend and extended its online networking sites with LinkedIn and Twitter.

- In May 2009, INTA attended its first OHIM Administrative Board meeting as an observer, along with four other trademark users' organizations in Europe (AIM, BUSINESSEUROPE, ECTA, and MARQUES).

Today, INTA provides services to its members and the public in three main areas:

- **Information and Publishing.** INTA has a collection of resources, which include country portals, trademark cancellations, country guides and others. Additionally, INTA has two in-house news publications, available in print and online: The Trademark Reporter, a bi-monthly scholarly journal that explores all aspects of trademark law, and the INTA Bulletin, a bi-weekly newsletter that provides up-to-date news on Association issues, trends in trademark law practice and procedure.

❖ **Education and Training.** INTA offers numerous conferences, forums, roundtables, workshops and e-learning programs that bring trademark professionals together from around the world to discuss trademark issues, intellectual property law and practice.

❖ **Policy Development and Advocacy.** The Association, often in cooperation with other national, regional and international intellectual property organizations, is the voice of trademark owners worldwide and focuses on taking public policy positions and protecting brand owners' rights.

INTA's largest event is the Annual Meeting, which dates back to 1878. The Meeting attracts participants from around the globe, and it consists of five days of networking, educational and professional development opportunities, as well as committee meetings and exhibits.

Trademark Counterfeiting Act of 1984

The Trademark Counterfeiting Act of 1984 is a United States federal law that amended the federal criminal code to make it a federal offense to violate the Lanham Act by the intentional use of a counterfeit trademark or the unauthorized use of a counterfeit trademark. The act established penalties of up to five years imprisonment and/or a $250,000 fine ($1,000,000 fine for a corporation or other legal entity) for selling or attempting to sell counterfeit goods or services. It increased such penalties for a second or subsequent conviction under the Act.

Trademark Act of 1870

Trademark law dates back to the age of President Ulysses S. Grant starting in the late nineteenth century with the Trademark Act of 1870. The Trademark Act of 1870 was the first trademark act passed in the nation and grounded trademark protection into Article 1 of the U.S. Constitution. The Trademark Act covered many different aspects of trademark law but failed to cover trademark counterfeiting. After much protest from merchants and manufacturers around the country, Congress amended the Trademark Act to make counterfeiting a crime. This however was short lived, as the case U.S. vs. Steffens in 1879 ruled that Article 1 of the Constitution could not serve as a basis of authority and thus making the Trademark Act of 1870 unconstitutional.

All trademark acts after the 1870 one, including the 1881 Trademark Act and the 1946 Trademark Act (The Lanham Act), make no mention of the trademark counterfeiting provision of the 1870 Trademark Act.

By the 1970s, counterfeiting was costing U.S. companies billions of dollars upwards of $100 billion in the years leading up to the Trademark Counterfeiting Act of 1984. Unless the counterfeiting manufacturer was large enough, little could be done to prosecute illegal counterfeiters. Most counterfeit manufactures were small companies that once a civil suit was filed against them, would virtually disappear. Lack of penalties for counterfeiters also meant that products could be sold that were not safe and up to regulatory standards including medications, cosmetics, and machinery parts.

In October 1984, after much lobbying by industry groups, mainly the International Anti-Counterfeiting Coalition (IACC), President Ronald Reagan signed into law the Trademark Counterfeiting Act of 1984. Senator Charles Mathias Jr., the Chairman of the subcommittee on Patents, Copyrights, and Trademarks of the Senate Judiciary Committee sponsored the Act. In enacting the Trademark Counterfeiting Act of 1984, Congress sought to provide trademark owners with more powerful weapons against persons involved in trademark counterfeiting, including protection of not only intentional copying of trademarks, but also entire products as well. Those who were in favor of the Act were pleased with it while those against it claimed it was "manifestly unfair," "heavy handed," and "overreaching."

Penalties under the Act

> "The Senate and House bills both aimed at accomplishing three primary changes in the law: First, creation of criminal penalties for intentionally dealing in materials that one knows to be counterfeit; second, authorization for mandatory or virtually mandatory awards of treble damages and attorneys' fees in civil counterfeiting cases; and third, authorization for ex parte court orders for the seizure of counterfeit materials when it can be shown that the defendant would be likely to attempt to conceal or transfer the materials."

The Trademark Counterfeiting Act of 1984 made it illegal for anyone to intentionally traffic or attempt to traffic goods or services knowingly using a counterfeit mark, which is defined as "a spurious mark and spurious designations (1) used in connection with trafficking in goods or services (2) identical with, or substantially indistinguishable from, a mark registered for those goods and services on the USPTO's Principal Register (whether or not the defendant knew the mark was registered) and in use and (3) the use of which is likely to deceive, confuse, or cause mistake on the part of the consuming public." These counterfeit goods include numerous things such as labels, stickers, wrappers, charms, cases, tags, and patches.

Originally under the Act, the penalty for being convicted for trademark counterfeiting was a fine up to $100,000 and a prison sentence of up to five years plus paying attorney fees to the trademark owners. These penalties were later amended and called for a fine of up to $2 million and/or imprisonment for up to ten years, with large companies being fined up to $5 million. If charged more than once for trademark infringement, individuals can be fined up to $5 million and/or be imprisoned for up to twenty years while corporations may be fined up to $15 million. Counterfeiters of safety-sensitive products, such as pharmaceuticals, would get the maximum penalty set forward in the Act.

Ex Parte Seizure

One of the most powerful provisions under the Trademark Act of 1984 is that of ex parte seizure. Under this part of the Act, an aggrieved party may seize the counterfeit goods, business documents, and machines used that the counterfeiter has without notice to the counterfeiter. The section on ex parte seizure amends the Lanham Act, creating stronger remedies in civil cases involving the intentional use of counterfeit trademarks.

Trademark registrants may apply for an ex parte seizure through the courts without notifying the counterfeiting party. The courts, however, will not grant the ex parte seizure unless:

- ❖ The applicant knows where the goods to be seized are located;
- ❖ The ex parte seizure will show that there was in fact trademark infringement;
- ❖ An ex parte seizure is the only order that is adequate;
- ❖ The applicant specifies the time period the seizure will occur within a limited time frame;
- ❖ The seizure is not publicized;
- ❖ The harm to the trademark holder is greater than the harm to the counterfeiter;
- ❖ Immediate harm will occur without the seizure to the trademark holder; and

❖ The person obtaining the order provides security to cover the damages the adverse party may suffer due to the ex parte seizure.

The second provision of the Trademark Counterfeiting Act of 1984 deals with damages that may be recovered against users of counterfeit trademarks; treble profits or damages (damages awarded in an amount that is three times the amount for which the wrongdoer is found liable for), whichever is greater, and reasonable attorney fees.

Counterfeiting Today

Counterfeiting is still a large problem in the world economy today, one that has mushroomed into a machine that doesn't give signs of letting up any time soon. The garment industry is one of the largest areas of counterfeit goods. Louis Vuitton estimates two to three million counterfeit Louis Vuitton pieces are produced each year, about twice the number of genuine products they manufacture. Because of this, Louis Vuitton spends upwards of five percent of its revenue fighting off counterfeiters; about fifteen hundred actions/civil proceedings. According to the International Trademark Association, between 1991 through 1995, apparel and footwear companies lost twenty-two percent of their sales, around $2.1 billion, due to trademark counterfeiting.

Anticybersquatting Consumer Protection Act

The Anticybersquatting Consumer Protection Act (ACPA) is an American law enacted in 1999 and established a cause of action for registering, trafficking in, or using a domain name confusingly similar to, or dilutive of, a trademark or personal name. The law was designed to thwart "cybersquatters" who register Internet domain names containing trademarks with no intention of creating a legitimate website, but instead plan to sell the domain name to the trademark owner or third party. Critics of the ACPA complain about the non-global scope of the ACPA Act and its potential to restrict free speech, while others refute these complaints.

Before the ACPA was enacted, trademark owners relied heavily on the Federal Trademark Dilution Act (FTDA) to sue domain name registrants. The FTDA was enacted in 1995 in part with the intent to curb domain name abuses. The legislative history of the FTDA specifically mentions that trademark dilution in domain names was a matter of Congressional concern motivating the Act. Senator Leahy stated, "It is my hope that this anti-dilution statute can help stem the use of deceptive Internet addresses taken by those who are choosing marks that are associated with the products and reputations of others."

TRADEMARK PROTECTION AND PROSECUTION

Overview of the ACPA

Under the ACPA, a trademark owner may bring a cause of action against a domain name registrant who (1) has a bad faith intent to profit from the mark and (2) registers, traffics in, or uses a domain name that is (a) identical or confusingly similar to a distinctive mark, (b) identical or confusingly similar to or dilutive of a famous mark, or (c) is a trademark protected by 18 U.S.C. Section 706.

A trademark is famous if the owner can prove that the mark "is widely recognized by the general consuming public of the United States as a designation of source of the goods or services of the mark's owner.

"Trafficking" in the context of domain names includes, but is not limited to "sales, purchases, loans, pledges, licenses, exchanges of currency, and any other transfer for consideration or receipt in exchange for consideration.

In determining whether the domain name registrant has a bad faith intent to profit a court may consider many factors including the following, which are outlined in the statute:

1. The registrant's trademark or other intellectual property rights in the domain name;

2. Whether the domain name contains the registrant's legal or common name;

3. The registrant's prior use of the domain name in connection with the bona fide offering of goods or services;

4. The registrant's bona fide noncommercial or fair use of the mark in a site accessible by the domain name;

5. The registrant's intent to divert customers from the mark owner's online location that could harm the goodwill represented by the mark, for commercial gain or with the intent to tarnish or disparage the mark;

6. The registrant's offer to transfer, sell, or otherwise assign the domain name to the mark owner or a third party for financial gain, without having used the mark in a legitimate site;

7. The registrant's providing misleading false contact information when applying for registration of the domain name;

8. The registrant's registration or acquisition of multiple domain names that are identical or confusingly similar to marks of others; and

TRADEMARK ENFORCEMENT

9. The extent to which the mark in the domain is distinctive or famous.

The ACPA does not prevent the fair use of trademarks or any use protected by the First Amendment, which includes gripe sites. Additionally, the domain name registrar or registry or other domain name authority is not liable for injunctive or monetary relief except in the case of bad faith or reckless disregard. While Section 1125 protects trademark owners, 15 U.S.C. Section 1129 protects any living person from having their personal name included in a domain name, but only when the domain name is registered for profitable resale.

The ACPA also provides that the trademark owner can file an *in rem* (directed towards a piece of property rather than against a person) action against the domain name in the judicial district where the domain name registrar, domain name registry, or other domain name authority registered or assigned the domain name is located if (1) the domain name violates any right of the trademark owner and (2) the court finds that the owner (a) is not able to obtain *in personam* (directed against a person rather than towards a piece of property) jurisdiction over the person who would have been a defendant under 15 U.S.C. Section 1125(d)(1); or (b) through due diligence was not able to find a person who would have been a defendant under 15 U.S.C. Section 1125(d)(1) by sending a notice of the alleged violation and publishing notice of the action. This provision is rarely used, however, because many trademark owners can achieve the same results through a Uniform Domain Name Dispute Resolution Policy (UDRP) proceeding.

ABOUT THE AUTHOR

New book by California lawyer, Ann Carrington, Business Structures and Incorporation — How-To and Do-It-Yourself. Carrington has brought her expertise as a lawyer to numerous startup businesses. A graduate of Lincoln Law School, she spent her career in the heart of Silicon Valley. Ann Carrington is also the author of two other books: Trademark Protection and Prosecution and Writing Winning Business Plans and Investor Presentations. Working in corporate law for more than 20 years, she had written many articles about business processes and procedures, corporate governance, and legal matters. Along the way, she became fascinated by the large number of "mom and pop" businesses not properly structured, protected, or planned because of lack of knowledge or money to afford an attorney; subsequently, she spent time organizing her articles, and the main information in her books is loosely based on those articles.

ABOUT AUTHORSDOOR GROUP

AuthorsDoor Group is an imprint of The Ridge Publishing Group, and publisher of the Roadmap Strategies for Startups series by Ann Carrington: (1) Business Structures and Incorporation, (2) Trademark Protection and Prosecution, and (3) Writing Winning Business Plans and Investor Presentations; the EntrepreneursOpen series by Melania Patterson: (1) Independent Publishing Website Platform, (2) Independent Publishing Must Haves: Blogsite and Social Media Platforms, and (3) Independent Publishing with Amazon, IngramSpark, and Others; and The Millionaire Mindset series and four Companion books by Lori Ann Moeszinger: (1) The Millionaire Writing and Publishing Mindset, (2) The Millionaire Marketing Mindset, (3) The Millionaire Sales and Advertising Mindset, (4) The Millionaire Branding Mindset, and (5) The Millionaire Public Relations Mindset. For more information, visit our website at https://www.AuthorsDoor.com.

ABOUT THE RIDGE PUBLISHING GROUP

The Ridge Publishing Group is an up-and-coming American worldwide book, film and board game Company. It's positioned to become the largest theology teaching resource in the world in terms of books, textbooks, documentaries, board games and card decks. The Ridge Publishing Group owns the trademarks and copyrights of the Guardians of Biblical Truth Publishing Group and the New Narrated Study Bible series; the Hoyle Theology Publishing Group and the Hoyle Theology Encyclopedia seminary textbooks series (independent study program); Documentaries in Print Publishing Group and the Defending the Faith – Two Worlds, Lost World, New World series; and Educations in Games Publishing Group and the Heaven's Seminary board games and card decks. For more information, visit our website at https://www.RidgePublishingGroup.com.

www.ingramcontent.com/pod-product-compliance
Lightning Source LLC
Chambersburg PA
CBHW071600080526
44588CB00010B/971